PARIAHS

PARIAHS
HUBRIS, REPUTATION AND ORGANISATIONAL CRISES

MATT NIXON

First published in 2016 by Libri Publishing

ISBN: 978-1-909818-80-4

Cover and design by Carnegie Publishing

Printed in the UK by Short Run Press

Libri Publishing
Brunel House
Volunteer Way
Faringdon
Oxfordshire
SN7 7YR

Tel: +44 (0)845 873 3837

www.libripublishing.co.uk

Trust in corporate institutions is on the decline – yet we lack consensus as to why, much less how to respond. Most analyses are trivial, general, or both. Enter Matt Nixon's *Pariahs* – an "insider's" book that is informed, thoughtful, and above all, contextual. Nixon brings to bear the perspectives of an HR executive, a classicist and a consultant, all of which enlighten. While rooted in UK examples, American and other audiences will have no trouble recognizing truly global themes. We can't fix trust until we understand the problem; this is a unique and special contribution to doing so.

Charles Green, author of *The Trusted Advisor*

***

In *Pariahs*, Nixon looks at an issue we all find fascinating as long as we are mere observers: organizations which become outcasts. Writing in clear flowing prose, he draws on ancient history and current examples to take us beyond the headlines. A great book!

Christian Stadler, Professor of Strategic Management, Warwick Business School

***

Nothing changes unless behaviour changes. We know that to be true. The behaviour, and ultimately the performance, of every institution on earth is determined by the behaviours of individuals. But Nixon has dissected this reality and examined not only the behaviour but the psychoses and neuroses that lie deep inside any human system. With compelling clarity he has drawn a red thread between an excess of ego, the resulting manifestation of that in large organisations and the truly awesome implications for organisations and the societies that they serve.

Colin Price, Global Managing Partner, Leadership Consulting Heidrick and Struggles

***

Matt Nixon asks unusual and intriguing questions on how the flouting of social norms can lead organisations to "pariah" status... if you feel your organisation is teetering on the brink of "pariahdom", seize this book and act on the recommendations.

Naomi Stanford, Organisation Design Consultant and author of the *Economist's Guide to Organisation Design* and *Organisation Culture*

***

This book covers really important topics. It's interesting how the words of our predecessors several thousand years ago are a very useful frame for addressing some of the complexity of modern business life. Anyone who has been touched by the changing waves of corporate activity – or is in a job where they are likely to be – should read *Pariahs*.

Barnaby Briggs, MD Plexitas Consulting, former Head of Social Performance, Royal Dutch Shell

***

In *Pariahs*, Matt Nixon provides both diagnostics and treatment advice for a fatal disease in the corporate world – systemic culture failure. With skill and sensitivity, he peels back the layers of the behavioural breakdowns that lead to such failure – often a combination of weaknesses in culture, governance, structure and process. At the Pariah stage, the sight of a corporation's innards isn't pretty; but for a leadership team which has recognized the need to act, Nixon shows the way to a lasting cure. A timely leadership book for our turbulent and fragmented era, in which an honestly lived corporate purpose is more vital than ever.

Björn Edlund, former Head of Corporate Communications at Royal Dutch Shell plc, ABB Ltd and Sandoz AG

***

Pariahs is one of those books with the strength to convert the unconverted. For business leaders that already understand that ethics, sensitivity and sustainability are winning qualities of 21st-century companies, Matt Nixon's *Pariahs* is a guide that will strengthen their resolve. However, for the majority of CEOs that opt for egocentric styles of leadership over the health of the wider system in which they operate, Nixon's analysis of corporate reputation costs, as well as opportunities for change, will be an eye-opener difficult to ignore.

Alejandro Litovsky, Founder/CEO, Earth Security Group

***

Pariahs reads as well as Dante's Cycles of Hell and yet offers hope. Matt Nixon's convincing account shows how greed, exploitation and tyranny cannot be sustainable and how they will meet their inevitable downfall. It shows how high-flying, derailing CEOs and corporates – like real pariahs, "proprietors of the soil" – become the *"disinherited sons of the earth"*; until and unless with time and endless frustration, they may rise again, sustainably. Nixon's account illustrates the enormous costs of such vicious "Pariah" cycles. This book is a healthy warning to all industry.

Professor Erik de Haan, author of *The Leadership Shadow*, Ashridge Business School

***

Matt Nixon offers a compelling analysis of the life cycle of a firm from success to hubris and then to disaster. This lively text, full of stunning examples, pictures for the reader the constant draw to hubris for people and organisations from classical antiquity through to the present day. A fantastic book from a thoughtful corporate insider.

Professor John Thanassoulis, Warwick Business School, University of Warwick

***

This book is a compelling read for both business and human resource leaders who want to question and understand how to influence the reputation and culture of their company. The insights from Matt, based on his first-hand experiences and broader observations, provide unique insights into the fragility of an organisation's reputation and a framework for deciding on relevant interventions.

Geraldine Haley, Global Head of Executive Talent, Standard Chartered Bank

To my family

Contents

Acknowledgements

THIS BOOK COULD never have been written without the dual privileges of time and resources that enabled me to reflect, focus and write. I am therefore very grateful for the long sabbatical in 2014 during which most of the writing was completed. The unmatched resources and staff of the London Library were also critical to getting the necessary research and writing completed. All authors should have such conditions to work in!

Some of the core ideas of the book owe their origins to my education as a classicist, and discussions or debates about the meaning of hubris decades ago with my classics teachers: the late Peter Croft in York, David Miller in Bristol, and subsequently my tutor, Richard Rutherford, at Christ Church, Oxford. Studying Greek and Roman thought left me with deep-seated habits in my thinking that have proved invaluable most of the time, at least where wider thinking, thoroughness, accuracy and compassion have been valued. There was a long hiatus after these early studies until the period when I started to have real, live conversations with consulting clients, and later colleagues in Shell and Barclays, about the impact of power on individual and corporate decision making. I am particularly grateful to the many thoughtful and challenging individuals I worked with over a decade in both firms where I was an executive, particularly to the four CEOs I worked with directly (Jeroen van der Veer and Peter Voser at RDS, Bob Diamond and Antony Jenkins at Barclays) and senior leaders in their executive teams, from whom I learned every day as they handled extremely difficult challenges and tradeoffs. At

Shell, I was particularly fortunate to work in a very able and thoughtful HR and OE team: my thanks to all of them for what they taught me about my own leadership (and its many failings and limitations!). Special thanks to Roxanne Decyk, Hugh Mitchell, Björn Edlund, Harry Brekelmans, Jeremy Bentham, Garmt Louw, Nick Putnam, Vincent Docherty, Ian Jones, Jim Tebbe and many others too numerous to mention in countries around the world. At Barclays, many thanks to Richard Haworth, Matt Hammerstein, David Wheldon, Lawrence Dickinson, Mike Aldred, Stephen Whitehead, Jon Harding and Mark Burton. I'm also grateful to Anthony Salz and all those involved in the Salz Report, and to the teams running the subsequent culture change efforts for sharing concerns and practical issues as we negotiated some very difficult moments together.

A project such as this, asking difficult and uncomfortable questions, requires a certain amount of courage, and hence encouragement from others, if it is to see the light of day. I am very grateful to Alan Richardson for the initial push to go beyond musing about these topics over a few pints. The inimitable Jenny Robinson gave the lifecycle its first public outing at a memorable client dinner and Mollie Bickerstaff helped improve it greatly through the addition of the idea of catharsis for successful metamorphosis. Phil Mix helped me secure the initial opportunity to speak about the lifecycle with the faculty at Ashridge and since that first talk I have been greatly helped by many colleagues there, including Erik de Haan, Dev Mookherjee, Roger Delves, Lindsey Masson and Vicki Culpin.

Many people have been kind enough to encourage and help the project along in various ways by providing platforms to test out the ideas, sharing their practical advice on publishing, and reading and commenting on drafts of the text. I am hugely grateful to several of the colleagues mentioned above and also to Elsbeth Johnson, Ian Gee, Charlie Green, Colin Price, Andrew Hill, Barnaby Briggs, Christian Stadler, Chris Beer, John Thanassoulis, Ale Litovsky, Geraldine Haley and Naomi Stanford. I am also grateful to the staff of the Managing Partners' Forum for providing a platform for debate and discussion.

As the book has moved closer to its final shape, Paul Barnett has provided invaluable advice on connecting the ideas to a wider marketplace. My publisher, Paul Jervis, and his team have provided detailed and helpful support in slimming down and finalising the text, and I am hugely grateful to Libri for taking on this book when others were not so brave.

The book draws heavily on a wide range of primary academic literature in many fields, and I must attest to the deep debts I owe to these real scholars for their work and clarity of thinking, far superior to my own. The bibliography notes the texts that I have drawn on most heavily and, if nothing else, I hope I have gathered some good sources for those interested in these topics.

Everyone who works in the emerging "field" of hubris in the UK is indebted to the work of David Owen and the Daedalus Trust. Lord Owen has not only been good enough to provide the foreword for this book, but was also personally most encouraging at a key point in its early genesis. My thanks to him and to Geoff Marlow for providing the initial introduction to the Trust and being another supportive voice when I lacked confidence.

Finally, I must thank those closest to me. Firstly my wife Terri, for supporting what must have seemed at times a quixotic and strange book. She also read the very first draft and was characteristically clear about where things could be improved. Most importantly, she provided the encouragement and support that are vital to any author lucky enough to receive them. My parents provided – and still provide – the inspiration to study, think and lead a life that is the opposite of hubristic. And my children, who one day may appreciate why I wanted to write this book, provided moments of unalloyed joy and, occasionally, some good reasons to go back to the library!

Foreword by the Rt. Hon Lord Owen

MOST BOOKS AIMED at improving organisations tend to focus on what others do to be successful. It is rare to find one that dwells on, and deeply analyses, crises and failure as the basis for learning what to do differently. It is extremely rare to find such a book written by someone with credible first-hand experience in organisations that went wrong. Especially when those organisations are of the scale and importance of Shell and Barclays. *Pariahs* is therefore to be welcomed as an unusual contribution to the literature of leadership.

Matt Nixon clearly wrestled with the title 'Pariahs' – but I think the shock nature of the word has an arresting quality that neither exaggerates nor trivialises. The ready acceptance by big companies of others' distrust, fear and scorn is something that we should be concerned about in a civil society, and it is anger at this corporate cynicism and indifference that drives this book.

Changing the status quo requires changes in how these organisations are led. Leaders are the ones who must take on this challenge, and I am pleased to see that this book rightfully places collective and leadership hubris as a major and under-diagnosed symptom of cultures that face imminent crisis.

I have been writing and speaking about hubris for many years now, and since 2011 I have been chairing an organisation – the Daedalus Trust – that both funds hubris research and brings together practitioners and experts from many fields to share their findings and observations. Although my own research stemmed from my interest as a medical doctor – trained as a neuro-scientist – in the physical and mental health of political leaders, my interest now is as much about how we can extend our understanding into leadership in other fields, particularly business. I am staggered how many millions the financial service industry puts into funding research on risk: in complex model building, actuarial studies and statistical research, whilst continuing to neglect behavioural and neuro-scientific research. It is as if they want to go on ignoring well-established descriptions like "animal spirits" and "irrational exuberance" and are afraid of facing themselves. This neglect must end. There is an unfilled appetite for research into these areas because funding is so difficult to attract.

The damaging conditions that make politicians prone to what I term *Hubris Syndrome* are most certainly present in large companies, banks and even public-sector institutions, and I was therefore delighted to know that Matt Nixon and others are taking this emerging body of learning into the mainstream of how we are developing future leaders.

Pariahs explores in detail how hubris causes tremendous damage, seen through the eyes, in this author's case, not of a doctor, but of someone who is an experienced management consultant. These professions are not entirely dissimilar: their successful practitioners know that clever diagnosis is insufficient for healing, and that the patient's willing involvement in the cure is essential for success.

The Barclays story in particular is a fascinating one, and Nixon writes from an almost unique vantage point, having worked first with Bob Diamond before the LIBOR crisis enveloped the bank, and latterly with his successor, Antony Jenkins, as he attempted to fix its cultural problems.

Jenkins involved the top leadership of the bank heavily in the definition and shaping of its values and with the detailed description of the behaviour that was going to be expected at various levels of leadership.

Nixon makes no secret that the list of values that Jenkins promulgated (Respect, Integrity, Service, Excellence and Stewardship) attracted cynicism and scepticism from many. Perhaps not surprisingly, given that the mnemonic RISES is, as the author puts it, "resonant in the context of banker remuneration". But his account helps us understand the magnitude and difficulty of the challenges of 'fixing' corporate cultures that have grown over many years, and in conditions where the rewards for success for the bankers, or the price for failure paid by others, are so large.

Barclays was indeed lucky to have as well the commitment, knowledge and foresight of Anthony Salz, whose 37 recommendations, in his important review of the bank's business practices conducted after the LIBOR scandal, included numerous references to alignment with purpose and values. Nixon was at the heart of taking these recommendations into the day-to-day operation of the bank, so his observations on how to do this are particularly relevant.

As Barclays changes its leadership yet again, it will be interesting to see whether they ever achieve the catharsis and forgiveness of Nixon's "true metamorphosis" stage in the *Pariah Lifecycle* or are doomed to repeat the cycle once more.

It is probably easier for start-ups or organisations at the beginning of their organisational cycle to build purpose and values in from the start, but they face other challenges. There are advantages in an organisation having a depth of knowledge and experience that only comes over decades.

Nixon notes this need for wisdom and experience too. I think he's right to say that many of the future crises for these young, fast-growing companies may turn out to be connected to the complex issues that surround the ethics and legal status of personal data and privacy. Again, we should worry that there will be widespread hubris in the leaders of big companies such as Google which will exacerbate the problems.

Fortunately, the author has a far wider experience than just Barclays. One of the pleasures of this book is the hope he finds in a wide range of organisations for salvation, from McDonald's through to Network Rail, as well as his fair-minded scepticism whether all is well in the NHS, the BBC or the charity sector.

Knowing what makes an organisation prone to pariah crises, and how to tackle at its root the interlocking nature of the changes that are necessary to remove pariah status, is the core of this book. Thoughtful, detailed and carefully written, it deserves a wide take-up among the thousands of people who are embarking on careers in business, as well as those who are already well-established leaders and those who supervise or govern them.

Introduction

IN THE LAST few years, whole industries seem to have been in perpetual turmoil, as scandals repeatedly rock their worlds. These stories are headline news almost every day and have included:

- Deliberate cheating to evade emissions tests by car makers
- LIBOR and FX manipulation by bankers
- Falsified drug testing, bribery and corruption by Big Pharma
- Newspapers tapping phones of the famous, dead or otherwise newsworthy
- A drilling rig explosion that spilled millions of barrels of crude oil
- Operation Yewtree's paedophile investigations into entertainers employed by the BBC
- Cover ups over high death rates in hospitals
- Horsemeat sold as beef in our supermarkets
- The collapse of high-profile charities.

The list of wrongdoing, incompetence and failure of governance and oversight can seem never ending. These crises have involved well-known and trusted brands from the private sector such as Volkswagen, Barclays, GlaxoSmithKline, BP and Tesco, as well as the BBC, NHS and others in the public sector, and charities including Kids Company in the UK. It is not always obvious what has gone wrong to cause these problems, but there is no disguising the widespread impact on many stakeholders, and the catastrophic loss of trust and sense of betrayal engendered by these crises.

This book has its origins in my curiosity about how organisations I had worked for came to suffer crises such as those mentioned above. These crises inspire deep emotional responses, and organisations including my own often became so disliked that they were treated by some as pariahs, to be publicly despised and berated. Suffering such public ignominy alongside my colleagues, I became particularly interested in what ordinary employees, as well as leaders, could do to protect their brands and fix the problems they faced.

This curiosity began as a longstanding background interest during my time at Royal Dutch Shell. My role in leading on organisational effectiveness across the company required me to get to grips with how a complex web of pressures had led to what became known as the Reserves Crisis shortly before I arrived, and the legacy that crisis had left in its wake. In that scandal, Shell's reputation as a dependable, well-managed company was heavily damaged, and the events led directly to massive changes in the structure, leadership and culture of the company. These changes lay at the centre of my working life for the next six years, as I worked all over the world with the CEOs and senior leadership of one of the world's most complex and challenging organisations. In that work, Shell's many reputational issues and its long, complex legacy (for good and bad) were never far away from our leaders' minds, whether in Nigeria, Sakhalin or Houston. Working with these teams, as well the leaders of the HR, Finance, Government Relations and Communications functions, was eye-opening for me. I came to understand how far from reality was some of what one read in the newspapers, but also how closeness to that very complexity could blind people to the validity of the views of others, who might be less well informed but highly influential. It also happened that, during my time in the oil industry, one of our major competitors suffered two major accidents of such size and scope that we spent a lot of time and effort trying to learn from them, and the terrible impact they had on that company's standing and reputation in the world.

If my Shell experience had not been stimulating enough, my next role, as a managing director in the HR leadership team at Barclays, threw me even more into the heart of challenging reputations and associated leadership dilemmas. Again, I joined an organisation that was no stranger to controversy, in this case one which operated among unresolved tensions and issues stemming from the recent financial crisis. Quite soon after I joined, Barclays' reputational issues became far more acute because of the LIBOR crisis. As another set of senior leaders lost their jobs and their personal reputations, I again became closely involved in the investigations and analysis of what had gone wrong and why, as well as what we could do to fix the problems. I wrote the first draft of the terms of reference for what became the Salz Review, assisted the review as the chief point of reference for HR data requests, and subsequently co-led a key workstream in the bank's work to put things right, while also leading our work on directing talent management for the top 150 leaders of the bank. Simultaneously, I was helping my colleagues who were responsible for developing changed values and behaviours, and preparing responses to the Parliamentary Commission on Banking Standards. I also represented Barclays on the Professional Standards Committee of the Chartered Banker: Professional Standards Board, an industry body that pre-dated what is now the Banking Standards Board.

These roles gave me a somewhat unusual level of privileged access, and hopefully some insights, into multiple aspects of the issues discussed in this book. These involve the strategic challenges at board level, the practical workings of complex global organisations, the decision making and personalities of senior executives, the political and policy issues of national and international governance and oversight, and the views of NGOs and protest groups opposed to the status quo. I was not a key player in any of these areas – but I was directly advising the executives making the biggest decisions, and the work was consistently fascinating and challenging to me. I won't discuss much of the details of my own work in this book for reasons of confidentiality, but inevitably it's these experiences that underpin my views. Certainly, I hope it's clear in what follows that I have huge respect for the leaders with whom I worked, who frequently operated under pressures that most people literally can't understand or imagine. A number of questions about the nature of the issues of reputation and how we were handling them occurred to me during this busy decade of my life. But, such was the pace of the work, there was never sufficient time to answer these questions to my own satisfaction. It was only in 2014, when I was finally able to take a sabbatical, that I had the luxury of spending serious time thinking and writing about the issues in greater depth.[1]

The questions that were troubling me included:

- Why do some organisations seem to become "pariahs" and lose their trusted reputations – at least with certain stakeholders or constituencies? Is there an increasing trend towards the press and public, including customers and even investors, deciding that certain organisations, even whole sectors and industries, deserve pariah status? If so, does that matter?

- Can we stop organisations becoming pariahs? Is it predictable who will become a pariah? What are the conditions that increase the risks? What can leaders and those who govern or regulate at-risk organisations do to lower these risks?

- After an organisation becomes a pariah, what can be done to regain reputation and become acceptable again to the majority of stakeholders? Is it possible to be "forgiven"? Or do you just have to live with the fact that not everyone will love you, and get on with business as usual?

- What's going on for those working in pariah organisations? What narratives exist within these organisations that enable people to work for them in good conscience? How do people inside the organisations cope with the challenges from others who may question their choices?

Many of these questions were also on the minds of external observers as scandals enveloped one trusted institution after another. Almost all of them were posed at times in the social media, if not spoken aloud by organisational critics, and their repercussions for the organisations concerned and their people are being felt daily. Certainly I had found myself having to answer such questions, both explicitly and implicitly, from friends and acquaintances. This wasn't always a comfortable experience, and at times I felt emotions ranging from shame (as embarrassing or disgraceful details were revealed about my organisation and its actions) to anger and frustration (at those whose criticisms were often ill-informed, partisan or simplistic), as well as an overwhelming desire to enable a better, more constructive dialogue to take place between these organisations and their detractors.

As I thought more about what we had done (right and wrong), it seemed to me that in particular the picture of widespread criminality, immorality and incompetence painted in the public narrative was at odds with what I observed every day in the boardroom and down through the operations of the businesses with which I worked. The people with whom I worked directly were not venal and corrupt. They did not set out to damage the firm's reputation. The vast majority were thoroughly honest, capable and decent, and hugely shocked and horrified when genuine wrongdoing – let alone criminality – was discovered. I became fascinated by one question in particular: were I and my colleagues simply self-deluding, unwitting pawns on the chessboard of a system that had bad outcomes regardless of our good (or at any rate, not evil) intentions? Or were we unfairly maligned victims in a game of reputation where some exterior forces (particularly the press and the NGO pressure groups) often seemed to have the power to control our reputation and damage us without regard to truth or fairness? In short, did we, collectively, deserve to be treated as pariahs, or was this just a convenient narrative for public consumption, unworthy of those who understood the real complexities?

Perhaps inevitably, both stories are partially true. You can seldom see your own role in the system in full and we are all prone to self-justification.[2] This especially holds when a lot is riding on being right and timescales for decision making are compressed. Yet it's also clear that there has been a growing need in the media, for both commercial and political reasons, to find scandals and stories; and that a fast-paced, transparent Twittersphere is hungry for gossip, scandal and intrigue, and less keen on nuanced detail, complexity or fairness to those doing difficult jobs under considerable pressures. Balanced judgement seems at times to play no real role in modern life. But there didn't seem to be a usable set of guidelines for those leading, governing or advising organisations to help them avoid becoming pariahs, or handle things well if they suddenly discovered themselves in trouble. Aside from the shrill NGO and press criticisms, what could actually be done differently? And was anyone really trying to stop pariahs being formed or were they benefiting from having clients who were always in trouble? Perhaps, I thought, this was where my own experiences could add some value to the discussion.

It's clearly insufficient to avoid "difficult" sectors in a world in which complexity is increasing – one of the interesting features of all the scandals in the list above is that they all occurred in industries that are critical to the functioning of our modern societies. Nor is it sufficient just to demand "moral" behaviour from leaders (though clearly that is desirable). There is more to solving this issue than just issuing the advice "don't be evil".

This book examines these issues in three sections. In **Part One – Introducing Pariahs**, I start to define the problem we are trying to solve by defining what a "pariah" might be (which my definition does not confine to the private sector) and the reasons why the number of pariahs is on the increase. We also look at why this increase is a real problem for a society struggling with the issues of trust.

The concept of labelling organisations as pariahs is controversial and I accept that I may not convince everyone that it's necessary. Others will possibly even find the term offensive or excessive. Even for those who are not won over by my arguments, I think we need to decide what the alternative reality is; and in either case, we need to decide whether the status quo is acceptable given the prevalence of scandalous crises such as those described above.

Part Two – the core of the book – is devoted to a detailed examination of the **Pariah Lifecycle**, explaining the conditions necessary for organisations with such challenged reputations to form and thrive; the hubris of their cultures and leadership; the different forms of crisis that recur; and the terrible nemesis they create for themselves. Finally, this section looks at what can be done to change after such crises, and whether such changes are real and lasting, creating a possible catharsis. Even readers not fully convinced about "pariahs" should find value in these chapters in considering where the roots of damaging crises lie, and how they might be resisted beforehand or addressed afterwards.

Part Three – Dealing with Pariahs looks at two other aspects of the pariah organisation that I felt worth studying. It starts with some attempts to predict the future and show that there will inevitably be further pariahs as we continue with the trends identified in Part One. I then spend some time looking at the vital role that the employees (not just the leaders) can play in both causing and stopping an organisation becoming a pariah, and finally share some overall conclusions and suggestions. Many of these observations are true of organisations generally, regardless of pariah status. I have also included ideas at the end of each chapter in Part Two for what can be done to address the issues raised in that chapter. Readers in a hurry should perhaps start with Chapter 3 and then dip into other chapters that are of particular interest.

This is a very wide-ranging subject and, although this is not a short book, I won't have done every area justice. My intention has been to draw attention to the issues and start the necessary dialogue among practitioners and leaders about taking the requisite actions. Throughout this book, the influence of the classical thought of ancient Greece and Rome is present, and both in the terminology of my models and occasional quotations from ancient authors I have deliberately tried to show the parallels between the problems of managing power in those empires and the issues of contemporary power and politics. This is not meant to be showing off, but it is hopefully showing *something* – that even 2,500 years ago, people were struggling with the impact of power. In the very first democracy, it's unremarkable that power was a subject of intense interest to those who were wielding it for the first time. In the age of social media and new forms of democratic expression, perhaps we can learn from the ancient Greeks what it means to take seriously the subject of power, and what it can do to you.

It is my hope that this book helps readers think differently about how we can build healthier, more sustainable organisations that are worthy of our trust, and that it provides some actionable ideas on how we can reduce organisational and individual hubris and the risks these pose to the world.

Notes

1   My original intention was to publish this book in 2015. In the time between writing the first major draft and publication, numerous scandals and crises have broken, and several excellent books have been published that are relevant to this topic. Where possible I have tried to read the latter and incorporate their thinking into my work, but inevitably this is a fast moving stream and some developments came too late to be fully digested.

2   There is a huge and growing literature around our psychological and neurological inability to see ourselves and our own actions in an objective fashion. One accessible summary is Fine, 2006.

PART ONE – INTRODUCING PARIAHS

1

Defining Pariahs

pariah (pə'raɪə; 'pærɪə) n
1. (Sociology) a social outcast
2. (Sociology) (formerly) a member of a low caste in South India

[C17: from Tamil paraiyan drummer, from parai drum; so called
because members of the caste were the drummers at festivals]

WHAT MAKES EITHER a person or an organisation into a pariah?[1]
This book sets out to give this term a novel, defined, shared meaning
that can become widely accepted and understood. Although a lot of people
are somewhat familiar with the term, it doesn't yet have either universal
appeal or shared meaning in the context of management and organisations.
I am using deliberately provocative language here to lay claim to what may
become a new variety of the term in the dictionary. But I believe this is a
crucial new concept: we need a label for organisations that many see as *going
too far* and whose reputation has become widely unacceptable.[2] If we fail
to label these organisations more clearly as being beyond the pale, we are
colluding in the problems they create in the world, and also failing to explain
how they could become better led and governed.

We have no problem labelling failing organisations in other ways (e.g.
when aspects of financial performance are subpar). Why should reputational
failure not be equally clear? What I am *not* doing is trying to create another
term of abuse for protest groups to throw at large organisations. I firmly
believe pariah status is neither permanent nor incurable, and in this book I

try to propose strategies for both prevention and cure. But first, we need to know what we are curing.

Two Key Claims

I will start by making two claims:

1. **Pariahs exist and their numbers are on the increase**. We are creating an increasing number of pariah organisations, whose reputational challenges are related to their leaders and workers and the choices they make within a societal context.

2. **This is bad for us**. This trend is bad for our societies as it becomes widespread. We should resist its growth, as it is inimical to social trust and mutual interdependence.

In this preliminary chapter, I define what makes an organisation a pariah and why it is bad to have a growing number of them in our societies.

Pariah Definition

Let's start with a proposed definition:

> **A pariah organisation is well known, but is more infamous than famous. It has become – permanently or temporarily – stigmatised as unacceptable to many stakeholders in the society in which it operates because it has violated the norms of that society.**

A useful way to start looking at potential pariah organisations is to imagine a continuum for stigma.[3]

At one end of the spectrum, over on the right of the table, are organisations which everyone seems to agree are low risk and which enjoy positive reputations across a wide variety of groups. At the other end of the spectrum, on the left, are organisations and perhaps whole industries that are so stigmatised as to be no longer acceptable to significant groups of stakeholders. Two things are immediately clear. Even at the most blameless end of the stigma spectrum it's possible to imagine someone who might dislike the organisation in question, perhaps for highly personal reasons. So it's going to be tough to be in the same place on this spectrum to all observers. At the other end of the spectrum, it also seems clear that being a high stigma organisation isn't a sustainable position: sooner or later you risk tipping over into excess and losing your licence. And again, perhaps one will be unacceptable to some observers while being in a different place to others.

Table 1: The Stigma Spectrum

EXCESSIVE	HIGH	MEDIUM	LOW
Constant and/or catastrophic crises threaten reputation	Frequent and/or major crises threaten reputation	Some crises raise issues about reputation	No major recent crises or reputational challenges
Societal disapproval hits an inflection point that makes it impossible for supporters to continue; political support evaporates	Many significant societal groups disapprove of the organisation's existence as well as many or most of its activities	Some focused and influential societal groups and individuals disapprove of the organisation or its activities, in context	Few or no groups or influential individuals disapprove of the organisation or its activities in any context
Press and social-media commentary becomes overwhelmingly toxic, irrational and vindictive	Press and social-media commentary typically or mainly negative	Some growing negative press and social-media commentary	Press and social-media commentary is consistently positive

So it's not going to be easy to place organisations, even on such a "simple" scale. Just as with nation states, where the concept of pariah is the subjective construct of other countries (albeit perhaps for very good reasons), so too perhaps for organisations. Some organisations are able to maintain great reputations as "admired companies" and "great places to work" even as others protest their very existence. And this duality – of being excellent in some ways but denigrated in others – lies at the heart of what I think is the denial by many organisations of their true status and hence their true risks. As long as some key groups love you, it's possible to deny that one is a pariah to others.

My claim is that a pariah is, in essence, seen as unacceptable by at least some significant part of its host society, and hence becomes increasingly dependent on other elements of that society (typically government, customers or investors) for security and protection. Once the balance swings, and if this protection is lost, so too is the organisation's licence to operate, along with its reputation. If we believe this point, then we have to accept that putting up with a bad reputation becomes a risky act, one that we shouldn't easily accept as inevitable. Along with this definition, I think we have to accept that working for pariahs (either established or emergent) is a risky business too. By attaching themselves to a pariah organisation and its brand, individuals risk connecting their own reputation to that of the brand, and its fame or infamy. And it's this risk that can exacerbate some of the behavioural issues that we witness in the pariah landscape.

Crime and Punishment – Pariahs as Outcasts and Exiles

Before we look at our proposed definition in more detail, it's worth reminding ourselves how ancient and deeply rooted in human society lie the concepts of disapproval, exclusion and punishment implicit in the concept of a pariah. Although the word "pariah" is a term from the Indian caste system which became widely used in British and then other forms of English in the late eighteenth and early nineteenth centuries, the idea I am discussing in this book is independent of culture or nationality. At its heart lies the notion of certain individuals being outcast, in the sense of being unacceptable social company even whilst (regrettably) still necessary to the functioning of a society. And that idea is a universal concept in all societies, even if we struggle to name that concept to our satisfaction today.

Becoming an outcast is a serious matter in any society. It's a form of punishment that goes back a long way into pre-history and our tribal origins. The wandering tribes of Israel described in the Old Testament of the Bible (circa 720 BC) illustrate how whole groups as well as individuals might find themselves refugees from their original homelands in the Bronze Age. Later on, exile became a powerful political weapon for the emerging city states of Greece. In ancient Athens – a society from which many of the key concepts in this book are drawn – tragedians often showed the ultimate end of the protagonist not as death, but as the living curse of being an exile from society[4] in a foreign land. In Euripides's play *Bacchae,* for example, Kadmos laments his fate:

> "Child, what a terrible disaster we have all come to – unhappy you,
> your sisters, and unhappy me. I shall reach a foreign land as an aged
> immigrant."

Bacchae 1353ff

For the Athenian citizens of the fifth century BC, the idea of losing state-hood, belonging and the associated social support system was the worst of imaginable blows, perhaps even worse than death. This was no stale meta-phor, confined to the stage and mythology. Athenians were familiar with exile as a real punishment, either imposed by rulers or self-imposed to avoid the risk of more unpleasant punishments (including death).

Some scholars[5] argue convincingly that increasing use in fifth-century Athens of a process known as ostracism was itself a powerful symbolic shift of power to non-elite citizens in the democracy. Instead of one or another power elites forcing each other into exile (as had happened previously and continued to happen elsewhere), the citizenry each year decided whether to conduct an ostracism, in which they could vote for someone to be exiled for ten years. If they did decide to ostracise, the nomination of candidates was a serious business. Names were inscribed on shards of pottery (in Greek, 'ostraka') and counted at a giant meeting in the agora of the city. If at least 6,000 votes were cast, the ostracised individual had to leave Athens. Prop-erty and income were maintained, and on return citizenship continued as normal. The purpose and significance of this rather unusual political process is still debated, but almost certainly it was designed to contain and manage tyrannical tendencies in strong leaders, and to enable the voting citizenry (all male and excluding slaves) to exert influence over those who were over-reaching themselves. Much has changed in our societies since then and those in political disfavour in Western democracies rarely now find themselves losing their citizenship.[6] But for many in the contemporary world, exile – whether voluntary or involuntary – continues to be a tool of political elites as well as displaced masses. However, neither exile nor ostracism have any place in our contemporary Western legal systems. In Chapter 7 on nemesis, we will consider whether pariahdom has in effect replaced these concepts for us.

Punishing Crimes and Wrongdoing

In the modern world, we do of course have a clear set of punishments for illegal or forbidden behaviour, usually dealt with through the court system (criminal or civil). The sanctions we can impose via the courts or other regu-latory bodies take different forms as the seriousness of the offence increases:

1. **Warnings** (formal and informal) to individuals or organisations

2. Types of formal proscription or **barring** (e.g. removing or suspending a licence to practise in a profession; bans from the Stock Exchange; bans from holding directorships; Asbos or restraining orders)

3. **Fines** (again, for individuals or organisations) small or large

4. Custodial **prison sentences** (of varying lengths and in varying types of prison)

5. **Corporal punishments** (such as whipping or cutting off limbs)

6. **Death.**

Three things should be noted here: firstly, that **the most severe punishments for individuals (denial of liberty or worse) are worse than the punishments for organisations**. Only people can be deprived of their liberty or life by the state and its judicial system.[7] Organisations can be warned, banned or fined, but not locked up or killed.[8] Some people may feel this is a matter for regret, but that's how it works. We cannot vote to have a company shut down, although we have power as consumers or shareholders as well as citizens to boycott or protest against them, and as voters we can influence government policies and pressures on regulators. So there are metaphorical similarities, but the only direct cognate of imprisonment is the actual removal of a licence to operate, which is a very rare occurrence indeed. By and large, organisations continue to exist and operate despite their transgressions, albeit with reputational damage sustained. However, we should note that the corporation has, at least in US law,[9] some of the same rights as a person – a controversial reality for over a century. Some see this as an asymmetry which should not exist without stronger expectations on the side of the corporation regarding its obligations and duties. Recent innovations such as the B Corp[10] in the US are clearly a step in this direction.

What happens when reckless behaviour has endangered not just a corporation's stockholders but wider society? In some cases, individual leaders or workers can be shown to have broken the law (e.g. by being negligent) and are successfully prosecuted. But these cases are the exception. The organisational punishments (whether direct fines or increased costs, lost revenue and so forth from reputational damage) are in effect taken by the stockholders and customers, not the executives who made the mistakes. Executives may lose their jobs, with or without payoffs, and may not easily work again. But it's only where they are paid heavily in company stock that executives face personal ruin; for most, there is still a structural imbalance which encourages them to take excessive risks. This problem, known as agency theory,[11] is well documented, but remains essentially unsolved in current limited liability companies. Only in partnerships or as sole traders do the downside punishments for failure truly match the risks. For public-sector organisations, it's even harder to fail permanently if funding continues; perennial lack of delivery does not always lead to the required operational improvements in government agencies (think of the recurring issues in benefit offices, passport agency, post offices and so on). Stakeholders become frustrated at delivery failures, but the organisation is not put out of business by them as might be the case in the private sector.

The second thing to note is that **it's not just the law courts that manage the punishment of organisations and their leaders/professionals**. For example, we allow a wide range of regulatory bodies (including, in the UK, those set up by Royal Charter or statute to manage their own professions, as well as the state-managed regulators) to act in a quasi-judicial fashion around wrongdoing in professional contexts, and these have power to fine and restrict the licence to operate of individuals and organisations alike. Recent history, particularly of the banking industry, has suggested that such professional bodies, even those with a statutory basis, may not be well positioned to manage effectively the people and leaders on whom we depend. In the most ludicrous of examples, at the time of writing, the CEO of the Royal Bank of Scotland at the time of its government bailout in 2009, Fred Goodwin, was still a member of the principal banking professional body[12]. It's obviously quite hard to dislodge those who won't accept purely social pressure to leave the profession (Goodwin had not been convicted of breaking any laws and, despite the fate of RBS, few believe that he was technically incompetent, in the narrow sense, as a banker). Where the professional bodies lack the statutory powers to investigate independently, it can be hard to take tough action. This is a polite way of saying: don't believe that medieval, national systems of self-regulation will be particularly effective in dealing with the problems of complex, global organisations. Partly because of frustrations at the lack of legal sanctions or effective professional bans, the press and social media have started to take action themselves in terms of naming and shaming those accountable for issues and crises, and this in turn has led to an increasing interest from our parliamentarians in the investigation of topical issues. One senior civil servant client I knew well was required to testify before no fewer than four separate such select committees in a calendar year. This was good for transparency and accountability, but not for her health or ability to perform the leadership role required of her. We therefore need to resolve the problem of stakeholders wanting to punish the unpunished organisations (and by extension, their leaders and employees) yet lacking the means to do so.

Thirdly, we should note that **we no longer have any established judicial concept of exile, for individuals or organisations**, although self-exile is common enough. At the height of his unpopularity in 2009, Fred Goodwin did reportedly flee the country for a while, "sheltering in the South of France and Switzerland with various friends." (Martin, 2013, Chapter 14) This is relatively unusual: most of those who leave these shores do so for reasons other than shame or infamy alone. It is perhaps ironic that one of the principal recent uses of the term "exile" is in the context of "tax exiles", a term for those driven to leave their own country by high marginal tax rates. Certainly, those organisations or individuals seeking to minimise tax burdens without such exile face an increasingly hostile press and public anger – they now become individual pariahs. But real exile is not a punishment available to our judiciary. Once granted, either at birth or by a process post-immigration, citizenship and its privileges are hard to remove, as the Home Office discovered in 2014 when it tried to get radical Islamic cleric Abu Hamza out of the country.[13] In this context, some of the arguments about EU and US extradition treaties have recently raised important questions about the role of the UK state in protecting its citizens even where there is prima facie evidence of them having transgressed laws elsewhere.[14] Lacking the judicial punishment of exile, I think we replace it with other forms of social ostracism, treating organisations and individuals as beneath contempt, protesting against them, insulting them online and generally trying to make our disapproval felt. This is an important component of the dynamics of how we create pariahs.

In all these cases, one of the core concepts behind the punishments is an increasing degree of *social disapproval* within a given society, usually formalised by those in power. The state (or authorised agency) is removing something valuable from the individual (status, wealth, freedom to work, freedom to socialise with peers, ultimately freedom to be in the country), and thereby inducing some degree of shame. The fine may be paid, the prison term or suspension served, but the stigma usually lasts – we will see later in the chapter on nemesis why this may be a useful practice. In the case of individuals, we insist on open declaration of criminal conviction long after the sentence is served or the fine paid. Why is this? Obviously, because we attach shame in our culture to having transgressed the law. It is less obvious that we should continue to punish people beyond the letter of the law (e.g. by discriminating against those with criminal convictions in employment decisions or provision of benefits). However, the general point is clear: those who are punished are also punished *socially* by the tribe for their transgressions. We humans are profoundly social beings, constantly defining ourselves via our relationships to each other, and the latest neuroscience research underlines that even for the most introverted or independent minded of us our status in the tribe is always under review.[15] Where the social aspect of punishment ceases, then typically so does the acceptance of the justice of the punishment, and obedience to the original law or rule transgressed also reduces. For example, few of us these days feel much shame in being fined for a trivial parking offence and we may even express surprise and outrage at being caught and punished. At an organisational level, the same holds true: although organisations cannot be locked up or put to death, they can be put out of business if their partners or customers refuse to do business with them, provide them with cash or support their share price, charter renewal or application for licence to operate. Losing too many of these supporters is fatal, but some organisations seem to accept – too readily – that they will be treated as pariahs by key constituencies. This book is going to suggest that this is a big mistake.

Pariahs as Exiles

Given the failings of the judicial and non-judicial systems to punish organisations and leaders to our satisfaction, we are creating new forms of punishment for organisations and individuals, especially for leaders. These punishments – in the form of negative commentary, social exclusion, as well as boycotts and other more formal protests – are tantamount to a form of internal ostracism or exile. They are, importantly, *social* punishments that transcend those for criminality or transgressions of rules that can be shrugged off or paid for by investors. And it's become massively easier for us to exercise such punishment on those who displease us, thanks to technology, and in particular the rise and rise of social media.

Inside organisations, so much attention is being paid to the non-social punishments (e.g. fighting court cases, negotiating fines) that the price being paid in social punishments is not always considered, or even noticed, unless it seems to be affecting customers or investors directly. We are so worried about being put to death, we hardly notice that we are increasingly internally exiled and ostracised. So social punishment is seen as less serious than the existential threat posed to the organisation by an outright ban on its activities, but it's the thin end of a long wedge. We should not succumb lightly to reputational threats, and as citizens we should care deeply whether such social punishments are being administered fairly and appropriately. If I am right, then what is happening is that pariah organisations are being socially ostracised by certain stakeholder groups within the society in which they operate. And if that is true, then it's no surprise that the pace of ostracism and pariah creation is increasing, given the power of social media and the democratisation of information and reputation management.

Characteristics of a Pariah

Above we defined a pariah organisation as one that is "well known, but is more infamous than famous. It has become – permanently or temporarily – stigmatised as unacceptable to many stakeholders in the society where it operates, because it has violated the norms of that society." Let's characterise what that might mean in more detail:

1. **Well known** – people from a wide range of stakeholder groups recognise the organisation and know (or think they know) what it does. It's hard to imagine how an organisation could be a pariah and not be well known, at least to those operating in their space. Paradoxically, perhaps, truly faceless (as opposed to just dull) leaders do seem to attract pariah status in some circumstances, although usually less so than those who are famous – there is a multiplying effect when infamous organisations have infamous leaders. So a pariah (and any pariah leader) needs to be recognisable. This characteristic of pariahs is directly linked to the genesis conditions described later in this book.

2. **More infamous than famous** – there is a *net negative* view of the organisation's reputation among detractor groups. At least some groups may question the organisation's very existence and are vocal about asking for it to be shut down or cease its core activity. The central basis for this negativity is usually some combination of the illegality, immorality, hypocrisy and/or socially damaging nature of the organisation's actions and activities.

3. **Stigmatised as unacceptable to many stakeholders** – fairly or unfairly, pariah organisations are generally known for breaking laws and rules; behaving in ethically dubious ways (such as lying, cheating and otherwise being deceptive); hurting people, including innocent third parties, or the environment. Even if they can't be proved to have done any of the above, at least some stakeholders believe they have transgressed enough norms that they can no longer be tolerated. These transgressions are directly linked to the different types of crisis (financial, operational and behavioural) described in Chapter 6.

Pariah Relativism – Who Decides?

Some people don't like using the term "pariah", because it seems too absolute. A spectrum of more or less stigma as described above is conceptually easier to accept. But my point is that this is all in the eye of the beholder. You and I may be able to agree that some organisations with difficult reputations are, in fact, very useful, albeit run in ways of which we disapprove. But someone else might have a much more fundamental objection to the same organisations. The term is thus inevitably relativistic and what the sociologists might term "constructed".

In his book *Difficult Reputations* (Fine, 2001), the American sociologist Gary Alan Fine suggests a way to look at these relativities. He suggests that the identification and reputation on which we individually and collectively rely has four domains:

+ **Personal** – the circles of personal intimates who actually know the person (or organisation) in question. Personal reputations emanate from these intimate groups, but we modify our behaviour for others in these settings because "of the options that reputations open and close, and because these reputations allow us to conceive of our selves in particular ways." In other words, we face complex social pressures inside organisations that impact our ability to challenge each other, even where we know what is going on.

- **Mass-mediated** – in an age of media saturation, high status is bestowed not only by formal role but by celebrity dictated by the press – where "the media help to determine who we should know about and care about". Leaders have to recognise that if they want to be of very high status, they will become media personalities.

- **Organisational** – organisations have reputations too, which are often closely linked to the reputations of their CEOs. Fine notes that "In a country where a corporation is legally a person, the existence of corporate reputations that mirror celebrity reputations should not be surprising." We attach our own reputations as individuals to the name on our business card.

- **Historical** – at some point knowledge of others becomes "institutionally sanctioned" as part of "settled cultural discourse" and a reputation is then sealed. Where the facts, or the interpretation of the facts, remains contentious, we may try to pacify or ignore the argument by skipping over the issue (as with the subject of the Civil War in the southern states of the US). These days, history seems to be written very quickly, and not always by those who know the facts or the personalities involved.

Thus a few of us are in a position to make personal observations based on our own knowledge of an organisation or its leaders. Many or most of us may feel we know about the organisation and its leaders via media presentation. And over time we may all start to accept certain narratives about the organisation and its leaders as though they were historical facts. But where the story gets difficult, all too often we gloss things over or ignore them, and it's left to our detractors to tell the story instead. This is seldom a good idea. As organisations become larger and more complex, it's small wonder that the personal basis of trust and reputation that we used to rely on in our transactions with each other becomes replaced by a more mass-mediated – but potentially fickle or false – set of reputational truths, moving these days into accepted "history" at breakneck speed. This is one of the dynamics that is accelerating the formation of pariahs around us: we simply can't keep up or form our own opinions about so many issues and organisations, but others are all too keen to tell us what to think. If the organisations don't get to grips with the difficult or controversial parts of the story, then others are happy to do it for them.

Creating History

Another helpful contribution from Gary Alan Fine's work is the following set of three models for evaluating historical figures (or organisations):

- The **objective** explanation assumes a world of facts, which if understood would be accepted by others. In this model "Truth is a fundamental building block of reputation". In this interpretation, if we all knew what *really* happened in detail behind the scenes in an organisation and why, we would be able to draw a fair and balanced view of what the reputation ought to be.

- The second model is **functional**: certain roles are needed in society and reputations evolve to fulfil these. "The reputations of villains and deviants help to establish the boundaries of society. These status hierarchies are expected, if not universal, features of group life." In this reading, pariahs are inevitable because we need them to wear the black hats so we can spot who the 'baddies' are in our shared cultural narratives.

- The third model sees reputation as **socially constructed**: "reputa-tions are a result of the socio-political motives of groups that gain resources, power, or prestige by the establishment of reputations." In this reading, reputational "entrepreneurs" establish reputations for others and these critical interventions establish the memes around which subsequent dialogue revolves. Fine suggests that this third model is the one to favour, for "Construction occurs at every point – in naming the problem, in marshalling statistics and other forms of evidence, and in deciding who can legitimately speak to the problem."

These distinctions (or versions thereof) are familiar to any serious literary critic or social scientist of the last fifty years. Yet many quasi-historical, news and contemporary non-fiction accounts seldom seem to recognise any but the objective approach. In other words, we prefer to behave as though there is "a truth" out there, and that we can divine it (so long as we have sufficient data). Most of the business leaders I have worked with also – consciously or unconsciously – take this view, and hence are surprised if other modes of evaluation seem to be at work instead. This is particularly true of those who are highly rational and data-driven themselves – engineers, quantitative bankers and technology leaders are particularly prone to making errors in reputation management, partly because they simply believe they have more data than others (or at least that no-one else has better, more compelling data) and hence are in a better position to judge their own innocence than the press or an outraged customer or NGO.[16] Those with more experience of the press and politics (including the wilier business leaders and most politicians and civil servants, as well as those in the presentational industries) are more aware that reputation might be socially constructed, or at least that some form of functional model is operating around them. They certainly know objective facts don't win all arguments.

As we will see, some pariah leaders can become quite enamoured of the functional model: Michael O'Leary at Ryanair is a past master at casting himself, albeit tongue in cheek, as a highly visible "hate figure" CEO, and plays with the press and its need to have such bogey-men characters. Conversely, Richard Branson is the darling of the PR professionals for his genius in casting himself as a whacky, against-the-odds, "let's do it", balloon-flying, rocket-ship hero. Many think both of them are equally flawed figures and neither seems to command too much peer-group respect from other CEOs I have known. But the point is that they are leaders who are savvy and aware of the way they and the brands they represent are being presented via the mass media. They choose to rely on that medium to get across their messages and reach their target audience, the punters who buy seats on their planes.

Defining pariahs, then, is not going to be an exact science (although I do believe we can potentially diagnose those at risk or already in pariah state). But we should not let the difficulty of naming the problems of excessive stigma prevent us from taking it seriously and tackling it.

Reputation and Reality

There are some clear emerging themes relating to reputation. A typical viewpoint is that of the Centre for Reputation at the Oxford Saïd School of Business. Four main claims are made: that **reputation is relational** (you have a reputation for something with someone); that organisations and leaders have **multiple reputations** with different groups; that we increasingly rely on third-party **intermediaries** to drive our reputations; and finally, that reputation's importance lies in its **signalling power**, its ability in a world of great complexity to simplify what view to hold about an organisation, brand or leader. I think there is much good sense here and none of these claims is wrong. But it is in the last claim that there is the greatest risk. If one believes only in the medium and the message, and not the reality behind it, the opportunity grows for a say–do gap to grow. As we will see, this is particularly problematic given our penchant for strong brands and clear identities for our leaders.

Table 2: Reputational Orthodoxy

CLAIM	IMPLICATION	ACTION	MY VIEWPOINT
Reputation is Relational	Get relationships right and you can influence reputation	Build relationships with stakeholders directly, especially customers, regulators, investors and government	*True, but remember you can't always control or contain who chooses to relate to or with you*
Multiple Reputations	Reputations can be managed differently with different groups	Create messages and communicate differently with different audiences	*True, but excessive balkanisation is problematic; don't leave all synthesis to the CEO and the board*
Reputation Intermediaries	Some people's views matter more than others in determining reputation	Get close to and influence the influencers (especially press, government and social-media influencers)	*True, but in the age of Twitter you may be surprised at where critical positive and negative intermediaries arise*
Signalling Power	What matters is the signal and who shapes it	Invest heavily in signals and signallers (i.e. brand/corporate affairs/comms)	*What matters is the truth that lies behind the signal; you can't always cover up for bad actions*

If we don't accept that there are any absolute pariahs (just different degrees of reputational challenge or stigma, judged by different stakeholders) we might still find it useful to describe what constitutes achieving that extreme status, even if we think it's only in the eye of the beholder. But if we are a little braver, and prepared to accept that at some stage, pariah status among multiple stakeholders is indeed to *be* a pariah, then we have to act on that understanding. By naming the issue, we make acceptance of the status quo less possible. Even if the status quo is stable and well understood, we should not accept it if we have organisations that are losing trust with many key stakeholder groups. My hope in this book is that by naming and, carefully and with thought, deftly shaming and fixing pariah organisations, we may be able to head off harmful crises and contribute to trust and mutual understanding in our increasingly complex, globalised societies.

Established Pariahs

Within the ranks of pariah organisations, there are clearly some that have been used to their status for a long time, often in industries where difficult reputations are normal across the entire sector. I suggest that we call these organisations "established pariahs", to distinguish them from organisations which are drifting towards that status but have not themselves yet accepted and absorbed the permanence of their situation; or indeed, which may be only temporarily in trouble. The latter are perhaps "emerging pariahs".

There are some key features that characterise established pariahs:

1. Their core business is, or can be, **harmful to people and/or the environment** under certain conditions: established pariahs are doing dangerous stuff, with real capacity to do damage to society, people and property. If it were not so, we wouldn't care so much about them.
2. They are therefore usually (heavily) **regulated** by government: established pariahs are used to managing around politics and regulation. If they are not regulated literally, then this is controversial (for example, see the current furore about newspaper regulation).
3. They face sustained, vocal, cogent opposition from pressure groups which seriously oppose their existence: ASH for the tobacco industry; Greenpeace and Friends of the Earth for the extractives and nuclear industry; GRASP or Gambling Watch UK for gambling; Hacked Off for the Press. **Your industry doesn't belong on an established list if there isn't a permanent pressure group against it.** continued

4. This NGO or pressure group critique is picked up and echoed by mainstream press and, often, disgruntled investors: **pariahs face continuous negativity in PR and reputation**, and their brands are frequently used in sophisticated ways against them.[17]

5. They consequently **deploy sophisticated PR, CSR**[18] **and reputation management** capability aimed at targeted audiences to manage and deflect criticisms: for established pariahs, this is permanent war, not a temporary crisis. They are adept at reputation management, if only defensively, and staff up accordingly.

6. Critically, they accept that not all stakeholders can or will be won over to their point of view: **established pariahs are good at marginalising detractors and at soothing those who are on the fence.**

The best reason to favour the term "established pariahs" is that these organisations are invariably close to the Establishment itself – that is, to the nexus of power, money and influence at the centre of any society. This is not intended as a controversial political point, simply an observation about how established pariahs survive, by tending their reputations carefully with those on whom they absolutely depend for their licence to operate.

Notes

1　The original etymology is based on a word meaning "to tell something", as the caste members made public announcements, preceded by banging their drums. In Indian society, the word "pariah" became widely used by the British to describe (inaccurately) members of several low-caste groups and was often falsely applied to those who are now known as Dalits (untouchables). The term – as with others I use in the book – has evolved beyond its original meaning and usage, and I will use it in the general idiomatic sense of "social outcast". See Viswanath, 2014.

2　Other words I considered and discussed with publishers include "unacceptable", "outcast", "toxic" and "disreputable". None of these seemed to me to capture the social exclusion and distaste I have felt as accurately as the term "pariah" does.

3　I am grateful to Rowena Olegario and Tim Hannigan from Saïd Business School for our discussion on the relationship between stigma and pariahdom.

4　The theme of exile is frequent as a punishment in classical Greek literature. See, for example Sophocles, *Oedipus Tyrannus* 1516ff; Euripides, *Medea* 1236ff and throughout, also *Bacchae* 1350ff; Aeschylus, *Coephoroi* 3ff. Also see Plato, *Crito* 52d in which Socrates prefers to accept an unjust death at the hands of the state to a dishonourable exile.

5　See Forsdyke, 2005. We also know from archaeological sources that ostraka were often pretty rude about their subjects.

6   The UK does still remove voting rights from convicted prisoners.

7   At the time of writing, 32 US states had the death penalty; 140 countries worldwide, including the UK, did not.

8   Governments, regulators, investors, customers or voters can remove literal and figurative licences to operate, deny revenue, capital or investment and hence cause organisational demise. But this is a figurative death.

9   Personhood for corporations was established in US law in the nineteenth century in Supreme Court rulings. Outside the US, the legal concept of personhood for the corporation is less well established, but there is also a longer tradition of multi-stakeholder models that explicitly question the primacy of the corporation's owners.

10   B Corps are for-profit companies certified by the non-profit B Lab to meet rigorous standards of social and environmental performance, accountability and transparency. See http://www.bcorporation.net/what-are-b-corps

11   See Jensen and Meckling, 1976

12   A fascinating exchange on this topic, and why the Chartered Institute was unable to expel Goodwin, took place at the Parliamentary Commission on 14 January 2013. See: http://www.publications.parliament.uk/pa/jt201314/jtse-lect/jtpcbs/27/130114.htm

13   Abu Hamza, a controversial Islamic cleric, was born in Egypt and also had British citizenship. Egypt decided to revoke his Egyptian citizenship in 2010, and the UK was not prepared to make him stateless. Abu Hamza was tried and convicted for terrorist offences, and imprisoned in the US in 2014 as a UK citizen. He was sentenced there in January 2015 to life in prison without parole.

14   The European Arrest Warrant essentially mandates EU countries to cooperate in extraditing those accused of certain types of crime; the Extradition Act 2003 implemented both the EAW and the UK side of the controversial UK–US Extradition Treaty of 2003 which provided non-reciprocal rights to the US to extradite those suspected of contravening US laws in the UK. There were heated political arguments in late 2014 about whether Parliament was being given the opportunity to vote on the issue.

15   See Lieberman, 2013.

16   The *locus classicus* for this type of management error is the row over Shell's decommissioning of the Brent Spar Oil storage buoy in the North Sea in 1995. Shell had decided after careful examination of the options that sinking the spar in a deep part of the sea was the best solution. Greenpeace disagreed, occupied the buoy and organised a huge and high-profile campaign of boycotts and pressure across Europe. Although Shell held its ground initially and secured UK government backing for its decision, it subsequently reversed this decision and towed the Spar for onshore demolition. Much later, Greenpeace accepted that Shell had been correct and had indeed chosen the best method, but by then it was too late for Shell's reputation. Few know that Greenpeace admitted they were wrong on this famous campaign, of course.

17 A notable recent example is Greenpeace's use of Shell's jaunty "Let's Go" slogan in a sophisticated attack in 2012 featuring bogus websites, press announcements and social-media competitions. See http://knowyourmeme. com/memes/events/lets-go-arctic-hoax-campaign

18 Corporate Social Responsibility – this much-derided term is, thankfully, falling rapidly out of favour as organisations realise how false it looks to isolate efforts from the mainstream of what their organisation does for a living.

2

The Case for Concern

Why Does Being a Pariah Matter?

The reasons for wanting to avoid the social, political and economic costs of being a pariah organisation may seem obvious. But clearly many organisations continue to survive for long periods of time despite qualifying as pariahs under our definition. Does that mean pariah status is not really important or, at worst, a matter for "reputation management" alone? My claim is that all stakeholders – customers, employees, investors, governments, regulators and wider publics – should have an interest in reducing and even minimising the number of pariah organisations in existence.

Being an established pariah in particular has hidden costs in terms of at least five major factors:

- Licence to operate
- Regulation
- Revenues and pricing
- Talent attraction, engagement and performance
- Damage to trust.

Licence

Firstly, being a pariah is problematic because pariahs have a less stable licence to operate than non-pariahs. Being highly unpopular with vocal and influential groups requires extra time and attention (and cost) to be paid to political lobbying, press and social-media management, and advertising to correct misconceptions of factual inaccuracies spread by opponents. We have observed above that actual removals of explicit licences to operate are very rare – but they do happen. In the wake of the Deepwater Horizon disaster, BP was forbidden to bid for deep-water licences in the US, and there was talk of forcing it out of business altogether in the USA.[1] Many organisations that have been "on the naughty step" recognise that they may face debarment or contractual renegotiations with clients and governments, as well as customer anger and social scorn for their behaviour.

Regulation

Regulators are harder on pariahs than others, as they need to show that they clamp down harder on those with records of infringements or prior failures and crises. Where most actors in an industry seem to be poor performers (as with banking), there is still a range. The FSA (formerly the UK banking regulator) reputedly saw the banks it regulated on a two-by-two matrix. According to a source:

> We always had a sort of "evil matrix" when it came to the banks. HSBC was generally competent and good, RBS was incompetent and evil, Lloyds was incompetent and good and Barclays was competent and evil.[2]

Guess which banks got the toughest regulatory scrutiny from the FSA?

Revenues and Pricing

Pariahs may face having to reduce prices to attract or retain customers. If low pricing is their normal business model this may not be an issue, but if they seek to maintain a premium positioning it is usually costly. Although PR professionals regard Tesco's handling of the horsemeat crisis in 2013 as highly competent, it coincided with stiff competition from discounters. Tesco is not reputationally in a position to take customers from higher-end rivals when it can't even guarantee its supply chain, and there is evidence that it had to discount heavily to remain competitive with the new entrants to the industry.

Talent

Pariahs should, in theory, also have a harder job attracting the best talent to come to work for them: there are layers of mistrust and risk aversion to overcome, and many candidates may reject them sight unseen. I say "in theory". The data I saw on this during my time in banking was, frankly, equivocal. Head hunters and graduate recruiters in the marketplace told us that there were barriers to getting some very good candidates even to engage at all. But we rarely had to look too hard or long to find well-qualified and capable people prepared to take on most roles. Clearly, pariah companies that can afford to do so usually attract industry insiders who ignore, overlook or simply don't care about the stigma attaching to the brand. (For example, some cynics argued that Goldman Sachs and other banks are attractive to gnarly traders precisely *because* they are so aggressively commercial.) And although there was a drop off in graduate recruiting applications in 2009, there has been little sign of a failure to attract the numbers of ambitious, able, top-quality undergraduate and postgraduate talent either.

A recent Universum study of ideal employers for students placed Goldman Sachs in third place (behind Google and Ernst and Young), with nine other banks in the top 50: JP Morgan 11th, Morgan Stanley 13th, BAML 23rd, HSBC 26th, Citi 30th, Barclays 34th, Credit Suisse 36th, Amex 40th and UBS 41st.

So is the "theory" looking a bit thin, then? I certainly don't believe in bending the data to fit the story, but this is a nuanced success. The worry for banks is that the intellectual quality and moral character, as well as the social diversity, of these candidates may not be as high as they would like. Banks worry that they are just efficiently attracting the smart but greedy (or at least money-oriented) at the expense of others who would, in the longer term, be better leaders and more visionary about fixing their problems. What we will later call mercenaries, rather than heroes or loyalists. We will all watch with more than casual interest to see whether the next generation of leaders in banks can outperform their predecessors.

Employee Engagement

Less obvious than some of these challenges is the ability of perennial pariahs to engage their own employees effectively and sustain high levels of performance. On the one hand, what at Barclays some dubbed the "Mill-wall effect" (named after the nearby East London football club, whose fans[3] have been known to revel in their unpopularity as a way to reinforce their own sense of belonging) can be at least temporarily effective in excluding negative external messages. Such an approach can, however, lead to a high degree of introversion and subjectivity, and is – in my experience – prone to high levels of doubt, rather akin to mass manic depression. So although at one level employees are highly engaged (for example, they may believe in the organisation's mission and purpose) this is undermined by self-critical doubts. Perhaps the detractors are right. Perhaps we *are* overpaid or not performing. Perhaps our industry is indeed a problem.[4] In the industries I know well, this engagement issue is acute at times of exceptional press pressure. When individuals have to defend their decision to work for a company to friends and family who ask critical questions, they may experience real doubt about whether this is the place for them.

However, our employee research usually revealed that such existential doubts were a background factor compared with the typical issues that always impact employee engagement: the quality of caring leadership, the opportunity to develop and grow, and job security and pay were far more often the concerns of the employees. But at the higher levels there is growing awareness in established leadership groups that they cannot rest on their laurels or ignore external critique. These realisations lead to interesting tensions as some groups are placed in positions where they almost have to be accountable to their own colleagues for what has gone wrong. Investment bankers don't like apologising to retail bankers; upstream oil guys don't like apologising to downstream marketers. It goes against the grain of all they have learned about status in their cultures. But sometimes it needs to happen.

Damage to Trust

This book won't spend a lot of time arguing the case that trust is highly challenged at the moment. But it's worth reminding ourselves that we are already paying a price for the scandals of the past and we can reasonably expect the declining levels of trust to continue if nothing changes. One of the best-established sources of data on trust levels across the world is the Edelman Trust Barometer.[5] The 2014 Barometer showed relatively healthy, slightly growing levels of trust in "Business" (58 per cent positive) but declines for "Media" (52 per cent) and "Government" (44 per cent). Business is far behind "NGOs" (64 per cent positive), but it's still interesting that in most geographies more people trust business than they do those who regulate and commentate on it.

Trust in leaders, however remains alarmingly low:

Table 3

TRUST TO DO THE FOLLOWING:	BUSINESS LEADERS	GOVERNMENT LEADERS
Correct issues within industries that are experiencing problems	26%	15%
Make ethical and moral decisions	21%	15%
Tell you the truth, regardless of how complex or unpopular it is	20%	13%
Solve social or societal issues	19%	16%

Table data from http://www.edelman.com/insights/intellectual-property/2014-edelman-trust-barometer/

These data support the view that trust in individuals, and their competence and trustworthiness, is in a poor state; and this undermines their brand aspirations. It seems to me a cause for very serious concern that there is such a large gap between views on trust in business organisations (which are poor enough) and their leaders (which are terrible). If a leader had scores like this on an internal employee engagement survey, you would probably fire them – or at least put them into intensive coaching. It's small recompense that business leaders outperform government leaders: the figures for both are too low to be sustainable. So this data is actually not only disappointing but surprising – a useful distinction all too often forgotten.

Ultimately, the impact of being a pariah over time, as most established pariahs will attest privately, is to weaken the will of the organisation in an important way, and to reduce its capacity to withstand further crises and challenges. Either an organisation accepts – even embraces – its pariah status, as budget airline Ryanair appears to do; or it lives in a form of semi-denial, stuck between the unavoidable truths of some of its failures and the idealisation of what it wants for itself (or even believes to exist). This is not a sustainable position over long periods of time, as cognitive dissonance builds up and dissident "truth tellers" and "whistleblowers" become more vocal. In the end, this unsustainability is a good news story which we will visit in greater depth in Chapter 11, as it suggests that, eventually, pariahs must either reform or fail.

Notes

1 For four years after 2010 BP could not do any work for the US government.
2 Quoted in *Evening Standard* 1 March 2012 (before the LIBOR scandal). http://www.standard.co.uk/business/cityspy/city-spy-barclays-lives-up-to-taxing-reputation-7498819.html
3 Sample Millwall song lyrics from the terraces give a flavour: "Fight, fight, / Wherever we may be / We are the boys from Bermondsey / And we hate you all / Whoever you may be / We are the boys from Bermondsey."
4 See Luyendijk, 2015.
5 http://www.edelman.com/insights/intellectual-property/2014-edelman-trust-barometer/

PART TWO –
PARIAH LIFECYCLE STAGES

3

Pariah Lifecycle Model

Essentially, all models are wrong, but some are useful.[1]

S O SAID THE British statistician George Box[2]. He certainly knew what he was talking about – no single statistical model can capture the complexity of every aspect of the real world. But a useful one helps those who want to understand the world or are searching for where to change it. The same is true – even more true, perhaps – for models of organisations and how they develop.

This chapter sets out a model to describe the lifecycle from birth to death (or rebirth) of pariah organisations. The rest of this book examines these lifecycle stages in detail, and considers at each point how we can reduce the risks to avoid creating or re-creating pariahs. I offer this model not as the only way to explain what goes on in the world of complex organisations and reputational failure, but as a way to connect the behaviour and choices of leaders, particularly where these involve hubris, to ultimate personal and organisational nemesis. The lessons implied by the model may be helpful to several fields of inquiry and study, both in terms of economics, leadership theory and the practical work of organisation development and organisational effectiveness where I have spent most of my career. I am hopeful it can provide insights which will reduce the prevalence and frequency of pariahs.

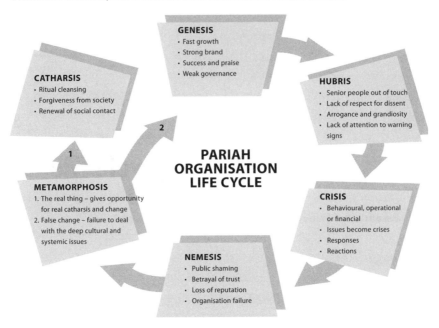

GENESIS
- Fast growth
- Strong brand
- Success and praise
- Weak governance

CATHARSIS
- Ritual cleansing
- Forgiveness from society
- Renewal of social contact

HUBRIS
- Senior people out of touch
- Lack of respect for dissent
- Arrogance and grandiosity
- Lack of attention to warning signs

PARIAH ORGANISATION LIFE CYCLE

METAMORPHOSIS
1. The real thing – gives opportunity for real catharsis and change
2. False change – failure to deal with the deep cultural and systemic issues

CRISIS
- Behavioural, operational or financial
- Issues become crises
- Responses
- Reactions

NEMESIS
- Public shaming
- Betrayal of trust
- Loss of reputation
- Organisation failure

Figure 1 – Pariah Lifecycle Model

Genesis – Beginnings

Pariahs don't arrive from nowhere, fully formed. They have their genesis, their beginning, and it is here that the seeds are sown for what happens subsequently. In this book, I suggest that there are four genesis conditions that enable the hubris of a true pariah to develop. These are:

- Fast growth
- A strong brand
- Success and praise
- Weak governance.

These are related issues. Without some success there is no trusted brand, and thus no disappointment and derision resulting from the promises broken and trust lost. And without apparent success and a degree of pride, it is not possible for organisational or individual hubris to develop. The success may be very limited, and occur only in the eyes of some beholders, but there is some form of "winning" going on before the fall from grace occurs. And if all this success and growth is governed by wise boards and regulators, much of the risk can be reduced and controlled successfully.

In their earliest stages, pariah organisations may look no different from those that will become non-pariahs. But they might well look different from failed organisations which simply have bad business models, or failed execution, or became irrelevant to their markets and customers, including those who are failing but still hold a place in people's hearts (think of these as the anti-pariahs – organisations that fail through a lack of success, despite their strong brands). Jim Collins focuses on these organisations in his book *How the Mighty Fall*[3]. Collins also posits a stage of Hubris as critical to organisational failure (for him it is the first stage of established industry success stories as they move towards irrelevance), followed by Undisciplined Pursuit of More, Denial of Risk and Peril, Grasping for Salvation, and finally Capitulation to Irrelevance or Death. So perhaps hubris will turn out to be doubly problematic! Certainly it's important to remember that, without the right strategy, getting culture right is insufficient for success. Pariahs may also be formed via the re-formation of organisations that went before, either through a formal process (such as merger, acquisition or re-organisation) or informally via some form of inflection point in the organisation's lifespan. This point will be important to note when we discuss the concept and possibility (or otherwise) of catharsis and metamorphosis later in the model.

In this book, I assume that for very many organisations we might consider to be pariahs, the seeds of their pariah status were in effect sown in the previous incarnations of their structures (for example, the rapid series of mergers and acquisitions which Lord Browne achieved at BP), as well as the prior experiences and beliefs of their leaders. In some cases, these previous lives may have been extremely successful (the organisation was performing brilliantly but the world changed the definition of success). In other cases, there is a distinct sense of going through this cycle repeatedly. Antony Jenkins, then Barclays CEO, alluded to this risk when he talked in March 2014 of why the bank was paying higher bonuses in a year of declining performance[4]:

> You get into something of a death spiral. Your brand deteriorates and you can move very quickly from being a first tier player to one in the second or third tier if you don't protect the franchise.[5]

To some extent then, all organisations are – wittingly or unwittingly – creating the genesis of their next pariah cycle all the time. As we will see, the shrewdest, most thoughtful and best-led are able to observe what they are doing and avoid crisis and nemesis. But many are not able to do so, and it is only much later that they realise where the roots of their crises really lay. And for some organisations and leaders, there is sadly never such a realisation, even after they have become defunct. In those cases, I observe that there can be a potentially lethal transfer of ignorance and lack of insight from company to company. And it is often via the transfer of leadership that this occurs. For this reason, we should be very interested in the issue of how to bring in leaders from outside an industry sector, and how to value diversity of all kinds as a source of protection against these challenges.

Hubris – Arrogant Overconfidence

So, given it's almost inevitable that some of the seeds of pariah status exist, what else has to happen to engender a crisis? The second stage in this model is that of hubris.

The term is quite well understood and increasingly common in modern leadership literature, yet is still infrequently analysed with any precision. Perhaps this is because leadership authors wanting to sell books or consultancy prefer to concentrate on positive language and attributes, rather than on analysing failures and disappointments.[6] This is a shame, as often failure can be just as instructive as success.[7] Fortunately, the quality of work done on individual hubris in leaders is high and I hope that, if the term becomes more fashionable, this quality will not be diluted, while insights on preventing and managing the condition will increase.

Hubris is, in Greek thought, naturally paired with nemesis. But not invariably so: the concept is complex and evolved considerably over time. Nevertheless, the idea that hubristic behaviour does not ultimately go unpunished in the world is an attractive one for those who like to see moral retribution. In this model, I take what I hope to be a common-sense view of hubris as a form of individual and collective arrogance, intimately connected to power,[8] the need for and perception of success (see the chapter on genesis), all unmitigated by old-fashioned virtues such as modesty and self-doubt, or by modern leadership virtues such as listening to wise advice, self-knowledge and self-regulation.

Of course, I do not believe all the top leaders of pariah companies are hubristic. Far from it: most of the leaders I have known have usually been wise to the risks of hubris, and worked hard to weed out and contain hubristic behaviour in others, even in themselves. Still, there is a clear sense in which leaders and even junior staff in some pariahs can be *collectively* hubristic, and that even personally modest and self-regulating individuals can act hubristically as they do what they think is required by their organisation.[9] Arrogance, contempt for others, a lack of emotional intelligence, a refusal to believe one or one's organisation can be in the wrong: these are not features confined only to the boardrooms of successful, competitive organisations. They become ubiquitous in the culture, sometimes across a whole industry.

Of course, it's the boss who sets the tone and decides what kinds of behaviour are tolerated and rewarded. At RBS before its near-demise and government bailout, Fred Goodwin was notable for his intolerance and cruelty. He was well known for his sarcastic and demeaning treatment of senior leadership at daily meetings known as "morning beatings" by some:

> "Fred was your classic bully" said one of his most senior executives…
> "I think he had no capacity for compassion. I really mean that."[10]

The key point about hubris is that it reduces the level of honesty, openness and critical, thoughtful debate in the organisation. Hubris always knows best, so it doesn't listen to or tolerate dissent. Superior intelligence, coupled with the trappings of power and success, can lead even the naturally reasonable to become at least temporarily unbalanced, and hubris can affect whole company cultures. Fred Goodwin was the CEO, but he was by a very long way not the only person suffering from hubris in the Scotland of 2008, let alone the global financial services industry of the time. Those who seek to blame him and him alone for RBS's failings are missing the point that hubris occurs in a context, and that is a context of power. It was for the board and the regulators to control and manage Goodwin's power at RBS (or Bob Diamond's at Barclays, come to that). If they did not do so, the blame lies with them and their politician friends, too, for letting the hubris grow and thrive, and for rewarding it. So it's vitally important we dissect hubris and how it can be avoided. In fact, I suggest it's the single most important part of the model for those who want to help organisations avoid pariah status.

Crisis – Point of Failure

Much has been said about crises and what causes them (although the specific link to hubris seems to be somewhat novel). Having experienced some of the most serious practical and reputational crises imaginable, the most experienced pariahs in certain established industries – such as tobacco, pharmaceuticals and mining – have become relatively skilled at preparing for and managing through modern crises.[11] The same cannot be said for organisations or industries new to crisis. Because they are less aware of the Pariah Lifecycle – having not yet seen and survived it – they are usually in denial that they are in it. So the crises that then ensue are a surprise to the afflicted organisations who are not prepared to deal with them effectively. And yet, a very high percentage of crises are not just predictable in theory, but actually are predicted from within the pariah organisation.[12]

Organisations which try actively to plan for and predict crises are, of course, still surprised, and nastily so; but they are inherently better able to adjust crisis response plans and leadership emotional responses, press handling, communication cascades and so forth than organisations that never expect any form of crisis. It's worth noting that substantial organisational learning has at least occurred at this level (i.e. preparing for the next crisis) if not always at the level of preventing crisis in the first place. In Chapter 6 below, I set out some of the different types of crisis that may occur and the damage that can be done by inept crisis management. I also draw some conclusions on the impact of hubris on crisis management and, most critically, the ability to learn from your own and others' crises. I also contrast crises in pariah and non-pariah companies.

Nemesis – Downfall

The tragic necessity of a relationship between hubris and nemesis runs deep, and continues to fascinate students of both individual and organisational pariahdom. It's no accident that Ian Kershaw's magisterial biography of the greatest pariah of all, Adolf Hitler, was published in two volumes respectively titled *Hubris* and *Nemesis*. And yet, we find that this word is very little analysed or mentioned in management or leadership literature.[13] In talks I have given recently, I have challenged some professional services firms (lawyers, auditors and consultants) about whether they might perhaps be locked into a model that rewards them too handsomely for repeated crises, so that they cannot be the agents of change who stop a crisis occurring. It's critical to my model that hubristic organisations face their nemesis, eventually. However, we might observe that experienced pariahs in particular seem adept at shrugging off repeated nemesis events without experiencing actual organisational failure. Although their organisational learning does seem to result in a tempering of hubris and arrogance in subsequent cycles, the fundamental sources of pariah status remain active.

In Chapter 7, we look at the nature of nemesis, and observe that it is during the nemesis phase that the critical decisions are made which lead to ultimate organisational failure or a successful metamorphosis and even the ultimate aim of catharsis – societal forgiveness.

Metamorphosis – Change

Metamorphosis is perhaps one of the more familiar terms in this litany. We learn in school biology classes of this wonderful feature of nature, in which an animal changes from one physical state to another – a magical series of shifts that gives us butterflies from caterpillars, frogs from tadpoles, and so forth. No wonder it's a popular metaphor. But how difficult is it for organisations actually to achieve a real metamorphosis? After the nemesis phase comes the opportunity for real organisational learning and change. In Chapter 8, I examine how different organisations have approached post-crisis learning, and the dangers of the speedy but superficial response. In doing so, I stress the role that leadership plays in setting the tone, the importance of accepting responsibility (and how this differs from legal blame), the need for visible change (and how this must not be merely symbolic but genuinely indicative of new norms) and the difficulties of staying in uncertainty long enough for learning and change to occur. We will also see how easy it is to end up back in the loop again, having learned little at the organisational level.

Catharsis – Cleansing and Redemption

In Chapter 9 we examine the concept of catharsis. 'Catharsis' in Greek means a ritual cleansing, with strong religious connotations not unrelated to the rituals of cleansing described in the Old Testament. Without such a stage of deeper forgiveness and the sense of expiation that it entails, we cannot move on, cannot leave the sins of the pariah in the past. Central to this stage is the concept of a relationship between the organisation and its detractors or critics, and the opportunity for emotional as well as intellectual closure on the past. Symbols and symbolic actions take on central importance here, as do the concepts of trust and, of course, forgiveness. This is perhaps the most unusual feature of my model compared with most others that you may see. Again, it's rooted in the learnings of the first democracy in Athens, which was coming to grips with new legal and other forms of control over power that replaced clan-like behaviour, ostracism and other types of exile. What they understood, and we must re-learn, are the conditions for effective self-knowledge, apology and forgiveness within a social as well as a judicial process.

This model is quite simple in concept: a circle which is doomed to repeat unless clear action is taken to achieve forgiveness and enable organisations and their leaders to change their context. The rest of this book goes into each stage of the lifecycle in more detail, and discusses what can be done to reduce risks for organisations, their leaders and those who govern them.

Notes

1   Box, 1987, p.424
2   Box also put it thus: "Remember that all models are wrong; the practical question is how wrong do they have to be to not be useful." (Ibid., p.74)
3   See Collins, 2009. I formulated my model before reading Collins' book.
4   In the case of Barclays, the challenge was (and at time of writing, still is) how to avoid the reputational pressures from the previous business cycle laying the seeds of tomorrow's demise. By paying up for the investment bankers' 2013 bonuses, Jenkins was attempting to lock in key players and send a message to those he wanted to keep after the major restructuring of the investment bank a few months later. But in doing so, he took a calculated risk that he would create an even worse reputational problem for himself with investors (as a spendthrift slow to cut costs) as well as anti-bank or pay detractors (as not 'getting it' on pay). Both groups disliked the high-pay culture of the bank (as did the Barclays Board) but Jenkins felt that to cut pay directly in line with performance when competitors were openly stealing US staff would be suicidal for the bank.
5   http://www.telegraph.co.uk/finance/newsbysector/banksandfi-nance/10676908/Barclays-We-paid-bonuses-to-avoid-death-spiral.html
6   *Good to Great* has sold well over 4 million copies; *Built to Last* has remained a huge bestseller with similar sales numbers. It's less clear whether *How the Mighty Fall* has sold so well, but it is certainly much less well known.
7   See Syed, 2015, Chapter 1.

8 "Hubris is specific to a context of power". See Petit and Bollaert, 2012, p.271.

9 Salz (2013, Paragraph 2.18) hinted at some of the frustrations picked up in interviews with Barclays stakeholders and employees:
"The institutional cleverness, taken with its edginess and a strong desire to win (particularly in the investment bank), made Barclays a difficult organisation for stakeholders to engage with, especially where those stakeholders were themselves dealing with unprecedented issues. It stretched relationships with regulators and resulted in them and the market questioning some of Barclays' financial information, especially its valuations of illiquid assets, and its control systems. Barclays was sometimes perceived as being within the letter of the law but not within its spirit."

10 Quoted in Martin, 2013. Another passage runs: "If there was an issue or a problem, Fred was more interested in finding a victim and having them crucified. The bollockings were pretty much daily. The new chief executive didn't favour shouting, or at least not very often. His preferred approach once again was the remorseless application of logic, to expose the complete ineptitude of his victim. The assault then culminated in withering sarcasm or laconic asides about their endless capacity for incompetence. 'Fill in the complaints book on your way out of the door,' he told a senior executive who was leaving his office after a particularly bruising encounter."

11 It is no coincidence that one of the best recent works on reputational crisis management lists a number of employees of established pariah industry companies in the acknowledgements. See Griffin, 2014.

12 See Bazerman and Watkins, 2004.

13 An interesting exception is a paper written by a defence analyst for the CIA in the '90s, who explicitly connects the concepts in analysing America's "bad guy" enemies such as Castro and Saddam Hussein. See Ronfeldt, 1994.

4

Genesis – Beginnings

gen·e·sis [jen-*uh*-sis]
noun, plural **gen·e·ses** [jen-*uh*-seez]
an origin, creation, or beginning.

"The Space Shuttle concept had its genesis in the 1960s, when the Apollo lunar landing spacecraft was in full development but had not yet flown."

Opening sentence of the Introduction: Report of the Presidential Commission on the Space Shuttle Challenger Accident, June 1986
(Rogers, 1986)[1]

PARIAH ORGANISATIONS AND their crises have to start somewhere. It's not inevitable that every organisation will become pariah, and of course most don't. But it's perhaps a puzzle what the conditions are that make an organisation prone to pariah crisis and it can be a surprise how far back in time one has to go to identify the genesis conditions. In this chapter, we will examine how pariah organisations get started and how some of what makes them great also contributes to hubris and nemesis later on. In researching this book, I reviewed not only the crises I knew well from personal experience but also many others, from many industries and sectors, about which I could locate detailed analyses. Whilst looking into how these organisations had come to grief, certain themes started to emerge at the system level. This is not a scientific study, however. It is merely a narrative theory with (hopefully) some explanatory power.

It seems to me that in the genesis phase – however short or long that might be – the following four characteristics emerge. It is from these four characteristics that the hubris and cultural problems evolve which cause crises and make subsequent change very difficult. These characteristics are:

+ **Fast growth** – organisations that grow too quickly create phenomenal stresses on themselves, and it can be impossible for learning and leadership to keep up. This makes it harder to avoid crises.

+ **Brand prominence** – prominent organisational brands make promises that the organisation cannot subsequently keep. This means crises are more critical and public than would otherwise be the case.

+ **Success and recognition** – the very success that is necessary to enable the organisation to survive and thrive can start a turbo-charged feedback loop that seeds future hubris. It becomes hard for successful organisations to hear dissent or believe that success won't continue.

+ **Weak governance** – those who should be regulating the organisation and keeping leaders on the straight and narrow fail to do so. This is the principal enabler of hubris, the next stage in the lifecycle.

Before we look at these claims in more detail, let's think a bit about how some of the best-known established pariahs got started and try to see if their origins provide some validation of this theory.

Established Pariah Genesis

As we observed in the previous chapter, the origins of a pariah organisation can be in a new startup or in an organisation that continues the work of predecessors. In any merger, acquisition or organisational restructuring, if people remain from prior organisations I think it's clear that many elements of the organisational culture will also continue. We may perhaps be sceptical whether pariahs necessarily have an "innocent" pre-lapsarian era which preceded their loss of reputation and trust, but it seems a concept worth exploring, for organisations and individual leaders alike. In that analysis, there was a time when the activities of Royal Dutch/Shell (as it then was) or Barclays were not causing such angst and upset as they are wont to do today. Our job, then, is to look for a moment of original sin,[2] a point after which their hubris grew.

Most of the established pariahs mentioned in the first chapter have been in existence for a surprisingly long time. In that regard, they are poor advertisements for my claims for the lethal toxicity of pariah status – it seems to be a rather slow-acting poison in their case. Shell, for example, has been going for well over 100 years. Barclays has its origins in a banking partnership from the late seventeenth century and has been trading under the Barclay name since the mid-1700s. There have been a number of studies of long-lived companies. Christian Stadler in his book *Enduring Success* (2011) conducts an analysis which certainly gives some clues as to the rather conservative values you need to follow if you want your company to survive for many centuries. British companies that have achieved the rare distinction of being over 300 years old include C. Hoare (private banking), James Lock (hatmaker), Shepherd Neame (brewing) and Fortnum & Mason (retail). Stadler points out that if this is a reasonable *potential* life expectancy for a firm (and there are quite a few much older companies in the world, including a Japanese innkeeping company called Hoshi that was founded in 718 AD) then we should be troubled that *actual* average life expectancy is only 12.5 years.[3] The equivalent in human terms would be a world in which we *could* live to 100 or more, but on average we all died aged four or five years old and hardly anyone made it to adulthood, and the maturity of judgement and wisdom that accompanies our ageing. Of course, companies are not people and so the analogy may be false. But even those who support a vigorous Schumpeterian[4] model of creative destruction must surely wonder whether things have gone too far for capitalism when they see such statistics.[5]

Celebrating and Learning from a Centenary at Shell

When you are as old as Shell, it might seem hard to get back to an innocent, simple, original time. But there are ways to do so, not least by paying close attention to the history and origins of the company. I led a team running Shell's senior leadership meetings and we were tasked with working out how to celebrate the centenary of the organisation in a suitable fashion in 2007. Two things stand out for me from our work for that meeting. The first was that, in purely human terms, we were able to find our way back to the firm's beginnings in only three "leaps". Those who were senior leaders with careers of thirty or more years in the company were themselves able to recall being taught about Shell and its culture in their first days by similarly long-serving veterans, who in turn had worked with some of the original founder leaders. By this example, we could show them the incredible depth of legacy and influence that they created for those they led, and those who in turn would be led by those people over the next century. Thus Shell could find its way back to its humble origins in a British shipping company and a Dutch oil-exploration company, not just in terms of our business, but also our leadership and our culture and values. The second thing I remember about our centenary meeting was how difficult it was to tell such a long story in a fair way; there had been considerable controversy in the company's history and it was hard to get the balance right without seeming to collude in some corporate whitewashing, even for our internal audience.

Perhaps the most difficult issue historically for Shell is the way that one of the most critical first-generation leaders, Henri Deterding, was supportive of the Nazis during the 1930s, before his sudden death from angina in 1938. But there was so much else to say about wise, careful growth over many decades, which seemed to me to outweigh giving undue weight to highly contested claims about one leader's behaviour.[6] The precise nature of the Dutch Shell involvement in supporting and financing Nazi activity both in the Netherlands and Germany in the 1930s before Deterding's death, and during the war as part of Dutch collaboration, remains highly contested by historians. Similar issues exist for most large companies operating at that time in these locations: some degree of collaboration was needed to survive and, in many cases, that collaboration was enthusiastic. GE, Kodak and Coca-Cola all have significant Nazi issues in their past, as do more obvious examples such as Allianz and Hugo Boss.

continued

My point is this: if you have been around a long time and grown accordingly, perhaps you have had more chance to make mistakes and hence to have had both good and bad influence on the world. That said, where ambition is limited and there remains a clear focus on a single business (as is the case with all of the British tercentenarians mentioned above) then there doesn't seem to be much of a pariah effect. What one does see in the Shell example, and also in other established pariahs, is that it's very important for healthy cultures to look honestly at their organisational origins, reminding themselves of why they came into being in the first place, and to reflect equally honestly on their great mistakes and ensure they are never repeated.

In many ways, though, pariahs probably don't look massively different from non-pariahs in these early stages. These characteristics are necessary but not sufficient for pariahdom to take hold. So an organisation might conceivably form, grow rapidly, be successful and well known, and have some experience with controversy and yet not become a pariah at all. However, my belief is that it's in these early stages (which might in the past have lasted for years or even decades, but now are typically much shorter) that the seeds of individual and organisational hubris are formed. I am also asserting that this hubris, described in the next chapter, is possibly the most important factor in enabling major reputational crises and organisational nemesis.

By looking at established pariahs, then, we can gain some helpful insights into what created organisational or leadership hubris. These genesis factors are likely to be present quite widely, and it's perhaps best to treat them as risk factors which start to mount up and may eventually prove unmanageable.

Fast Growth

The first genesis condition that concerns us is fast growth. Growth frequently remains an often un-argued-for good in modern commercial life, questioned seemingly only by those who have macro level concerns about sustainability and the environment.[7] But our conception of success, and our economic requirements for revenue growth that outpaces cost growth, make this a tricky norm to negotiate. We are struggling to discover how to manage sustainable growth in ways that make sense for the planet and humankind. But as well as these important issues – indeed, potentially as part of them – there are the questions of growth at the individual organisational level. Particularly in the private sector, we remain unclear how to solve the dilemma between, on the one hand, the need to create new organisations that can meet our needs, provide jobs and economic opportunity; and on the other, how to manage some forms of required decline if we are to achieve a sustainable balance.

The long histories of our favourite established pariahs are so extended that inevitably there are variations in growth. However, their very longevity and economic success are inevitably related to their ability to grow, at least over time, in a way that enabled them to compete successfully in successive eras. In their well-known study (Collins and Porras, 2005) of long-lived successful companies, Jim Collins and Jerry Porras examined the startup phases of several organisations we might also now consider to be pariahs. Their contention is of course that growth is not a bad thing and that the companies they favour as "great" demonstrate their greatness through their superior stock-market performance over time when compared to similarly long-lived competitor companies. I don't dislike Collins and Porras's analysis – it contains many good ideas about how to create a sustainable and successful enterprise. But what both *Built to Last* and its European counterpart, Stadler's *Enduring Success* (2011), make clear is that the faster growth periods of these companies are also the ones that are strewn with the most errors and problems. Or, more precisely, that after some of the key fast-growth stages there are crises which potentially threaten the organisation and which are related to the challenges that later mark out pariahs.

The key issues in the past seem to have been that fast growth strains many things in an organisation:

- The organisation's **physical ability** to meet external growth demands. This can result in very pragmatic issues such as running out of office space, struggling to manufacture sufficient products to meet demand or being unable to cope with sudden surges in website usage.

- The **learning ability** of the organisation becomes stressed in multiple dimensions. Fast growth reduces the time available to test things. This can reduce the safety of new technologies to the understanding of new customers or markets. Country entry and international growth also create massive gaps in learning as the nuanced understanding of other cultures, customers and suppliers is accelerated.

- On the **people** side, very rapid growth places a dual challenge into the mix: growing the workforce and growing leaders to lead the organisation. Wherever you have very rapid organisational growth you see the considerable challenge of bringing in sufficient numbers of competent new people to staff it up. Those people need to be ingrained in the purpose, values and culture of the organisation, to learn what it's all about, how it does things and why, to learn from mistakes and near misses of the past, as well as to do all the hard work of actually growing it further.

- At the same time, and critically for all of the above, **leadership** demands grow exponentially, typically far faster than the actual leaders of the organisation can reasonably keep up. It's as though an infant is being asked to learn to walk, then immediately to run a marathon, without the intervening build up.

So, although fast growth is generally presented, particularly in business, as a nice problem to have, we can see that many of the mistakes that result in pariah crises have their origins in the desire to keep up with growth paths that exceed the organisational capacity to cope. In Chapter 10 – Pariahs of the Future – we will see how the very rapid growth models of technology make these companies as prone to hubris (if not more so) as their "old economy" predecessors.

Brand Prominence

All of our established pariahs have big, well-known brands. Everyone, in other words, has heard of them. This prominence of the organisational brand (to contrast with a product brand[8]) is something that most organisations have always promoted. And there are sound reasons for doing so: it's important that others know who you are and what you do, and it's increasingly important in the so-called war for talent: if no-one knows who you are, people are presumably unlikely to want to work for you. But having a brand is not all good. Having a brand, deliberately or otherwise, sets up a bunch of expectations and implied or explicit promises to the outside world. That's not inherently a problem. After all, that's how brands are meant to work. And all those wonderful companies with 300 or more years of history, like Fortnum & Mason, are famous because they have delivered, consistently, on those promises.

But pariahs become pariahs because, for many different reasons, they are not able to deliver on their promises. As we will see, this creates complex webs of intrigue as pariahs seek to "thin slice" their stakeholder groups in the hope that at least some promises can be true for some of them, some of the time. But we will also conclude that the very impossibility of doing this effectively across a globalised organisational brand might make it a good idea to tone down or even turn off the organisation's brand, because of the risks it creates.

Success and Recognition

The third precursor condition for hubris created in the genesis phase of the Pariah Lifecycle is the very success and recognition that the organisation and its founders presumably seek. Organisations, like individuals (and including their individual leaders), are built up by the press and their own marketing efforts. Investors are thrilled that they have backed a winner and want to hear more about what a wise choice they have made, and how much more money they are going to make. One only has to look at a random article from *Forbes*, *Fortune* or *BusinessWeek* to see the sort of excessive adulation that is accorded routinely to companies coming to prominence. All too often, the exuberant praise (pun intended) turns out to be overstated, as the *Economist* noted when an Uber executive got himself in the news for all the wrong reasons:

> On November 17th [2014] it emerged that an Uber executive, Emil Michael, had said at a private dinner that the firm should consider spending $1m to dig up dirt on its critics in the media, in particular Sarah Lacy, the editor of Pando, a tech-news site. Mr Michael has since apologised. Travis Kalanick, Uber's boss, said on Twitter that his remarks showed "a lack of humanity and a departure from our values and ideals", but brushed off calls for Mr Michael to resign.
>
> Although it is hardly an excuse, the remarks were a reaction to a series of highly critical articles on Uber, in particular by Ms Lacy and her publication. She has argued that Mr Kalanick, known for his libertarian views and combativeness, is an example of Silicon Valley's "asshole problem", meaning that venture capitalists increasingly invest in entrepreneurs who know neither scruples nor social graces. Most recently, she accused the firm of "sexism and misogyny" because its

branch in Lyon, France, had offered to pair passengers with "hot chick" drivers. She says she has deleted the Uber app from her smartphone.[9]

As I originally wrote this piece, the latest Uber controversy was being debated and digested at warp speed on the Internet – as befits an Internet company. But even if this particular storm blew over for the highly successful Uber, questions now remained about its culture, its ethics, its attitude to women and a host of other things that may give users and investors, as well as potential regulators, pause for thought.

The question of interest to me is: has Uber become a super-successful, $62 billion valuation, 300 city, 58 country, $1 billion revenue a month company in a mere six years *because of*, or *despite*, a culture that clearly leaves a lot to be desired in terms of maturity and ethical direction? Are we watching a new pariah in the making or is this a case that disproves my theory? CEO Travis Kalanick, 39-year-old libertarian and founder of the company, had already established a controversial reputation for himself long before this crisis, and had not endeared himself to feminists by describing his newfound attractiveness to women as "Boober" in a public speech. Despite his immediate attempts to distance himself from Michael's remarks in a series of tweets, Kalanick was thus inevitably on the defensive. Already, Uber's success seems to have become an immediate precursor to hubris and hence crisis. It's hard not to see Kalanick as an example of a geeky, socially awkward, smart, deliberately annoying type trying to follow in the gilded footsteps of Bill Gates, Steve Jobs, Larry Paige and Mark Zuckerberg. And it's even harder not to feel that, in the hard-driving, caffeinated, sophomoric and still very male-dominated world of tech startups, hubris is practically a goal for too many; and that those who are older and wiser are not doing their job of holding back these heroes from their own self-destruction.

Weak Governance

Perhaps the most dangerous genesis condition, the hardest to diagnose and to treat sufficiently quickly, is weak governance. Whether it's at the company board or the industry regulator, it's in governance that the only real restraint on executives who must resist hubris occurs. If governance is weak and easily subverted, then in combination with the other conditions noted above, hubris can flourish. The good news is that, where fast-growing and successful companies have strong, active boards and alert, focused regulators, hubris can be avoided. At their best, boards and regulators deliver in three ways:

- **Attention to business model and strategy** – good governance has a broad and deep understanding of the ecosystem in which the organisation is operating and its potential impacts and challenges. Startups often have to make dramatic changes in direction in their early stages and boards have to remain alert if they are to add value as the models change. Selecting the right strategy is notoriously challenging and boards have to be able to rein in leaders who are wasting resources, damaging customer relationships or pursuing unjustified personal hobbies. Regulators too are in touch with more than how the existing industry works, but can imagine and steer the future alongside industry players.

- **Attention to talent and leadership** – the top boards and regulators of potentially dangerous industries pay huge attention to the selection and development of the right people to lead their organisations. Regulators actually police who gets allowed to occupy critical positions by managing qualifications and vetting procedures. The focus should be on what serves the organisation and the system, not vice versa. Good talent management is therefore a most powerful antidote to the potential individual hubris that leaders may experience as they are exposed to power.

- **Attention to the what and the how of execution** – good governance is attentive not just to what gets done (though that is measured and monitored carefully) but also to how it is done. The values that are displayed and cared about in the early growth stages set the stage for the future and are the basis for success or failure later on. Where little or no attention is paid to how the results have been delivered, it's pretty obvious that in a fast-growth, demanding environment operational, financial and above all behavioural crises will occur.

So getting the right board is incredibly important. It is in this area that we also see the origins of the deep rationale for separating a company's chair and CEO. The tension of that relationship is there for a good reason.

Inverse Genesis Conditions

Conversely, organisations which do not have these characteristics seem to be much less prone to later pariahdom. This is not something we should find surprising:

- Organisations that **grow slowly** are likely to be more cautious, have more experience at running the business at a given scale and have time to grow leaders who are ready for the next stage of expansion. The periods of slow but steady growth in the history of Shell and Barclays (or any other pariah company) are not typically the ones that seem to engender their reputational crises, unless they have become periods in which stagnation occurs (as was the case at Shell with the reserves crisis).

- Organisations that **deliberately shun having a big corporate brand presence**[10] seem much less likely to become pariahs. It's not clear whether this is simply down to the difficulty this creates for NGOs in creating brand presence where it does not exist, and/or that more modest cultures are less likely to indulge in the behavioural or other failures which relate to pariah crises.

- Organisations that are **never successful** tend not to grow or develop brands very well. If there has been no track record of success, it's harder for press, NGOs and customers to be so disappointed later on and nemesis is muted. But although this may be a good recipe for avoiding pariahdom, it is clearly also not a great recipe for survival and indeed the lack of success may create issues which become crises later. This is not a route to salvation in the private sector, though some would argue this is less the case in the public or third sectors.

- Organisations with **strong governance** benefit from the wisdom and support they get, and their leaders are less exposed to the challenges of unrestrained power, such as having to pretend to omniscience.

I am not, of course, suggesting that we should not create fast-growing, well-known companies that take on risk. But we should be concerned that some elements of conventional capitalist success (or even success for organisations in the public or third sectors) are so well aligned with the conditions for later pariahdom. It seems very likely that what we are really describing here are the conditions for hubris, and it is this hubris that is the actual key to subsequent crisis and nemesis.

For this reason, we will focus in this book more on how we can avoid hubris than try to advocate a new post-capitalist sustainable economics. But that's not to say that we should not ask some big questions about the role of the limited liability company, the faceless Whitehall bureaucracy or the self-congratulatory charity in creating the conditions for their own subsequent demise.

RECOMMENDATIONS

1. Manage Genesis Conditions Mindfully, Especially Governance

We noted above the conditions for pariah genesis (growth, brand, success and weak governance). But an organisation that has no growth, no brand, no success and takes no risks, even with strong governance, is not going to be much of an organisation. So what to do?

Firstly, we should stop treating **very rapid growth** as an unalloyed good. The speed at which modern organisations can grow is unprecedented, thanks largely to globalisation and digital technology. Facebook, for example, grew from a dorm-room experiment in early 2004 to a 500-million-user social-media organisation in July 2010, some two years before its eventual IPO. There's nothing wrong in that, but we should not underestimate the challenges of scaling at such a fabulous rate. Organisations that grow exponentially need to be hyper-vigilant about the likelihood that they are creating risks, and must put in place the governance, learning, development and risk measurement that can – at least in part – mitigate them. In particular, they need to ensure that just as their operations, logistics and manufacturing capabilities have to scale up, so too does their leadership, its understanding of the world, its sophistication and savvy. In his book *In the Plex*, Stephen Levy recounts Google's astonishing challenges in staying ahead of spiralling demand as they build out its massive server farms in Europe. Before settling on a site in Belgium, a team examined an abandoned Soviet-era minibus factory in Latvia:

> In the center of the building was a giant pit, filled with some acidic
> liquid, and [Cathy] Gordon [the responsible executive] couldn't help
> but wonder whether any bodies were quietly decomposing in the stew.

The group went to the area where the power facilities were located, and it looked to Gordon like they were on an old horror movie set, a Gulag Archipelago version of Dr Frankenstein's lab. One of the hosts leaned over and spoke in a confidential whisper, heavy with Slavic accent: "Don't get too near those things," he said, "Basically we don't know if they could kill you."

(Levy, 2011, p.196)

Google has perhaps done better than any organisation in history at managing the physical and logistical challenges of its own non-linear growth. But this example shows how the need to work in new markets where one does not know all the risks makes it hard not to fly blindly. If rapid growth is not to become one of the signature issues in your organisation's reputational demise, it's vital to get ahead of the demand cycle and appreciate the range of challenges it will pose to your organisation in every dimension. This is particularly true of leadership: if leaders are not growing at the same pace as the organisation and its complexity, failure is inevitable. See Chapter 5 for some more specific recommendations on how to manage these issues.

Brand is perhaps the most tricky area on which to advise. It is so counterintuitive to tell ourselves that we should not set up powerful, global, well-known brands, when all around us they appear to be central to our lives. But if we accept the arguments in this book about the genesis of pariah hubris and crisis, we also need to recognise that creating strong organisational brands carries significant risks. Perhaps the most satisfactory solution is to separate the organisation brand (including the employee brand) from the subsidiary or product brands. Of course, this is not always possible, but it should be worth consideration for any startups hopeful for rapid success. Associated British Foods, for example, does this well. Few consumers know who they are, but they are highly aware of brands such as Ryvita, Twinings or Silver Spoon. Non-pariahs will find a way to construct strong product and organisational brands based on values to which they can stay true, maintaining their integrity. They will probably avoid making claims that are hostages to fortune, such as "Don't Be Evil". But they will face severe challenges, because brands are long on promises – it's what they are all about. As any parent knows, to promise (or even to appear to promise) is to risk creating disappointment. Keeping honestly to the promises you are making is not something that every organisation will be able to do.

Success is, as they say, its own reward. There is absolutely no way that we should suggest that it's a bad thing or allow others to subvert the genuine claims being made here. I am not against success, but I am against believing your own hype: there is a significant difference. And in particular, I think we should advocate careful consideration of what success is, how it should be measured and who gets to judge it. So I remain very suspicious about unbalanced praise and more interested in balanced criticism that can help you improve. Organisations that avoid pariah status will cultivate an ambivalent attitude to their own success. On the one hand, they will welcome it and want to understand how it has occurred. On the other, they will be somewhat paranoid about those who praise them to the skies (and so they should). To be admired is a fine thing. But seeking out admiration for its own sake is a value we should be suspicious of – it's a predecessor to aspects of hubris, particularly narcissism. We are human beings, so we won't get rid of it, but a fine start would be to put an end to all those ridiculous award ceremonies where everyone gives each other prizes, including those for "Most Admired". It's nice to have a black-tie party to celebrate excellence, but you'll know when you have admiration worth having. And it doesn't come in the shape of a lucite block sponsored by BigCo. It comes in the way your employees and their relatives speak of you, how customers rate your products, how the City rates your stock, how your regulator views you, how many people want to come and work for you and how long you stay alive as an organisation without shameful crises.

As we repeatedly see, the central virtues, the saving graces and antidotes to the precursors to pariah crises are the values of humility and integrity. I write those words with due concern for sounding preachy. But the risks are real. In the NHS's Mid-Staffs scandal,[11] it was the focus on the wrong outputs (waiting lists) over the right ones (patient care and outcomes) that was central to the issues faced. In banking, seeing success solely in terms of profitability, ROE and personal bonus outcomes rather than client benefits or any pretence at utility was equally disastrous. So, the battle over how to define these output measures, to be clear what "success" should look like, is absolutely critical. If success for the organisation is, truly, financial profit, then that is still fine, by the way. One can run a ferociously competitive financial organisation with high integrity and humility; I simply don't buy it that unashamedly seeking profit necessarily implies deceit and braggadocio. We have let recent events blind us to the centuries during which bankers were boring, staid and dull. There needs to be integrity between reality and what the organisation claims, what the brand promises, what people then do. In reality, no organisation of any sophistication or size can reduce its measures of success to only one or two things, and any search for such simplicity is doomed (though lucrative for consultants and accountants).

Whether one is a devotee of the *Value Imperative* (Kontes and Mankins, 1994) or the *Balanced Scorecard* (Kaplan and Norton, 1996) is not the only issue – it's about whether people realise that success is multi-faceted, that what one stakeholder group will cheer will be booed by others (or by the same ones at another time, when they tire of it); that to survive for a long time means adjusting success to the needs of the times, and all of this without sacrificing a sense of purpose and values. Small wonder we retreat to the measurable, to "metrics" and "KPIs" and particularly to financials as our success proxies. They are comparable, objective, fair. Or they are until we discover the profits have been manipulated, because everyone values profits just a little bit too much. The organisations that get this right will have to avoid running away (as too many do) from the complexity of success in their world. They will certainly have to deliver financial outcomes for owners and the City. But they must deeply acknowledge that these are not all there is and that profits are not real; they are virtualisations, models of real activities going on in the world that have implications for many people operating in their systems. Sadly, after years of fine talk, no discernible progress has occurred in accounting beyond the basics of Luca Pacioli's fifteenth-century innovation of accruals accounting. But we all know there is more to life than this, and that more can and must be done to redefine success beyond the basics of financial survival.

What to say about **risk taking**? Simply to start up an organisation is to take significant risks – ask any entrepreneur. (Actually, don't bother: they will likely tell you whether you ask or not.) But these need not be mindless risks. Organisations that want to manage risk taking need to take a professional approach to risk, which starts with taking risk seriously. It's not, as some seem to think, the act of some grey dullard to have a risk register or to calculate financial risks properly, to think actively about what can destroy your dreams and what you value. It's a mature act, and if this book is about anything, it is about advocating some maturity in how we run our organisations, especially the large, complex ones with the power to harm us. We are not children. The opposite of understanding risk is not youthful innovation: it's blind stupidity. And when we look at risk, we need to do so accepting the reality of randomness (including the possibility – the probability – that we have benefited from good fortune to have succeeded to date):

> Lucky fools do not bear the slightest suspicion that they may be lucky fools – by definition, they do not know that they belong to such a category.

(Taleb, 2001)[12]

Governance is perhaps the single most crucial area in which much can be done from the outset.

First, it's essential that organisations have boards that are fit for purpose. For larger public organisations, there are already copious requirements specifying how their boards should be formed and structured, what kinds of skills are required and even how their performance should be assessed. In the UK these range from formal codes[13] for the large FTSE companies to guidance covering trustee boards for charities[14] or even the boards of school governors[15]. The FRC code sets out the basic context for this guidance well and it's worth reading two key clauses in full:

2. The first version of the UK Corporate Governance Code (the Code) was produced in 1992 by the Cadbury Committee. Its paragraph 2.5 is still the classic definition of the context of the Code:

> Corporate governance is the system by which companies are directed and controlled. Boards of directors are responsible for the governance of their companies. The shareholders' role in governance is to appoint the directors and the auditors and to satisfy themselves that an appropriate governance structure is in place. The responsibilities of the board include setting the company's strategic aims, providing the leadership to put them into effect, supervising the management of the business and reporting to shareholders on their stewardship. The board's actions are subject to laws, regulations and the shareholders in general meeting.

3. Corporate governance is therefore about what the board of a company does and how it sets the values of the company. It is to be

distinguished from the day to day operational management of the company by full-time executives.

For private organisations, it's less clear what should be going on and who should be doing it. One of the ongoing challenges of managing the massive growth of tech organisations has been how to provide both the right kind of advisory and supervisory guidance and governance for founders and executives in the periods before, as well as after, their IPOs. So in many cases the problem here is simply that there isn't any governance in place. However, the 2015 Volkswagen emissions scandal demonstrated that, even where the much-admired German system of management and supervisory boards was in place, disaster can still strike. Having formal boards doesn't solve the problem. What matters is not just the right forms of governance (e.g. the separation of the duties of the chairman and the CEO), but the more tricky question of the right operation of that governance. Most critically it's no good having all the right people on the board representing diverse points of view if they are incompetent to ask the right questions and hold the executives accountable, or socially cowed into silence by the dominance of certain individuals. This is so obvious that it's practically a platitude. So why is it so difficult? There are many views, but if one looks across a wide range of crises and subsequent investigations, several themes emerge:

I.   **Balance of support and challenge** – boards and their chairs need to be constantly vigilant about balancing support for the executive with challenge. Being at odds is not only socially uncomfortable, but a reputation issue in its own right – and is usually fatal for the CEO in the long run. But getting too cosy, so you can no longer be tough on performance and getting hard questions asked and answered, is fatal for the board. On the whole, crises occur more because of the latter type of failure than the former (i.e. too often, the board *trusts* the CEO too much, rather than remaining politely sceptical). Time and again, from Lehman Brothers to Kids Company, dominant CEO personalities are not managed effectively by boards, and this difficult issue (what is in the best interest of the organisation as a whole – should we tolerate "rockstars" if they appear to be successful?) tends then to permeate down through the organisations in question. In other words, boards can and should create tensions with their executives, and be prepared to see the CEO leave rather than let them cause damage to that organisation and its reputation.

II. **Technical competence** – as organisations become larger, more global and more complex, it becomes harder and harder for executives to understand and manage them (as we discuss elsewhere in this book). But it's also hard for boards to develop the right capacity to stay ahead of the challenges that face the executive, predict and manage those challenges, and – critically – decide whether the CEO is the right person to lead the organisation. The CEO (rightly) has the dominant understanding of the operations and the complexities of the organisation; the board have to decide what the right questions are that will find out how things are actually operating, and how good are the CEO's plans for the future. This is one of the key reasons that historically CEOs have moved up to chair their own organisations: who better to hold the new executive to account than someone who knows the details of the organisation? However, this is a recipe for inbreeding and perhaps even wilful blindness. We need to be more prepared to train non-executives who did not start their careers in a given area on the key technical risks and how to probe for them, than to assume that only those who have worked in an industry are fit to govern it.

III. **Diversity** – having a diverse range of non-executives is now recognised as being vital for success. However, there can be tensions for boards in balancing improved diversity (e.g. on gender) with maintaining or increasing the technical experience base of the board (see above). It may be that in the future there will be more prescription on the formation of boards to require that there is indeed adequate representation from a wider range of sources – geographies in which the organisation operates, gender, race, professional backgrounds, perhaps even democratic requirements that allow stakeholder groups to become represented adequately. This will also force a greater emphasis on preparation, training and perhaps even qualification for board membership.

IV. **Rotation of talent** – boards need to be renewed and this is an issue that is recognised and managed in the public board codes mentioned above. Again, this is an issue of balance around rotating not just the chair and non-execs but also the CEO. In Chapter 11, I discuss three different types of employee: loyalists, mercenaries and heroes. We ought to be cognisant of the need to manage the balance of board membership in the same way, balancing the wisdom, experience and organisational memory of long-serving members with the challenge and disinterested objectivity of those who work as NEDs for a living.

V. **Board culture and effectiveness** – this is perhaps the most difficult area to define – it will be different for each board. But the phrase in the Code above about "setting the values of the company" needs to start in the boardroom. Board effectiveness is a subject about which there is no single emergent standard, and there are question marks over why the rigorous systems of 360-degree assessment and performance review so prevalent in the executive ranks are not always maintained across the governance group. The best boards are not just politely asking each other what they think of each other and the chairman or CEO. They are conducting systematic reviews of multiple stakeholder groups' views, in particular testing their performance in managing risks for the organisation. But this is hard stuff. It takes up time that could be spent on actually governing. Only when it becomes a mandatory and primary feature of the board's operations – as performance management is to the executive – will we see significant improvements in this area. When we do, I believe boards will have the opportunity to get substantial early warning and an extended set of insights into not just their own performance but also that of the CEO, and hence an early warning on development of hubris. But we will still face the risk that if the board itself is mono-cultural, and particularly if it is composed of individuals who are themselves hubristic (especially the chair), then this process solution won't solve the problem. It's very hard to mandate the self-doubt required for self-improvement.

VI. **Size** – finally, a short word on size. Large boards in theory allow more diversity, a wider range of technical input, and hence different and better challenges to cosy relationships among a group of like-minded individuals in a power clique. And it's more likely you can be quorate when some board members can't be there. But small boards can allow closer relationships of trust and mutual challenge rather than polite collusion. What's the right size? Most experienced chairs and board members think that effective boards are at their best somewhere between 7 and 15 people. But the key is not just how many people are involved. What matters is the effectiveness of the team, and the level of trust between the team members. Chairs should spend far more time than they do on these meta-issues about team functioning if they want boards to perform properly. And yet we still see away days and other attempts to help the board step back and consider their own operations treated as luxurious extras, not as essentials without which the board cannot function.

The issues surrounding regulatory supervision are similar, but with the added requirements to connect to both the narrow legal requirements and the wider political pressures of the day. For regulators, the central questions remain about their competence, their pace and their ability to follow through on their findings and concerns. These topics are not ones I will go into in depth here, but it seems clear from the issues surrounding industries as diverse as banking, oil and gas, and now automotive that all is not well. The sheer complexity of regulating global organisations using national regulatory models is particularly suspect.

Although it will be hard in the earliest stages to avoid all the risk factors of a pariah organisation, it can be done. The culture of the most pariah-proof organisations will be determined yet modest; proud in the right way of their own success, but aware and sceptical that no one measure can sustainably represent success; and thoughtful about the risks they take but not reckless about what could destroy them and others. This may sound like a counsel of perfection, but I believe sustainable organisations will create these foundation conditions for real, lasting success. To do so requires a little thought and work up front, but the benefits will last a lifetime.

2. Get Purpose and Values Right

Purpose and values have become very fashionable in OD circles lately. The literature advocating running organisations on the basis of purposive principles and supporting values is vast, and also as old as the modern organisation. Some of the longest lasting and most successful (by any metric) organisations turn out to have very clear senses of purpose, and perhaps even clearer values of how to behave, often deeply tied up with some concept – however folksy and antiquated – of sustainability, of lasting value. As Barclays faced its recent crises, commentators were lining up to remind its leaders that its origins lay in the venerable tradition of the Quaker movement and their values of honesty, integrity and plain dealing.[16]

Management consultants have not been slow to push for more purpose-centric organisations in recent years. Partly building on the success of the analysis in Collins and Porras's book *Built to Last*, consultant Nikos Mourko-giannis produced his book *Purpose* in 2006, well before the current raft of crises rose to a peak. In the book, Mourkogiannis suggests that the organi-sational purpose that drives great companies (he has little to say about the public sector, although he acknowledges the principles apply to these organisations as well) derives from one of four moral purposes (discovery, excellence, altruism and heroism), each of which has a particular associated philosophical tradition. Mourkogiannis's argument is that a clear purpose makes everything better in the organisation:

> An organization with a strong sense of Purpose does not just make
> people feel better. It also creates a strong sense of direction and obliga-
> tion. Indeed, it raises morale at least partly because it creates this sense
> of direction. This combination of energy and direction makes it effec-
> tive at stimulating action.

> (Mourkogiannis, 2006, p.122)

In recent years, many others have joined Mourkogiannis in proclaiming the importance of organisational purpose[17], typically in the context of sustain-able, multi-stakeholder, long-term and ethical leadership. The new consensus, the zeitgeist of modern business literature, has become very friendly to notions of purpose and values. Why is that? Have we discovered the Philoso-pher's Stone at long last? Or is it just the latest craze that will soon fade and be replaced with a reversion to a focus on hard performance and profits in a never-ending cycle of novelty? In the absence of any viable control-group experiments, who knows? Hopefully, we can get to some eternal truths around managing complex human organisations which last beyond a few months or even years of validity.

To test the claim that purpose and values matter and are worth installing in your organisation, let's look at the recent history of values-based organisations, at least from a UK perspective. Running organisations for purpose not profit was not exactly the hallmark of the post-1979 Thatcher era, which increasingly under Major and then Blair and Brown became obsessed with running even public-sector organisations on the basis of efficiency and effectiveness (or so they said). However, by the 1990s it had become all too clear that some of the corruption and incompetence that Northcote-Trevelyan had sought to root out in their original nineteenth-century reforms[18] were recurring, notably in Parliament itself, but potentially throughout the sector. In 1994, John Major set up the Committee on Standards in Public Life in response to the growing tide of public revulsion and anger at "sleaze" amongst politicians.[19]

In his speech on establishing the Committee, Major said:

> It is important that the public have confidence in our system of public administration, our methods of making public appointments, the conduct of people in authority and the financial and commercial activities of public figures. It has always been the wish of this House that British Government, Parliament and administration should be entirely free of malpractice and I am determined to ensure that that is so.

The terms of reference for the Committee were:

> To examine current concerns about standards of conduct of all holders of public office, including arrangements relating to financial and commercial activities, and make recommendations as to any changes in present arrangements which might be required to ensure the highest standards of propriety in public life.[20]

Lord Nolan, the first chair of the Committee (which still exists) gave his name to the Nolan Principles for those in public office. It is from these thoughtful and well-constructed principles that many organisations in both the public and the private sectors in the UK and elsewhere have sought to create their own formalised value system:

Selflessness – holders of public office should act solely in terms of the public interest. They should not do so in order to gain financial or other benefits for themselves, their family or their friends.

Integrity – holders of public office should not place themselves under any financial or other obligation to outside individuals or organisations that might seek to influence them in the performance of their official duties.

Objectivity – in carrying out public business, including making public appointments, awarding contracts, or recommending individuals for rewards and benefits, holders of public office should make choices on merit.

Accountability – holders of public office are accountable for their decisions and actions to the public and must submit themselves to whatever scrutiny is appropriate to their office.

Openness – holders of public office should be as open as possible about all the decisions and actions they take. They should give reasons for their decisions and restrict information only when the wider public interest clearly demands.

Honesty – holders of public office have a duty to declare any private interests relating to their public duties and to take steps to resolve any conflicts arising in a way that protects the public interest.

Leadership – holders of public office should promote and support these principles by leadership and example.

When the Nolan principles were launched in the first report of the Committee in 1995 they were perhaps not fully appreciated. Most of the reaction at the time came from MPs who were worried about being portrayed as venal and corrupt, or losing control of self-regulation.[21] After six months of work, the Committee reported and found that:

> We cannot say conclusively that standards of behaviour in public life have declined.[22] We can say that conduct in public life is more rigorously scrutinised than it was in the past, that the standards which the public demands remain high, and that the great majority of people in public life meet those high standards. But there are weaknesses in the procedures for maintaining and enforcing those standards. As a result people in public life are not always as clear as they should be about where the boundaries of acceptable conduct lie. This we regard as the principal reason for public disquiet. It calls for urgent remedial action.[23]

It's impossible to read these words now without a wry smile, knowing what turgid times were ahead for MPs, the NHS, civil servants and others in "public life". There were to be no quick fixes here. So should we regard this effort as a failure? A recent report[24] of the Committee recognises the challenges, but also the ongoing value of having the Nolan principles:

> In the face of these changes, our research shows that public support for the seven principles endures. These principles are not merely theoretical concepts, they have practical consequences for ordinary people in receipt of public services. The public must feel reassured that for example safeguarding or educating children, caring for the elderly, or security arrangements at our prisons, are carried out in line with these expected behaviours.

In other words, as we observed in the first two chapters, expectations are ahead of reality on delivery, but that does not mean reality is worse than it was before. The process of challenging public servants continues to this day and has now spread to the private sector. The underlying base belief is that, on the whole, people are honest and decent, but they need to operate in an environment which makes it very clear what the rules are, and to be unambiguous about clarifying expectations up front. Only where they do so, and where their leaders are clear about upholding a culture which can make these values real in decisions and behaviour, can you expect trust to build between the electorate and those who serve them. We might raise eyebrows at whether execution against the Nolan principles has been adequate, given the many scandals and crises referenced across the public sector in recent years from government department IT project failures to NHS governance failures and police/press corruption. But the fact that delivery is difficult does not make the principles ignoble or not worth aspiring to. In fact, that's the point of them.

The disasters of the 2008–9 financial crisis and the heavy criticisms that came in their wake have reignited interest in the notion that organisations, and companies in particular, should think hard about their purpose and then align everything else (including corporate "values") with that purpose. One of the most high-profile efforts to get purpose and values right was launched at Barclays by the new CEO Antony Jenkins soon after he took on the role after Bob Diamond's departure in the summer of 2012 (the project was first publicised externally in early 2013 when the new strategy was launched). Jenkins was convinced from his experiences taking over an ailing Barclaycard, and subsequently the retail business for the bank, that the most important first task for an incoming leader is to clarify the purpose of the organisation as the north star by which all subsequent actions and decisions could be grounded. Given the crisis that had just occurred in the bank when Jenkins took over, it struck some as bold and brave to take this approach, but to a great extent he was following the zeitgeist established in the UK after Nolan. This was the sort of thing that the Establishment now required and it would have been a curiously bone-headed executive who could not have seen this after watching his predecessor's demise. In July 2012, a *Guardian* article had (rightly) poked angry fun – on the day of Bob Diamond's resignation – at the gap between the bank's corporate social responsibility reporting and the realities of its actions:

> The Barclays Citizenship Report and 2015 strategy lack credibility because the company has failed to live up to the opening statement that it has a "clear sense of its business purpose – to help individuals, communities, businesses and economies progress and grow."
>
> Is this the same company that manipulated interest rates for its own gain and hoodwinked small businesses into buying complex insurance that they did not need? Surely not.
>
> What Barclays' behaviour shows is that its culture, and that of many other banks, is rotten to the core in some areas of their business. Greed and fear have run riot and the idea of being in service is left to the bank's branch cashiers and community departments.[25]

So it was understandable that the launch of the new purpose and values six months later, though welcomed, was treated with some scepticism. Anthony Salz's report (published some months later, in April 2013, but reflecting the views of the time that produced the Jenkins purpose and values statements) noted – rather casually, as though no other view could possibly be true – that:

> Public opinion also tends to be more generous to those organisations that seem to be trying to do the right thing, or that have an appreciable social purpose.

> (Salz, 2013, 2.4)

Salz noted that, whatever was written in HQ-authored reports, the bank lacked purpose or values:

> But the overriding purpose at Barclays in the lead up to the crisis and beyond was expressed in terms of increases in revenues and profits, return on equity and competitive position. The drift in standards was manifest in the events that set the context for this Review.

> (Salz, 2013, 2.13)

And later:

> We believe that the business practices for which Barclays has rightly been criticised were shaped predominantly by its cultures, which rested on uncertain foundations. There was no sense of common purpose in a group that had grown and diversified significantly in less than two decades. And across the whole bank, there were no clearly articulated and understood shared values – so there could hardly be much consensus among employees as to what the values were and what should guide everyday behaviours. And as a result there was no consistency to the development of a desired culture.

> (Salz, 2013, 2.15)

Salz's 37 recommendations included numerous references to alignment with purpose and values. So there was essentially a consensus already when the bank went down this route that there needed to be meaningful, deep-seated and well-engineered changes in this area, not just bland PR claims in a few documents that most of the bank's employees would never see. Jenkins was certainly not democratic in the process of setting organisational purpose: he would subsequently tell Barclays top 150 executives that the purpose – "helping people achieve their ambitions – in the right way" – was not negotiable. Although the purpose was not created by a democratic process, it was more than just a personal whim. Such a purpose, as we observed above, aligned well with what many external stakeholders, including politicians, wanted to hear the bank saying. It was also sufficiently flexible (or if you prefer, vague) to remain meaningful for each of the very different banks that comprised the Group at that time, ranging from retail bankers in Africa to some of Wall Street's most aggressive traders.

It's worth pointing out that the multiple cultures Salz encountered at

Barclays might be encountered in any organisation that had grown multiple businesses across the world, and in particular where these had grown partly through acquisition of third-party organisations (such as Lehman or ABSA, the African bank). The difficult question, which Diamond had encountered as soon as he became responsible as CEO for the whole group and not just for Barclays Capital, was how you could successfully demonstrate to a hostile Establishment (by which I mean government, regulator and press) that the universal bank model could work culturally. One of the key claims in the recommendations of the Independent Commission on Banking was that ringfencing would enable cultural separation:

> The UK retail subsidiaries would be legally, economically and operationally separate from the rest of the banking groups to which they belonged. They would have distinct governance arrangements, and should have different cultures.

(Independent Commission on Banking, Final Report, p.11)

Diamond and many others disputed the assumption that you could not find a common set of cultural norms that could arch across the different banking businesses of a single institution. But he was swimming against the tide: the Establishment narrative was already set in 2011 that innocent, wholesome, retail banking needed to be protected from rapacious, nasty investment banking culture.[26] At times it felt like a "heads you lose, tails they win" debate. If you accepted that the cultures were indeed tough to merge, then those pressing for tough ringfencing or even full separation gained ground (which Bob Diamond certainly didn't want to happen – he had after all fought tooth and nail against the ICB to try and avoid ringfencing of any kind). Conversely, there was a worry – particularly in the investment bank – that any attempt to create a single common culture would create a bland, lowest-common-denominator culture suitable for neither business. This worry also affected all the other universal banks.[27] So the idea was to launch some common cause across all the businesses and geographies, to force the issue on what external expectations were, to drive what could be done consistently and together, and to challenge explicitly those who were claiming the investment bank could never really sit under the same roof as the retail bank. Many other large organisations had done similar work, and hence there was a rich wealth of experience on how to drive such programmes.

Unsurprisingly, the decision to launch a purpose-based organisation faced a degree of external and internal cynicism. Jenkins knew this would happen and he therefore involved the top leadership of the bank heavily in defining and shaping the values that would support the purpose, and the detailed behaviours to be expected from those who had such values at various levels of leadership (so they could be explicitly assessed, developed, measured and rewarded). The resulting list of values (respect, integrity, service, excellence, stewardship) also attracted scepticism and cynicism from many, not least when it was realised that the mnemonic RISES was, shall we say, resonant in the context of banker remuneration. The work completed since then to embed these values in a meaningful way into the expectations, goal setting, behavioural assessment, leadership potential and so forth for leaders throughout the bank is generally regarded as unprecedented in its pace and completeness. If nothing else, most people acknowledge the response was thorough and well engineered, and I am proud of my colleagues who have done this very demanding work at tremendous speed. As such, it's a serious attempt to achieve a real metamorphosis, not a false one. But the jury's still out on whether even the best work in this field, lavishly resourced, will suffice to challenge the behavioural norms driven by banking's legendary reward systems.

As I was writing this book, Jenkins was fired as CEO of Barclays, as a lack of strategic clarity and grip over the performance of the investment bank seemed to loom larger than progress on cultural change in the mind of the new chairman. Nevertheless, one of the key lessons the bank believes it has learned is not to be defined by its detractors, and to plough on to make the changes that have to be made. For example, it is now perfectly possible for a Barclays banker to get a zero bonus purely for behavioural failures even if he or she is "delivering" on other fronts. Whether the HR "plumbing" put in place is actually utilised to deliver this outcome is a matter for the board and leadership of Barclays, but at least it can be done if the will is there.

The Barclays story demonstrates how hard it is to fix cultures once they have become broken in critical ways. However, it should be far easier for startups or organisations clearly at the beginning of an organisational cycle of genesis to get purpose and values right. Here follow some further, specific suggestions that may be helpful:

Purpose should be defined in relation to those outside the company or organisation – so that it's explicit that the reason for the organisation's existence is *not* to serve the interests of its (senior) employees alone, or for that matter its owners' narrow interests. Inevitably, such a claim will create tensions against the natural forces, particularly economic, which encourage the opposite. But that is the whole point. An organisation that takes a purpose seriously thinks how to achieve it *and* deliver returns to shareholders, pay its executives in a competitive talent market and so forth. Good executives worth their salaries can figure out how to achieve these potentially competing challenges.

Values need to be relevant to the organisational purpose and context. However, given the dangers that we have noted, it's worth being explicit about reinforcing an anti-hubris culture. This might be by having a specific value, such as humility. Or it might be in the language used to support other values, such as "customer first". What matters is that everyone inside and outside the organisation feels they have the explicit language to challenge arrogant, hubristic behaviour before it becomes a norm. And unless behaviour is challenged from the very top of the organisation, explicit values are useless, and indeed become another reputational millstone around the CEO's neck.

Of course, there are very successful organisations with strong and healthy organisational cultures that have never written down their purpose and don't need to write down their values (they are not aspirational, they are explicit). However, given the pace of growth, and the globalisation and complexity we have noted in most industries, I suspect these will become rarities. What is more troubling is that there will be lots of pariahs with well-written (and, whatever the cynics tell you, well-intentioned) purpose and values statements but cultures that demonstrate daily a failure to align with the aspirations behind these statements. What are we to say about this phenomenon? I am reminded of those who are hyper-critical of people who fail to live up to the stated values of their religion or other moral belief system. Firstly, there are questions of degree: a single minor lapse for an individual against a sea of people behaving consistently well is a different thing than a widespread norm where values and principles always go out of the window. Sadly, I fear it's just tough. You have to get to a place where your organisation has zero tolerance for aberrant behaviour to survive the scrutiny it's going to get. If what occurs is indeed very rare, be prepared to prove it. But if you allow even a little horsemeat in some of your lasagne, or just two or three of your traders are on the fiddle, or your accountants mis-book a few lines of revenue... well, sympathy is going to be limited. Secondly, there is this persistent question about who gets to judge, and with what degree of empathy and kindness. By and large, the contemporary trend is for the wider public to do the judging, sometimes very harshly, and sometimes on very little information – even on false data. Here again, I am going to tell you to suck it up. Your best hope by far is to be in a constant dialogue with a wide range of stakeholders so that you can explain your point of view to them directly rather than relying on others (particularly the press) to be your reputational entrepreneurs (see Recommendation 8, in Chapter 6 below).

Given how harshly falls from grace are now viewed, some feel that purpose statements and values are hostages to fortune that we would do better to ignore. I don't agree. What we should *not* do is form them, publicise them and forget them. If you are going to have values, develop them properly, involving multiple stakeholders in forming them, and really plumb them deeply into how you hire, reward and manage your people, how you treat your customers and owners. Use them to set the tone for what follows and don't be put off by the inevitable setbacks you will receive when you are unable to live up to these promises perfectly. This all takes time, effort, and the support of good leaders and a strong HR department.

Alternatively, if you follow my advice about a low brand genesis being lower risk, it's possible that by not having a purpose or values you may imagine you can avoid charges of hypocrisy. After all, if you don't have a high-sounding purpose and fancy values, at least you won't disappoint anyone when you fail to live up to the promises... But you now face two risks. The first is that your external stakeholders may not be clear what you stand for, except implicitly via the organisation's branding messages. The second is that it's now unclear what will drive behaviour in your organisation (though economic pressures and the behaviour of senior executives will predominate) and how you are going to align external and internal expectations. Perhaps the most important issue is that you have nothing by which to course correct if behaviour or outcomes fall short of what's required. What is it exactly that this person did or did not do wrong (assuming no laws were broken)? If you have not been explicit on your expectations, you will at least face legal questions, even if you have the courage to fire or discipline someone for a transgression. The reality is, even if you don't hold with the fad of making purpose and values explicit, there are going to be some sort of implicit purpose, values and behaviours in your organisation, and these will show themselves during any crisis you experience. And perhaps they won't be what any stakeholders want to see, even if they aren't "hypocritical": they may be a purpose that barely recognises the need for survival, let alone sustainability or service to others, with the only values on display being those of selfishness, greed and self-preservation. Too late, then, to worry about culture or leadership.

So you're likely to face similar practical challenges even if you don't formally have these words in five-foot-high plexiglass in your lobby. I see nothing incoherent about having a very low corporate brand presence and yet still having clear principles and purpose. Let's not confuse doing what's easier and less hassle with what is ultimately best for the organisation. But if you *do* have them in five-foot-high plexiglass... well, that's a big branded statement and you'd better be ready to go all the way in your execution. Or face some dire consequences.

Notes

1 The Rogers Commission into the famous 1986 Challenger disaster (in which the twenty-fifth space-shuttle mission unexpectedly blew up shortly after launch, killing all on board) was correct to spot that the origins of the crisis lay in design concepts developed decades earlier, as well as in the more immediate challenges of developing new technologies to operate safely in such challenging environments.

2 I use 'original sin' here in its general usage of an action which is itself sinful. The Christian concept of original sin is altogether more complex and nuanced (and argued over) than that. There may be a case for arguing that large, powerful organisations are prone to the sins of Pariahdom by their very nature. For more on original sin, see Jacobs, 2008.

3 Recent studies suggest the life expectancy of Western companies is decreasing rapidly. BCG calculates that the five-year mortality rate for UK quoted companies is now 32 per cent.

4 Joseph Schumpeter (1883–1950) was a prominent Austrian political economist at Harvard. His theories on creative destruction are well known. Less well known is his belief that capitalism would itself be destroyed by a form of corporatism hostile to entrepreneurs.

5 Of course, those who benefit from the associated financial transactions are less likely to mourn the constant demise of companies old and new. But there is a price to be paid for such instability and unsustainability, and criticism of the system is growing. See, for example: http://www.economist.com/news/business/21567062-pursuit-shareholder-value-attracting-criticismnot-all-it-foolish-taking-long

6   The *Dictionary of National Biography* article on Deterding by T.A.B. Cowley states that "Although the evidence is weak that he actively supported the Nazi regime, he did propose certain schemes which conveyed that impression." What's not in doubt is Deterding's abiding hatred for Communism: Shell's oilfields in Russia had been appropriated after the revolution and he was unforgiving about such actions.

7   This is an area for deeper consideration. How do the collective, potentially hubristic growth ambitions of millions of organisations globally threaten our sustainable existence on the planet? See also Meadows et al., 1972.

8   For the purposes of this book, I am taking a simplistic view that organisational brand encompasses the name and associated brand of the parent company or organisation, and that product brands represent the named products, services or organisational subsidiaries within the parent organisation. The two may be synonymous (Ford/Focus) or not (Associated British Foods/Primark).

9   http://www.economist.com/news/business/21633833-uber-risks-consumer-backlash-over-its-tough-tactics-uber-competitive

10 We should note the difference between a corporate brand and product brands here. An organisation such as Cargill (2013 revenues of $213 Billion) operates in a low-key fashion while managing numerous products across the globe.

11 Mid-Staffordshire NHS Trust was at the centre of a major scandal involving high mortality rates and poor patient care. See Francis, 2013.

12 Taleb is a relentless critic of those who pretend to know things they don't, and in particular of those who overestimate their own skill rather than luck in becoming successful and rich.

13 In the UK, weak governance associated with former scandals led initially to the Cadbury and Greenbury Committee recommendations, and now to the FRC Governance Code. See https://www.frc.org.uk/Our-Work/Publications/Corporate-Governance/UK-Corporate-Governance-Code-2014.pdf

14 The Charities Commission website provides advice on trustee boards, people and skills. See https://www.gov.uk/guidance/trustee-board-people-and-skills

15 National Governors' Association guidance, http://www.nga.org.uk/Guidance/Legislation,policies-and-procedures/Model-Policies/Code-of-Practice.aspx

16 John Mann, MP, famously asked Bob Diamond at the TSC hearing on 4 July 2012 if he was familiar with these principles in a contrived, though effective, soundbite moment. Diamond either did not know or could not remember them.

17 The titles available are too numerous to list in full, but popular titles on Amazon include: *Common Purpose* (Kurtzman), *The Purpose Linked Organization* (Love and Cugnon) and *Lead with Purpose* (Baldoni)

18 The 1854 Northcote-Trevelyan report stimulated critical reforms of the UK Civil Service, establishing the need for recruitment and promotion on merit rather than patronage, preferment, purchase or length of service.

19 Major himself appeared at the time to be too boring for sleaze, but the nation was duly stunned to learn later on that he had himself had an affair with Edwina Currie. Nevertheless, we should applaud Major as one of the few

politicians to have really tried to address this issue seriously. His successor, Tony Blair, has the dubious claim to fame of being the only serving PM to be interviewed by the police (with regard to the sale of peerages and honours).

20 http://www.parliament.uk/documents/commons/lib/research/briefings/snpc-04888.pdf

21 The subjects of enquiry missing the point like this presaged the press's own reaction to the Leveson Inquiry in 2013.

22 This headline finding seemed to many a classic Whitehall whitewash. However, it was simply Nolan's honest view (and few came more honest, morally upright and honourable than Nolan). Importantly for our discussion, we were already witnessing in 1995 a change in transparency and standards of judgement which was outpacing the speed at which purification of people and process could take place. We should have no doubt that had the politicians of yesteryear had the same intense interest placed on their activities, there would have been just as many scandals, and probably a lot more, than we now witness.

23 http://webarchive.nationalarchives.gov.uk/20140131031506/http://www.archive.official-documents.co.uk/document/cm28/2850/285002.pdf

24 CSPL Annual Report 2013–14, published September 2014: https://www.gov.uk/government/uploads/system/uploads/attachment_data/file/358202/Annual_Report_241014_CSPL_Final__V2_.pdf

25 Has Barclays brought corporate responsibility reporting into disrepute? The fact that social auditors failed to expose the bank's rotten culture shows the limitations of independent assurance. http://www.theguardian.com/sustainable-business/barclays-corporate-responsibility-reporting-disrepute

26 This narrative was popular in the UK, but was always a poor fit with the facts: poor-quality lending decisions on home mortgages and a multitude of multi-billion-pound selling fiascos including PPI had their roots firmly in the retail sector.

27 Salz perhaps didn't do enough to say that the existence of multiple cultures need not in itself be a problem – Barclays could perfectly well have had multiple good cultures with good values appropriate to each one's business segment, and hence would have avoided the scandals that subsequently plagued it.

5

Hubris –
Arrogant Overconfidence

hu·bris [hyoo-bris, hoo-]
noun
excessive pride or self-confidence; arrogance.

"The worst president is closer by nature to the best than either is to anyone who has not gone through what it requires to become president."

George Friedman, *The Next Decade: What the World Will Look Like*

THE ROLE OF hubris in creating pariahs is critical. Without hubris, there would be no nemesis, no sense of justified comeuppance, and no meaningful difference between the pariah organisation and the non-pariah. Hubris is a complex subject worthy of deeper study in its own right. In this chapter, we will look at the concept's origins and some more modern interpretations, and make some observations about hubris in organisations as well as individuals.

Origins

The Greek word ὕβρις (usually transliterated as "hubris", which I shall use, and sometimes as "hybris") has as its primary definition in the great Liddell and Scott dictionary: "Wanton violence, arising from the pride of strength or from passion."[1] Although the case can be made that our current usage of hubris has evolved substantially since classical times, there is an important key point in this sense of the word, and that is its conjunction with *power* and the *use of power*. Classical scholar Douglas Cairns, in his article "Hybris, Dishonour and Thinking Big" (1996), provides a nice précis of Aristotle's definition of hubris (*Rhetoric* 1378b):

> Hybris, we are then told, requires the initiation of harm, and the pleasure of hubris lies in the thought of one's own superiority... Aristotle lends support to his insistence that hybris is fundamentally a matter of causing dishonour...

There is an important element of contempt in hubris, which manifests itself in the dishonour done to others. In the finely tuned social world of ancient Greece, status anxiety was rampant. But hubris is originally a more physically violent word than is implied in simple "dishonour". Another scholar, Douglas MacDowell, in an article on "'Hybris' in Athens" (1976), shows that the etymology of the word refers back to the noise that an ungelded donkey makes. The blatantly sexual references in some of the literature quoted show us that the outrage in the conceptual origins of the word are highly related to male sexual dominance of the crudest kind, and hence by extension even to rape. The Greeks realised better than we often seem to that rape is a crime of violence and abuse of power. Hubris is also often connected with the Greek word "koros" meaning "fullness" or "satiety". By eating or drinking too much (and the Greeks knew a few things about such excess), one becomes more hubristic. In an early society where a full stomach was unlikely to have been everyone's daily experience, it's interesting to see that hubris requires material prosperity. Indeed, MacDowell suggests that the three primary characteristics of those suffering from hubris are youthfulness, having plenty to eat and drink, and wealth.

Hubris, then, is always bad. It involves "taking from someone else a thing which belongs to him, or preventing him from receiving what should be his". It is "a matter of depriving him of the honour which is due to him." The very first recorded use of the word in Greek literature is in the beginning of the *Iliad*, where Agamemnon deprives Achilles of Briseis, a slave girl he has "earned" for his prowess in war. Without wishing to get into feminist literary theory, we cannot but note all these examples reinforce the rather obvious, crude maleness of hubris. In our recommendations we will examine further the role that improving the gender balance may have in insulating organisations from hubris; and this is also part of the case for diversity in leadership. Some readers will at this point be unable to restrain themselves from making connections and comparisons to contemporary organisations and leaders. Certainly it's tempting to draw some parallels between what I see as the growth of pariahs and a growth in hubris in leaders, and to note that those leaders are indeed getting younger and significantly better paid than their predecessors. There may perhaps be some universal truths here worth observing about moderation.

Certainly for the Greeks, the concept of hubris was contrasted with that of "sophrosune", an equally complex and untranslatable concept which has at its essence a natural balance and the avoidance of excess. Perhaps the best-known example of hubris in classical mythology is the story of Icarus, the son of Daedalus. Daedalus – a character of myth rather than history – created the labyrinth in Crete. Imprisoned there to protect his knowledge from the outside world, he crafted wings from feathers and wax for himself and his son Icarus to use in their escape. Icarus, overcome with the impetuosity of youth, flew too high despite his father's warnings, and the sun melted the wax that held the wings together. Before his father's horrified gaze, he plummeted to his death. Icarus was the victim of his own youthful arrogance and cockiness. Another oft-cited story is that of Oedipus. The naïve view is that Oedipus, by modern ethical standards, was unfairly doomed – in the story, his fate proves unavoidable, despite all his best efforts. But to a fifth-century Athenian audience it would have been symbolic that Oedipus's over-confident cleverness was no match for the workings of fate, and that he eventually is left ruined, exiled and powerless, a man who has murdered his father and slept with his mother (both exceptionally "unclean" acts for which it would be virtually impossible to be forgiven or cleansed of guilt).

In all these examples, one is left with what I think remains the central challenge in handling hubris in the modern context. Excessive pride and cleverness in the context of power, coupled with a lack of listening to moderating voices and advice, place our heroes (now the leaders of our complex organisations) into the path of crisis and nemesis, just as they always have. But can hubris be avoided? As we will see later, the punishments for modern leaders and organisations may not be as grisly as Oedipus's self-blinding or as emotionally wrenching as Icarus's death, but there are important lessons here about how hubris builds, and its negative impact.

Hubris as a "Male" Disease

In the classical world, we mostly see the world through what is now appropriately called the "male gaze". Ancient Athens and Rome were both "men's worlds" and – although we are now learning more about the role of women, and despite the fact that there were some sympathetic male authors (Euripides in particular) – we don't really know how women felt through their own words. But in discussing hubris with women while writing this work, I often heard comments along the lines of "It's all about testosterone, isn't it?" Certainly, it seems that the risk taking (look at Icarus), overconfidence, excess and violence at the heart of the concept of hubris are more easily associated with the male of the species than the female. And we read of studies which demonstrate that in competitive, "masculine" environments such as the trading floor, women also experience surges in testosterone, especially when they are winning.

Much has been written recently[2] on how men and women differ neuro-logically and biologically, and how this impacts behaviour. Inevitably, such work and the conclusions to be drawn from it rapidly move from the field of science to that of gender politics. For the purposes of this book, the point here is that we have always recognised that hubris is a very male disease, but of course not one that only men can suffer from. We will not solve the problems of male power and hubris by insisting that women who want to succeed must be the ones who are most like men, only more so. We will have to evolve a new theory *and practice* of leadership that bring in a humility and reasoned self-doubt, if only because our world just can't afford to suffer the damage that hubris causes it any more. So we will see that making the workplace, and in particular the boardroom and the C-suite, more gender neutral (or in other words, less purely masculine) may be one of the best simple ways of reducing the pariah risk for organisations.

Prime Ministers, Presidents and Hubris – the Owen Model

Lord David Owen, the former Labour Foreign Secretary, SDP founder and independent social democrat peer, is also a medical doctor. In recent years he has gone to considerable lengths to examine the historic behaviour of prime ministers and other world leaders, and has formulated a theory of "hubris syndrome" which he has explained in several articles[3] and most recently in a book.[4] Owen is clear that in certain circumstances, power can make certain sorts of personality prone to "impetuosity, a refusal to listen to or take advice and a particular form of incompetence when impulsivity, recklessness and frequent inattention to detail predominate. This can result in disastrous leadership and cause damage on a large scale." (Owen and Davidson, 2009, p.1,396) He proposes symptoms ("clinical features") of those suffering from hubris syndrome, many of which are common to those recognised in existing personality disorders:

Table 4 – Proposed Clinical Features of Hubris Syndrome

SYMPTOM	CORRESPONDS TO DSM-IV
1. A narcissistic propensity to see their world primarily as an arena in which to exercise power and seek glory	Narcissistic Personality Disorder (NPD).6
2. A predisposition to take actions which seem likely to cast the individual in a good light – i.e. in order to enhance image	NPD.1
3. A disproportionate concern with image and presentation	NPD.3
4. A messianic manner of talking about current activities and a tendency to exaltation	NPD.2
5. An identification with the nation, or organisation, to the extent that the individual regards its outlook and interests as identical to his/her own	Unique
6. A tendency to speak in the third person or use the royal 'we'	Unique
7. Excessive confidence in the individual's own judgement and contempt for the advice or criticism of others	NPD.9
8. Exaggerated self-belief, bordering on a sense of omnipotence, in what we personally can achieve	NPD.1 and 2 combined
9. A belief that rather than being accountable to the mundane court of colleagues or public opinion, the court to which they answer is: History or God	NPD.3
10. An unshakeable belief that in that court they will be vindicated	Unique
11. Loss of contact with reality; often associated with progressive isolation	Antisocial Personality Disorder APD.3 and 5

SYMPTOM	CORRESPONDS TO DSM-IV
12. Restlessness, recklessness and impulsiveness	Unique
13. A tendency to allow their "broad vision", about the moral rectitude of a proposed course, to obviate the need to consider practicality, cost or outcomes	Unique
14. Hubristic incompetence, where things go wrong because too much self-confidence has led the leader not to worry about the nuts and bolts of policy	Histrionic Personality Disorder HPD.5

Owen's analysis of hubris as a disease of power extends, therefore, to formalising it as a medical condition which can be diagnosed in others, or at least leads in that direction. Owen and his co-author, psychiatrist Jonathan Davidson, posit that at least three of these symptoms would have to be present for a diagnosis, of which at least one must be from the "unique" set. In his articles and books, Owen goes on to judge which leaders may or may not have suffered from this affliction and to set out his rationale for such judgement. This approach to history is fascinating, and what is perhaps most striking in reading his work is the sheer volume of presidents and prime ministers suffering from serious physical and mental illnesses. It's no joke to carry the burdens of high office, and of course the nature of these powerful roles often attracts extreme personalities and those with psychiatric dispositions towards hubris. We should also note that Owen is not the only one to have diagnosed extensive narcissism – a key feature of his diagnosis of hubris syndrome – in politicians. Hill and Youssey (1998)[5], for example, noted that politicians outscored librarians, university professors and clergy in narcissism.

There is some controversy about whether or not leaving power necessarily rids the sufferer of the "disease" of hubris. Some suggest that George W. Bush was a sufferer in office, but has regained a sense of reality in his retirement in Crawford, Texas; whereas others criticise Tony Blair for continuing to suffer from the syndrome long after he left the formal power of UK government. Conservative politician Boris Johnson opined in June 2014 that "I have come to the conclusion that Tony Blair has finally gone mad." The cause of this characteristically blunt assertion was Blair's claim in a TV interview that the collapse of Iraqi society was "always, always going to happen" and was not provoked by the 2003 invasion, the removal of Saddam Hussein and the subsequent occupation. We shall no doubt monitor Tony Blair with interest for signs of recovery, but hopes are not high. This conception of hubris as a disease of the powerful is at least superficially attractive, because it links problems of hubris to other ailments and frailties that all people may be prone to, and hence humanises and demystifies the problem of why tyranny occurs so frequently. It's also dangerous because it could lead to false or amateurish "diagnoses" for political or other reasons, and one could be worried that a less scrupulous and well-qualified individual than Lord Owen would be reverse engineering the disease, the symptoms and the diagnoses for non-medical reasons. Owen recognises this danger, but draws our attention back to the famous dictum of Lord Acton, who wrote in 1887:

> I cannot accept your canon that we are to judge Pope and King unlike other men, with a favourable presumption that they did no wrong.
> If there is any presumption it is the other way against the holders of power. Power tends to corrupt, and absolute power corrupts absolutely.

Owen rightly draws the parallels between political leaders and CEOs of large businesses, and of the banks in particular. This seems reasonable to me: large organisations certainly provide considerable vehicles for wielding individual leadership power, but there are many restraints on what a CEO can do, as there are for politicians.

Hubris Conditions

We discussed earlier why certain genesis conditions might make organisations prone to hubris. But what are the conditions that make individual leaders prone to hubris? If Owen is correct, hubris is in effect a personality disorder to which only some are prone, brought on by a heady cocktail of what I will call "hubris conditions" that are most easily available to those in the highest offices. While some focus on identifying those at risk, we may also want to think about what will trigger them to behave badly (knowing that high office will always prove attractive to narcissists).

What might these hubris conditions be? I would suggest that they include:

1. **A need for frequent, rapid decisions** – top jobs require a constant stream of clear opinions and decisions based on limited data and consultation. The pressure on decision making in senior roles is relentless and creates a comfort with forming decisions rapidly and often, even where certainty cannot be achieved or data is sketchy. Diffidence is failure in both politics and business if decisions take too long. It's easy to start to believe you are "good" at making decisions because you have to make a lot of them and many have turned out well (or at least OK). In selecting leaders, we deliberately seek out those who will "make a call" given limited data and exclude those who are less prepared to do so. That is fine, but we should be more careful about which decisions need to be left to the person at the top: in many cases it is healthier if the top leader is bound to listen more closely to advice and counsel, or even has to accept that certain decisions (e.g. key assumptions for financial models) are made by others *ex officio* and cannot be made by the CEO.

2. **Access to execution capability** – although there are limits, checks and balances, the formal devolved powers of CEOs, within their own company, to mobilise the resources and capabilities as they see fit are very considerable.[6] If what you want done is indeed done, eagerly and quickly, this can fast become an expectation and an entitlement. Again, in selecting and promoting leaders we tend to discourage those who do not leverage the resources at their disposal and delegate accordingly.

3. **Requirement to present oneself as a strong leader internally and externally** – our modern obsession with strong individual leadership, coupled with modern media capabilities and advisors, frequently results in what can look like personality cults in support of the broader mission. It is all too easy to conflate a given strategy for a business with the leader who happens to support it.

4. **Isolation for reasons of wealth and security** – few modern leaders are successful in avoiding the isolating effects of their office. Because of their fame, wealth and the need for effective security, they do not travel, mix or converse with their fellow citizens except in the most

contrived of situations. This has very bad consequences for their grip on reality, which soon becomes highly distorted.

5. **Isolation by nature of the office** – CEOs are famously "lonely". Even extroverts, surrounded by advisors and close colleagues, still have to make decisions alone. There are real barriers of access to leaders – their time is ultra-precious and access to them is carefully controlled by staff trained to push away those who will annoy or frustrate their bosses and make them angry or disgruntled.

6. **The glamour of power** – power can be intoxicating and the glamour of a fast-paced lifestyle, full of limousines, corporate jets, invitations to exclusive events and the company of other powerful people (and those men and women who are in turn attracted to such agglomerations of power), is notoriously seductive.

For those vulnerable to hubris, their existing tendencies to self-confidence (bolstered by being right a lot of the time), their high intelligence (which also often means being right before others have figured out the issue), their drive, their egotism (even outright narcissism), their need for praise, their manipulative natures and even their religious faiths[7] may combine with these conditions. Without these conditions, one might still have an extreme personality capable of hubristic leadership; but only with these hubris conditions can acts of hubris actually occur. There is much to ponder here, particularly for leaders and those who surround them as colleagues and advisors.

Hubris and Geopolitics

One other aspect of hubris I think worth commenting on is the growth of globalism. When organisations were largely national in scope (at most) then a degree of national elitism and hubris was inevitable. How much worse must things be now we have so many globalised, trans-national corporations and organisations? The potential for real power increases, while the important links to local social and societal norms reduce. It is all too easy for the biggest corporations (and NGOs, as well as the most powerful governments) to become frustrated with the petty parochialism of a given society or country, and its antiquated customs and laws. In his insider account of the rise and rise of Google, *In the Plex*, Stephen Levy gives us – perhaps unintentionally – a sense of how such tendencies emerge:

Qing Wu [a decision support analyst in Google's advertising division] calls Google "the barometer of the world." Indeed, analyzing the clicks of Google users was like sitting beside a window with a panorama on the world. You saw the changes of seasons – clicks gravitating toward skiing and heavy clothes in the winter, bikinis and sunscreens in the summer – and could track who was up and down in popular culture. ... [Hal] Varian [Google Chief Economist] himself once even did a study that compared Google traffic in individual countries to the state of their respective economies. Not surprisingly, Varian says, high GDP tracks closely with how much people use Google. His paper was titled "International Googlenomics".

(Levy, 2011, p.120)

I am not picking on Google. There is any number of companies who are doing the same thing (though none with as much data and ubiquity in mass markets as Google) and even quite junior staff can start to feel strangely powerful and influential as a result. Before you know it, this feeling of power, of knowledge about the world as a system, of having the power to influence and nudge it, can become arrogance and hubris. Rather than be fettered by the laws of the many nations in which you operate, why not be fettered by none (as in the case of the choice Shell made prior to the reserves crisis)? Or perhaps pick the rules you find most pleasing, as Amazon and Starbucks have done for taxation? Or play off different jurisdictions against each other, as the investment banks tend to do with London and New York? This grandiosity that trans-national power and influence can develop in leaders, coupled with the glamour of hanging out with the great and the good in Davos or Aspen or wherever, takes a lot of resisting. We should not decry these meetings or be unsympathetic to those who lead complex organisations and want to meet with the (relatively small) group of fellow leaders globally who can help them understand and influence their worlds, or who understand the peculiar stresses of their jobs. What we can do is ensure these events are extremely transparent and that we encourage CEOs to spend time with groups other than these super-elites. As we noted above, we should also – as shareholders, taxpayers and fellow citizens – show interest in whether attendance at these events is changing our leaders for the better or the worse.

How to Measure Hubris?

At the time of writing, there is no single well-established metric or measure for hubris, either in individual leaders or in organisations. There are some proxy measures we might use to help us:

1. Cultural measures on values (e.g. power dimension on the OCI instrument)
2. Individual measures of leadership (e.g. use of pacesetting or coercive styles of leadership, or aspects of commonly used psychometric instruments designed to pick up on aspects of narcissism or "dark side" issues of leadership)
3. Measures of fear or intimidation on employee surveys (e.g. "I am free to speak up")
4. Analysis of a given leader's speech and writing (increasingly feasible in an age of big data).

If I am correct, we should do more to identify and monitor measures which can give us early warnings of hubristic behaviour by leaders at all levels, but particularly at the top of the organisation. It is here that the board should be most interested in monitoring behavioural risks and challenging where required.

As I suggested above, removing trigger conditions could also form part of a preventative strategy. To do this effectively would also imply the ability to measure the right perceptions, such as the staff's view of how well connected the leadership are with reality, their accessibility and approachability, the perception of fairness and equity in the organisation, and the ease with which one can be heard (whoever one is and whatever is being said). But perhaps the single thing that organisations should do that could be most powerful is to measure and embrace criticism to improve performance. Most organisations either ignore or vilify their critics. However, it's usually our critics who have most to tell us about how we could get better: it's smarter to embrace the squeaky wheels. One of the challenges of all measurement environments is that, especially where we reward on the basis of metrics, there is a potential incentive to cheat the system. We know that banks which run to increase profits will tend to lend more, but do so on increasingly leveraged and hence risky capital base. We know if you ask hospitals to reduce waiting times they will deliver, but sometimes at the cost of careful diagnosis and treatment.

So it's necessary to design metrics that are at first sight perverse, at least for some. Reducing complaints may seem like the smart thing to do, but it may be that this will dissuade managers from asking for difficult feedback or making the complaint process clear and easy for unhappy customers; whereas it could be the greatest source of insights on how to beat the competition you'll ever get. So perhaps it's best to target an increase so you know you are hearing all the problems people have.

Collective Hubris vs. Individual Hubris

The leadership of organisations, even massive trans-national ones, should not be confused with the political leadership of peoples or countries. But there are inevitable parallels.

In his recent book, *The Myth of the Strong Leader*, Archie Brown makes the point well:

> "Strong" leadership is, then, generally taken to signify an individual concentrating power in his or her own hands and wielding it decisively. Yet the more power and authority is accumulated in just one leader's hands, the more that leader comes to believe in his or her unrivalled judgement and indispensability. The more decisions are taken by one individual leader, the less time that person has for thinking about the policy and weighing up the evidence in each case. Since there are only twenty-four hours in the day of even the strongest leader, that person's aides find themselves (often to their great satisfaction) taking decisions in the name of the leader. That is just one reason why the allure of "strong leadership" being exercised by a single person at the top of the political hierarchy should be resisted.
>
> (Brown, 2014, p.9)

Brown subsequently goes on to make the obvious points that democratic countries have attempted to set up checks and balances to deal with this very tendency. As leaders move away from service to their parties (or at least to their cabinets), they become more despotic and hubristic. Those who resist these trends and allow others to shine may, in the short term, be less glamorous, but potentially more successful when judged by history. In political government, we know that, taken to extremes, such unchecked power can have catastrophic impacts on people, with extreme examples of perhaps the ultimate negative impact – systematic genocide – documented during the twentieth century alone in Hitler's Germany[8], Stalin's Russia[9] and Pol Pot's Cambodia.[10] The ability of good people to do evil, especially in a social and cultural context, has fascinated psychologists[11] and philosophers, and will continue to do so.

continued

What we have learned about "groupthink" and bad outcomes in government must provide us with insights onto the human condition in other situations where great power is being wielded. Given that modern multinational organisations are so wealthy and powerful, it's only reasonable we should ask how they are to be inoculated against such abuses, just as we do with our governments. It won't surprise the reader to learn that I don't agree with the popular notion that all large organisations are inherently doomed to bad behaviour. However, it's clear that the same unquestioning psycho-dynamics which led to the Holocaust or the Great Purge can and do manifest within civilian organisations. The desire for acceptance, reward and preferment can lead to very bad outcomes. The NHS culture of management bullying of whistleblowers (seen in numerous cases, including Mid-Staffs) derives from misplaced loyalty to the organisation. Similar issues can be seen in banks, oil companies and other pariahs. I doubt this is a coincidence.

Hubris turns out to be a complex enemy. In some ways hubris, as the Greek tragedians knew, looks so good, so capable, so attractive. But we must train ourselves to be more suspicious and doubting, to recognise the dangers and to demand deep respect and humility in our leaders.

RECOMMENDATIONS

3. Monitor Status Broadly

Organisations can start their battle with hubris by improving the range of sources that they monitor to determine organisational performance. One of the defining features of the hubristic organisation is that it does not listen to those telling difficult truths internally. Enron, Worldcom, Lehman, BP, Shell and others too numerous to mention all had versions of internal whistleblowers trying to tell senior leaders about the issues that beset them, only to be ignored or actively suppressed. My first boss at Shell memorably told me that it was my and my team's job to be 'microphones' in the organisation, to amplify voices, views and signals that might otherwise not be heard by the powerful. We need to make it safer for people to tell the truth as they see it. This is a complex process, culturally speaking, and it goes far, far beyond the processes that are increasingly legislated for to support formal whistleblowers (e.g. in financial services or the NHS), important as these are. What I am talking about here is the need for leaders who are mature and developed enough to deal sensitively with those who disagree with them, to seek out alternative viewpoints and acknowledge them, and to explain carefully what their reasoning has been if and when taking a contrary decision. I am talking about organisations where the employee sensing tools are used seriously to improve things, not as self-aggrandisement for already over-compensated megalomaniacs. I am talking about organisations which create honest, not over-policed and corrected, forums for dialogue. I am talking about places where the town halls are full of real dialogues, not planted questions.

Secondly, we need to do a better job of listening, internally and externally. Too often the communications function pays lip service to such an aspiration but is obsessed with getting the "brand message" out; and thus sincere questions by others are treated as naïve or are immediately swamped with irrelevant material. Externally, the range of stakeholders encountered by the average manager is much too low to give a good sense of what matters for the health of the whole organisation. It's usually not until they reach their predecessor's office that most CEOs finally realise what a wide range of people they will have to deal with, from heads of state to regulators, Wall Street analysts to NGO activists, TV journalists to employee relatives, angry customers to frustrated suppliers. The list just goes on. Below the office of CEO, each of these characters usually has a specialist organisation to take care of them. Typically, a lot of these interactions are managed via people working outside the core operational areas of the business, frequently in corporate relations, government relations and regulatory relations type roles. This specialisation has the great merit of enabling proper person-to-person marking of key relationships and the development of the kind of individual trust that is critical to success. But there are downsides: in particular, the concern I have is that too many of the senior operational and functional leaders involved lower down the organisation are not aware of or involved in these conversations. It is thus only via the CEO that a real connection is made – and the CEO hasn't got time to do all the required connecting.[12] Also, the specialisation may mean critical stakeholders are ignored (because they don't fit the remit of any internal group, or have fallen out with some individual and ceased to engage with the organisation).

Finally, the distinction between issues and crises we note below in Chapter 6 may lead to complacency. If it's your special "job" to monitor an issue for the organisation and prevent it becoming a crisis, it can be tempting to show

how on top of your job you are by downplaying objections or concerns in a dangerous display of urbane bravado. Conversely, your specialist devotion to the subject may label you internally as a pointy-headed crank who doesn't understand the practical issues and thus prevent you raising concerns effectively with operational leadership. So we should be wary of excessive, extended specialism in our organisations. We should encourage extensive rotation of those intended for the most senior leadership roles in complex organisations through responsibility for functions such as government affairs, investor relations and regulator relations, to create the appropriate relationships, experience and mindsets well in advance of taking on the integrative leadership roles where these will all be needed at once.

On measurement, it's not my intention in this book to advocate the balanced scorecard against other ways of monitoring progress. But if you do nothing to monitor leading indicators, don't act surprised (or disappointed) when the downstream indicators are what they are. You need to understand the whole system you are in to get the financial and other outcomes you want and are accountable for. Organisations that are serious about heading off stakeholder dissatisfaction measure these levels, do something about it when they are outside parameters and reward the appropriate people for doing what needs to be done. This is an area where the gap between the most sophisticated of the established pariahs and the non-established is, frankly, vast. In many cases, I truly believe that had the established pariahs put such capabilities in place earlier, they would never have attained established status. And where they cheerfully measure poor data and do nothing, they usually have to repent at leisure.

In the most simple terms, to avoid becoming a pariah, you need to act like you already are one. A paradox, to be sure, but one to learn from.

4. Make Your Culture Unfriendly to Hubris

Let me outline the two main areas for change here:

As far as practicable, keep those prone to hubris away from power. This is not a trivial matter, given the predilections of the clever, charming, autocratic, narcissistic and downright psychopathic for leadership roles, and our own predilection for charismatic leaders. If we want to avoid the problems caused by hubristic leadership and the crises that it inevitably causes, we need to look more and more closely at how we select for senior leadership roles, how we develop and advise those who are selected, and the conditions we create for them in leadership. Wherever possible, we should be identifying those with severe personality traits that are dangerous, particularly those traits associated with narcissism, anti-social and histrionic behaviour, and either excluding them from senior roles or making sure leaders with these traits are highly aware of them and committed to managing them – and surrounded by others who can (sympathetically but firmly) guard against these traits becoming faults. Some organisations do a very good job of this. One hundred years of experience has taught Shell some good lessons on the price to be paid for letting headstrong, arrogant leaders have too much headroom, and it is therefore not only careful about selection of leaders but also about ongoing monitoring of leadership behaviour, with corrective interventions where required. Boards should also be doing more to demand transparency on how checks and balances are working to reduce the prevalence of those least likely to resist the temptations of hubristic leadership. Valérie Petit and Helen Bollaert write compellingly in their article (2012) on the topic of CEO hubris of the need to encourage "authentic leadership" attributes in leadership development programmes, working on four behavioural dimensions: self-awareness, balanced processing, moral action and relational transparency. I am convinced that with improved selection and development in place, whole industries could be made much more hubris-proof and hence less likely to generate pariahs.[13] Much work in this area has been inspired by the good work of the Daedalus Trust, a charity set up by Lord Owen and other senior leaders who recognise the challenge that hubris creates for modern organisations.

Make organisations safer by identifying and removing hubris trigger conditions. We also need to make organisations more deeply capable of withstanding the tyranny of hubris when it occurs (as it inevitably will at some level). I think it's here that organisational culture can be particularly powerful, especially with respect to how leaders behave. Humility in all things, connection with a wider network, scepticism about their own hype, and devolution of power and decision making – all have a part to play. We must put in place strong governance that ensures appropriate advice is given to major decisions and that the CEO delegates decisions to better-qualified specialists, not all of whom need to be direct reports. We can ensure executives remain grounded and connected to normal people, including their own customers and staff. We can put clear policies and limits in place to prevent the abuse of the company's resources. And perhaps here lies the best actual argument against soaring executive pay: there may be good reasons to limit very high short-term rewards, simply because of the role they play in encouraging damaging isolationism, socially and practically. Finally, we might usefully tone down the encouragements to CEOs to ape celebrity lifestyles. They don't need big sound and light shows at their own company leadership conferences. They don't need to let themselves be fêted and wined and dined as much as they often do. They don't really need to fly on private jets and, often, could use the tube or the bus with no actual challenge to their personal safety. It is a disaster for anyone's ego to be constantly ferried around by limousine, as numerous ministerial memoirs attest. If all these changes make executive life less attractive to some, I suspect it will be the right sort of leaders who still want to do the jobs. Those who are principally attracted to power, money and life in the elite might well have been those most prone to hubris. Writing this book has convinced me even more than before of the critical importance of humility in cultures that avoid pariah status, but this is clearly an area demanding more study if we are to demonstrate that humble cultures ultimately outperform hubristic ones.

But how can we really value humility in the culture? And can we do that in industries and organisations that need big "rockstar" individual contributors, those where a top 10 per cent performer is worth millions or billions more to the bottom line? Curiously, I believe we can. How can that be?

Firstly, it's worth saying that most cultures that highly value individual contribution (and pay accordingly) are usually in the position of being able to measure that contribution precisely. We all know how many goals (and "assists") the star striker scored for our team this season. And star traders have similarly precise measures available on their profitability, value at risk and so forth. In environments where the best are *so much better* than the average (and where the worst are failed out every day and cease to earn at all), it can seem inevitable that top talent is entitled to be immodest, to demonstrate the confidence needed to score the goals, make the trades and so forth. Certainly this is the argument that is usually used to defend relatively high pay in most sectors where it occurs. However, it's all too easy here to conflate confidence and hubris. As Nicholas Taleb says, many really successful traders fail to appreciate that (at least) some of their success is down to good luck.

> As the reader now knows, the fund manager can expect to be heckled by me during the presentation, particularly if he does not exhibit the minimum of humility and self-doubt that I would expect from someone practising randomness.

> (Taleb, 2001, p.151)

Hubris comes from two intertwined areas in these cultures: success and reward (aka money). The one that is most often written about is reward; the assumption being that more money creates worse problems directly, as a form of corruption. The arguments then begin again about both the absolute and relative amounts of money that are "right" to "allow" people to earn, as well as the (to my mind, more important) questions of whether people have actually done the right things to earn whatever sum they are paid. But it is not just how much that people are paid that makes pariah companies at the centre of debates about reward. It is that there is insufficient conviction that they are even getting paid for doing the right things. The Salz Report blamed HR for this at Barclays:

> The role of human resources (HR), and the design and operation of the ways in which the bank managed and developed its people, did less than we would have wished to underpin desirable behaviours. The HR function was accorded insufficient status to stand up to the business units on a variety of people issues, including pay. This undermined any efforts to promote correlation of pay to broader behaviours than those driving individual financial performance. This mattered, because pay was seen as the primary tool to shape behaviour. The lack of serious attention to the consequences of individual behaviours was also reflected in insufficient attention being given to personal development and leadership skills (as opposed to technical training). And there was too much emphasis on financial performance in recruiting, performance evaluation and promotion, with insufficient focus on values and behaviours.

> (Salz, 2013, 2.25)

But it also recognised that the perceptions and realities were not identical:

> We should point out that very many Barclays' staff are paid moderately and have minimal or moderate bonus incentives. It is unfortunate that the high bonus awards to a relatively small group of people indiscriminately impact the public perceptions of all bankers and bank employees in general.

(Salz, 2013, 2.17)

The report saw pay as a key cause of the financial crisis (and by extension, we could assume for the pariah status that Barclays and other banks now enjoy):

> Broadly speaking, we feel that the pay structures in banks have tended in the past to be too complicated, too easily gamed, too narrowly and too short-term focused, and too often resulting in overly generous pay outs. And these pay outs have tended inadequately to reflect risks, a genuine assessment of an individual's contribution or a fair allocation between employees and shareholders. It is also true, in the context of a competitive global industry, that it is particularly challenging to change radically the structure of compensation. Such change will take time.

(Salz, 2013, 11.12)

I won't quote all the Salz Report here, but the pay section is worth scrutiny. Essentially, Salz felt that although there was and is a case for paying lots of money to top performers, Barclays had paid for the wrong things (in particular, for revenue not profit; and for short-term not long-term value) and that all too often high pay had been awarded to people who had not even directly contributed to these measures, but had attained roles which allowed them to share in the pie:

> One interviewee observed that the scandal of banker pay was less that of the star performer, but of the mediocre banker who, under the umbrella of a star and benefiting from the franchise of a top investment bank, received disproportionate reward simply for being there.

(Salz, 2013, 11.17)

There seems to be no defence for paying huge sums of money to people who are adding limited value, especially if they have not achieved the objectives set for them. But the concern outside the industry is more widespread than this. It is, in essence, that no-one could deserve such large rewards, and that paying them at all is part of a hubristic culture that is bound to fail, not least because its employees are excessively focused on their own bonus and not on doing the right thing for clients. I don't accept that this is what happened at Barclays, necessarily, but there is no doubt investment bankers set huge store by their bonus. Significantly, they worry about the relative size of the bonus, as well as its absolute size. And, it is assumed, if the sort of people who go to work for an organisation such as a bank are principally there to get rich, or at least are first and foremost interested in money, then that must in turn lead to bad outcomes as they game the system to make it pay up. The extremes of this are LIBOR or FX fixing (i.e. breaking the law) but there must be other examples almost daily. Or so it seems.

It is therefore easy to convince people that such cultures are not only venal and corrupt but also inherently hubristic. For one thing, the high pay levels facilitate opportunities to cut executives and bankers off from normal existence. Lifestyle choices that start innocently enough (limousines to the airport to avoid the chance of not getting a taxi or the dangers of late-night subways) give way rapidly to habits, expectations and entitlements (limos everywhere, helicopters to the Hamptons, private jets, yachts and more) simply because these are individually affordable or corporately justified and normalised behaviour. Certainly one of the most dangerous aspects of high-pay environments is that they separate people from normality, elevating them beyond their fellow employees to a level where first access, then conversation and finally critical feedback are denied to them with any but a select few fellow gods and goddesses.

We can quite easily guard against some of these problems at the corporate level simply through thrift and humility enforced by policy. If executives fly the same class as everyone else for a given journey length, have the same car or taxi options when the company is paying, then they are still free to pay for more largesse on their own account. But then it will be clear who is paying, and leaders can set a clear example by not showing off their own wealth and discouraging it in others. As well as avoiding normalising excess on the corporate tab (and hence encouraging individuals to get into unaffordable habits that require vast bonuses to sustain them in their private lives), companies and their boards could do far more to ensure that the behaviours they say they want are hardwired into the performance management system. After Salz, Barclays created a system which explicitly required management to assess both the "what" and the "how" of individual performance against a set of behaviours directly related to the values.

But these explicit symbols of humility in a culture are crude ways to try and put the genie back in the bottle. It's far better never to let it out – and it's not for nothing that so many investors are aware that the opening of lavish corporate headquarters, the purchase of private jets and of course clearly self-oriented management pay awards are symbolic of the poor governance and weak board activity that prefaces a pariah crisis. How your organisation can show value to humility, and not for hubris, is going to be one of the key questions for boards in the future, as it should also be for stock analysts deciding where to invest. It's not clear whether we can legislate (or regulate) for it, but we can certainly make it a fashion where we live, one choice at a time. Everyone who takes the bus not the limo, who talks to the people bringing the coffee as well as the keynote speakers, who gives credit to the whole team and minimises their own role, who asks questions rather than making statements, who is curious and unsure at times – these are people we should value and promote more often to the positions of leadership.

5. Get Leadership Right

There are far too many books already about leadership and this never set out to be another one. So I will keep this section as brief as possible. There are some clear pointers from this book as to what great leadership might look like in an organisation that is less prone to pariah crises. Critically, wise leadership will focus on what is good for the long-term health of the organisation, not (just) for the success of individual leaders or one generation of leadership. It will demonstrate a maturity that contrasts with the juvenile narcissism sometimes seen in pariahs. Boards who want to ensure their executives are not storing up nasty pariah surprises for them will pay attention to balancing the technical skills, work ethic, social skills and intelligence traditionally held to be important with other virtues. And if they are serious about diversity and inclusion, boards[14] will discover another benefit of taking diversity and inclusion seriously in their talent and leadership planning and succession management.

Specifically, board nomination committees[15] should consider three areas in which their interventions can make a difference in the organisation, in conjunction with other shifts in the culture and led by the CEO and other executives: the definitions of what leaders need to look like and what they are supposed to be good at; a long-term, *multi-year*, consistent commitment to investment in leadership development and the production of a leadership cadre worthy of the name; and close attention to the details of how leaders are moved around the organisation, when and why.

5.1 Definitions of Leadership Potential and Leadership Capability

Leading complex organisations at the demanding pace of the twenty-first century, as we have noted above, seems to require almost superhuman qualities. HR departments and line leaders are under orders to discover (and help others discover) such capabilities at earlier and earlier career stages. To have a hope of developing people to take on the top jobs in a large organisation in their late 30s or early 40s (itself an interesting shift towards the cult of youth), we have to identify the likely candidates at an early stage. Usually this means finding young managers (typically but by no means universally graduate entrants) who can be developed into the leaders of tomorrow via programmes which expose them to increasing their understanding of themselves, and assignments that will test and develop them, as well as exposing them to the full range of the organisation's operations and challenges.

So how are we to achieve this feat of successful prediction and development? How are we to find those who may have the "right stuff" or, perhaps just as important, screen out those who will bring the "wrong stuff" into positions of power? Can we avoid hubris by careful selection and nurturing? Or are we doomed to keep repeating the patterns of the past – which, as Einstein so famously reminds us, will tend to keep producing the same results? In other words, if pariah companies turn out, at least in some cases, to have been quite thoughtful and careful about leadership selection and development, can we think of ways to do that selection and development differently to avoid crises? Let's start by observing what is standard practice in most large FTSE companies today. As well as looking for a track record of high performance in our high-potential future leaders, we try to identify what we believe will be the characteristics of the leaders we want tomorrow and select those who seem to have these characteristics, particularly where we suspect these characteristics are impossible or very hard to develop (such as certain types of intelligence as opposed to, say, public speaking skills, which can almost invariably be improved over time).

It remains controversial whether or not there actually are any truly universal truths on what makes leaders great, but decades of research and experience suggests that the following are all important in those who will make the "best" leaders: the brainpower to cope with the sheer complexity and volume of data, information and decisions; a high degree of drive, motivation and personal resilience to keep going and make things happen even in severe adversity; and interpersonal characteristics that make others inside and outside the organisation want to be led by the individual. Most of the large organisations I know well also increasingly select in and out on the basis of other attributes connected with their culture and values (for example, an individual's ability to show respect to others or devote themselves to client service). This increased focus not just on ability but on deeper aspects of what we may term "character" is a shift towards something that was always important in the past; and the return of these issues to the selection process is to be welcomed if it can be achieved without bias. But we have to be careful about over-selection, especially early in career. It's easy to find people who look like us and seem to share our own (blameless) values and attributes. The sharp, savvy, socially capable 23-year-old American man may look the part, but his quiet, more withdrawn female Pakistani colleague could turn out to be more capable in the long term. If we only promote and invest in the former, we have a self-fulfilling prophecy about success in the organisation that suppresses real talent.

Formalising the wrong attributes can be particularly dangerous. Many organisations select for high-potential programmes at least in part on the grounds of certain rather obvious types of "drive", often combined with "self-confidence" (which, mysteriously, men often appear to have more than women) rather than considering at an earlier stage why otherwise highly capable and emotionally intelligent potential leaders may be put off from leadership. "Not wanting" leadership roles is an automatic disqualifier from high-potential programmes, but we should spend more time wondering why so many people look up and decide not to join the ranks of the top leaders. In too many organisations, a good number of the people who want to be the leaders should be dissuaded and vice versa – and I don't think it's a coincidence that Plato spotted this same challenge. Boards and HR departments should be assiduously keeping as many minorities under consideration for as long as possible and ensuring these employees are getting fair access to opportunities in developing their skills to be competitive for roles. So what should be in any list of desired leadership competences or capabilities in a non-pariah organisation?

Well, we know some things to avoid. The rational research tells us that "charisma" is overrated in successful leaders of large organisations. Christian Stadler's work provides some compelling rationale for this view (see Stadler and Davis, 2013). In his book *Enduring Success*, Stadler argues that his empirical and statistical research supports four characteristics of successful leaders of organisations that survive for the long term. These are:

- They understand their company and industry
- They understand the hierarchy of tasks – listen, communicate, then act
- They understand their own limitations – they get the right people instead of trying to get things done personally
- They possess the skills but not the ambition of a politician, and put their own interests second and the company's first.

This is a pretty good list that stands up well to my real-world experience. We need people who are technically capable of understanding the complex machine they are running (and smart enough to do so). We need people who are emotionally smart and know how to listen to others before they drive on with their agenda, and have been skilful communicators and change managers beforehand. The third one – understanding one's own limitations – is particularly important and rare, especially in the larger and most complex organisations: we need people who have a well-developed sense of their own abilities and disabilities, and are smart enough to hire and enable other, better people to complement (not compliment!) their own skills. These are secure, well-grounded people who can laugh at themselves, not egotistical psychopaths using the organisation's resources to scratch their psychological itches.

And finally, we need people who have, sooner or later, developed a deep humility and a sincere desire to see the organisation succeed, and show the deep loyalty that their loyalist employees have the right to expect. The latter is a tough one to develop intentionally; it's all too easy for senior leaders, and

CEOs in particular, to confuse their own ambition for themselves with a love of the company to which they do, after all, give every waking hour devotedly. In the end, getting language and theory right – though necessary – won't be sufficient. It's going to take shrewd and potentially sceptical board interventions, balancing support for executives with a questioning and demanding mindset and active feedback that continue to push back on egotism and self-orientation. It's going to take relentless and consistent standard setting by the CEO in his or her own behaviour and tolerance for behaviour in others. It's going to take probing questions in talent reviews that challenge what we have seen in our own and each other's people. And it's going to take those outside the organisation holding leadership accountable to the promises they make, including promises about leadership.

5.2 Long-term and Intentional Leadership Development

In Plato's *Republic*, the author imagines a world in which the "best" people are educated as philosophers and, despite the attractions of the intellectual life, are willing – through a sense of duty to the city that educated them – to take on the tricky realities of leadership and governance.[16] It's not a bad metaphor for the challenge we face in developing the leadership to pariah-proof our organisations and develop a healthier, better society as a result. Then, as now, it seems that not all the "right" people sought power, and this classic work continues to cause surprise and consternation in readers due to the radical nature of the ideas it contains for the alleviation of this problem.

Perhaps the most radical of all – the notion that children should not be raised by their own parents but distributed by lot to other families,[17] so that everyone would encourage the common interest – still has the power to shock even someone who is lucky enough to be an adoptive parent, as I am. I doubt we can seriously advocate abolition of the family, however much families are at the root of inequalities and inequities of opportunity in society.

But Plato's point is a good one: if we want to educate people to lead effectively, we need to start early. Plato suggests a lengthy education, to be sure, with multiple stages at which only the "best" would be selected for further education and developed.[18] Future rulers would start in childhood by learning calculation and geometry through play (Plato would surely have been a supporter of Montessori schools). After teenage years devoted *solely* to physical training (with no intellectual training because "weariness and sleep are the enemies of study"), those deemed worthy would at age twenty start to be educated in such a way as to bring together the relationships of what they have learned in a "synoptic vision". Ten years later, at age thirty, the best of the best (those particularly "steadfast in learning, war and other lawful duties") are tested again. Only then, and with great care, will they be taught dialectic, as there is the gravest danger in allowing those with the wrong character and preparation to indulge in philosophising. After five years hard work arguing, the now middle-aged philosopher-king candidates are forced to rule in matters concerning war and the young. This final period of testing lasts fifteen years. Only then, aged fifty (as old people) would they finally be led to knowledge of the "good" and alternate further philosophical study with ruling, regarding governing "not something noble but necessary."

I don't think we should take Plato too literally in his programme for educating leaders. If we did, we would not let anyone under fifty run our organisations or countries, as they would not have the required wisdom.[19] That might not be the worst problem, though. The real issue would be that we would have a lot of leaders with only theoretical educations and no practical experience of running organisations until their late thirties: this is hardly ideal, even for those of us who are uncomfortable with the current paradox of younger leaders on top of ageing workforces. The problem of people with no practical governing or leadership experience being parachuted into very big jobs is becoming acute in our political system. It is often observed that none of the current major UK party leaders has had what most people would regard as a real job (unless David Cameron's stint in PR for Carlton counts). However, they all seem to have been exposed to dialectic at a dangerously young age... so perhaps Plato was right after all.

To be serious again, we might well agree that it would be very beneficial to the collective good if leaders were receiving a more effective and structured education and preparation than many seem to get. I say this, fully aware that a vast industry has grown over the course of my lifetime in the business schools of the world that purports to do just this. But it doesn't. There isn't room here to explain why a two-year MBA is never going to be adequate to cover all the many topics that a great leader needs to master. But even a life-time of repeat visits to business school may not suffice to cover the catalogue of capabilities we seek to develop in the leaders of tomorrow. Unfortunately, the best alternative that has existed to date is becoming deeply challenged.

For many decades, organisations like Shell and GE developed their own leaders, according to their own models of leadership, and as these models emerged and developed, so they updated their education and development of their highest potential recruits and mid-level managers. Alongside a technical development of capability sat the development of character, behaviour and a testing of decision making and emotional intelligence. This complex education system was and remains one of the hallmarks of the great learning organisations, and of course it is the confidence that comes from long-term investment in such systems that makes these organisations choose their own leaders over other options. They have come over the years to know these leaders "warts and all" in a way that no interview or assessment process can rival. They can combine the theoretical outcomes of simulations, assessments and tests with the data and feedback from 360-degree processes and performance management to give a rich picture of the leader. This picture, built up over time, provides, I believe, the best kind of contextually relevant data to help leaders improve their own leadership and performance, especially when it is done in a supportive environment in which leaders at all levels observe their peers and those succeeding above them doing the same. The problem is that, with the reduction in average tenures and the growth in specialist roles, there are fewer and fewer organisations with predominantly "loyalist"[20] senior leadership cultures. More and more leaders are there as explicit "mercenaries" to serve in a particular role and drive a particular agenda. At best, these leaders may be "heroes" who want to save the organisation, but the lack of deep appreciation of their entire history, motivation, drive, capacity, talents and experiences is always an issue for those managing senior talent issues.

Boards and CEOs alike tend to react to these real-world problems by asking for more data, which is usually created via careful analysis of biographies, psychometric profiles, references, interviews with the leader and their teams and superiors, and so forth. In the circumstances where little is known about the leaders in question (e.g. after a merger or with new hires) this is not a bad place to start, but it can never make up for years of institutional knowledge and understanding of how an individual has performed, behaved and managed themselves in multiple roles across a large organisation. One of the most underplayed tasks for members of the board, is a deceptively simple one: to get to know the organisation's talent. Tempting as it is, you cannot outsource this to third-party psychologists or to HR (though HR should also know the leaders of tomorrow well so they can help to support them). This is work that is frequently avoided, as other priorities are felt to be worthy of inevitably pressured time in calendars, or leadership team and board agendas. The best companies, and certainly ones that will avoid pariah status, have a commitment to the talent and leadership agenda over a long period of time which is backed by action, not just paperwork.

What else might we do? One idea that I have discussed with colleagues is that of a **leadership passport**. This would be a highly enhanced version of the traditional CV or LinkedIn profile, stored throughout one's career via a trusted third-party firm and made available as required to a current or potential employer. The passport would contain all the data and feedback collected on an individual over multiple jobs, including 360-degree profiles, test scores, views of assessors and so on. Access to the data could be controlled by the individual, but there could be a quid pro quo element where in the final stages of a selection process it became required to share at least some of these items. Data could in turn, with the permission of the individual and the organisation, be held as it builds up in the next employing organisation. Thus, over a career, all the "hard" data is not lost with each move, and if the platform used were properly connected to, say, LinkedIn (perhaps this should be where LinkedIn take their own platform) it would become pretty easy to engage former managers and co-workers in an honest and helpful assessment of talent.

Of course, there are many issues to be raised in such a technology, including: data ownership legal issues; the cautions of putting things on a "permanent record"; how to handle the most negative feedback and assessments; and how to note where the individual has successfully worked on a behavioural glitch. But in reality, where effective referencing still takes place (and believe me, it does, off the record and anonymously), such issues are rife anyway, as people try to avoid expensive hiring mistakes. Making such data transparent and clearly likely to be available to future employers might be a powerful motivation for some people to behave better, or at least to pay attention to the opinions of others. Which, as we've often noted, is a good thing for leaders to do... One of the positives and negatives of such an innovation would be that there would likely be considerable standardisation over time of which data, including tests and scores, were felt to be useful and widely used.

This is fine in many ways, but I would be concerned if it prevented organisations developing and innovating their own unique views of leadership, or how to assess people in ways appropriate to their needs. This is just not yet a science where we know enough to be confidently didactic like that.

5.3 Critical Promotions and Developmental Moves

Having put in place the right frameworks to support the identification and investment in the right people, and then driven forward a strong and consistent leadership culture over years, the next critical task to get right is to make sure that the right people are given critical promotions and developmental moves. Easy to say, but this remains one of the more mysterious areas in the HR canon. A non-pariah company that gets things right will be able to take bets on well-assessed potential, avoiding the pitfalls of betting on the usual, un-diverse suspects who look and sound just like the current leadership. Leaders in such a paragon organisation will be actively finding and sponsoring talented individuals, particularly from diverse populations, and helping them to understand the politics of the organisation and how to become suitably exposed to those who make the key decisions. In talent discussions about these people, more senior leaders and the board should be on the watch for signs of hubris; self-regard, self-promotion and a lack of respect for others will be seen as warning signs and may delay or negate promotions or other moves. Equally, those who actually deliver on the cultural values that the organisation says are important *must* be seen to progress and to get opportunities.

Providing the "stretch moves", which give leaders the breadth and experiences that accelerate their learning and understanding of their industry, is not easy, particularly in companies where the key roles are in "challenging" places far from the HQ. Banks find it much easier to fill key roles in London or New York, or even Singapore – a popular expat assignment – than in developing countries where daily life may be less easy for the leader and his or her family, and achievements take place far from the watchful eyes of the bosses. Mining and extractive companies are also beginning to find that leaders who would in the past have trustingly accepted roles in tough places are no longer prepared to live lifestyles seemingly fit more for nineteenth-century officials of the Foreign Office than to twenty-first-century executives with working spouses and children they actually love and want to see every day.

Women are often disadvantaged in these moves, not only because they don't want to take the jobs, but because people *assume* they don't want to take the jobs. So it's vital that there is an ongoing dialogue with all high potentials which not only encourages diverse, modest, self-effacing leaders to attempt such roles, but also to challenge traditional and sometimes unwarranted assumptions about how essential such roles are to career success at BigCo. I believe that deconstructing hubris is about deconstructing dysfunctional power, and that dysfunctional power is closely allied to a low-diversity culture in which everyone has far too much tied up in the status quo. If that is true, then it's only by taking away the barriers to diverse leadership that an organisation can thrive and be inherently able to withstand hubris from the inside before crisis occurs.

This is not the stuff of banal how-to guides. It's hard work and it takes years. Building the technical skills to lead cogently in industries traditionally dominated by white men is profoundly untrivial. But this work is beginning and we should support it wherever we can. And perhaps, if a whole industry cannot be led by anyone but white men, that is a pretty good argument against its ultimate long-term relevance and ability to survive in a world that will increasingly not look (or think) that way.

5.4 Performance Management and Reward

Reward remains one of the most difficult and emotive topics in my work. Whatever the quanta, we should do more to consider whether we are rewarding the right things and using the right mechanisms. Dan Pink (2011) makes some powerful points about the inadequacies of goal-based systems and contingent rewards for non-algorithmic (i.e. unpredictable, creative) work. His piece on agency theory explains a lot more about what is wrong with banker pay than those who worry about the large numbers involved:

> By offering a reward, a principal signals to the agent that the task is undesirable. (If the task were desirable, the agent wouldn't need the prod.) But that initial signal, and the reward that goes with it, forces the principal onto a path that's difficult to leave... There's no going back. Pay your son to take out the trash – and you've pretty much guaranteed the kid will never do it again for free... What's more, once the initial money buzz tapers off, you'll likely have to increase the payment to continue compliance.

So there remain big challenges for organisations such as banks where there is economic value for the owners in variabilising big employee costs along with profits (this is all that bonuses really are: an out-of-control cost-management/gain-sharing programme). Many believe that behaviour would improve dramatically – even if bankers were still paid a lot – if more of the total compensation were fixed. But to afford such costs, something would have to give. Either bonuses would go down everywhere – something very hard to achieve in a global talent market; or fixed pay increases instead, and you have to reduce the size of the industry to cope with the increased costs.

Quite apart from these entertaining arguments, we must consider what performance management should look like in a non-pariah organisation. The simple points to make here are:

A) Goals have to be the "right" ones, congruent with the aims and values of the organisation. It's no good saying your organisation has a purpose in supporting communities and then narrowly pursuing short-term profits regardless of community impact. Equally, it's no good pretending that subpar returns won't have dire consequences over time.

B) Performance has to be assessed regularly and skilfully at all levels. It should be clear to people what they are being assessed on, who does it, and how different aspects of their personal and collective performance are being judged. There are dangers to making systems too broad and clunky, and certainly more can and should be done to avoid judging outcomes in inappropriately short time periods. The current fad for "junking" performance management processes as too time consuming and difficult may turn out to be problematic if we don't find other ways to encourage honest discussions and feedback at more frequent intervals.

C) The alignment of rewards and performance must be done at a macro as well as micro level. It's depressing that you have to explain to some people their rewards are impacted negatively by the utter shipwreck of another part of the organisation as the economy tanks around them. But you do, and far better to be explicit upfront than face a lawsuit[21] later on.

D) We should spend less time on the hardware and more on the software of the performance management system. Many of us have invested countless hours of our lives trying to produce theoretically sound systems for allocating (finite) rewards, while the efficacy of the system hangs in large part on the competence of managers and leaders every day to set clear goals, make clear contracts with staff, monitor, support and coach their people and each other over the performance period, confront under-performance promptly, and to feed back results constructively. We know that if we invested 10 per cent of our bonus bill on training and capability building in these areas, the returns would pay back. And yet we still pretend everyone who is a manager is a capable performance manager... While HR departments rigidly separate the strong analytic capabilities of reward specialists from the expertise on human behaviour in OD or learning groups, I suspect this won't change much.

If we can indeed address the areas discussed above, we might do a great deal to prevent pariahs developing in the first place. We can set the broad context for the organisation by getting the genesis conditions right and taking purpose and values seriously. We can take a broad view on how we are doing from multiple perspectives, even if we disagree. We can build a culture that values humility above almost everything else. And we can put in place the HR plumbing to reinforce these points, particularly in terms of the leaders we select, how we train them, and how we assess and reward performance.

Notes

1   Other meanings include "an outrage", including physical harms such as rape or beatings, all the way through to more metaphysical harm.
2   See Baron-Cohen, 2004 and 2008; Brizendine, 2010; Walter, 2011.
3   Owen and Davidson 2009
4   Owen 2007
5   Also see Furnham, 2010, Chapter 5.
6   CEOs often express frustration to their intimate advisors that their orders and instructions are not followed. This is an important dynamic: effective and alert 'toe holders' will be able to distinguish between legitimate concerns and the inevitable letting off steam that must occur in private. But unthinking obedience of subordinates is invariably a bad sign and a precursor of hubris and crisis.

7   This is not to suggest for a moment that religious faith is itself a problem in leadership per se. In fact, having a belief system that engages with a greater power than oneself can be one of the best ways of avoiding hubris and malignant narcissism.

8   See Arendt, 1963. Once a system is thoroughly corrupted, it is not just the top leadership that is unable to tell right from wrong.

9   See Conquest, 2007.

10 See Short, 2007.

11 See Perry, 2013 for a revisionist critique of the famous 1960s Experiment 18 of Stanley Milgram, in which volunteers were encouraged to administer what they thought were painful electric shocks to other participants (actually actors) in an experimental "game". This review of the original data and other evidence has also questioned the extent to which protocols were followed and hence whether the results – which appeared to show that people are easily coerced into torturing strangers by social pressures – are to be trusted.

12 For a good discussion of the issues surrounding silos within organisations and their role in the financial crisis, see Tett, 2015.

13 See Stein, 2013. Stein's work suggests that narcissistic leaders can – almost simultaneously – portray both positive and negative characteristics; the dogged, determined never-say-die loyalism that inspires others, and the damaging, distracting and unrealistic failure to accept accountability.

14 They may in so doing have to give up some of the tenets of "good leadership" that worked so well for them in their own leadership journeys up the ladder and hence onto the board in question. Few FTSE boards are yet convincingly filled with the servant–leaders so many profess to encourage, although things will improve as diversity (including, but not restricted to, gender diversity) starts to have a real impact over the next few years.

15 Or their equivalents – trustees of charities and non-executives of NHS or civil-service organisations have similar responsibilities

16 Plato, *Republic*, Book VII 518b–521b, explains this challenge as part of a long and complex argument on education and virtue. The gist of this is that the people who would be "philosopher kings" to rule well would require a lengthy education in both intellectual matters as well as practical ones. Only then, when they were about 50 years old, would they be ready to judge for themselves what is good and steer their leadership towards it.

17 Plato, *Republic*, Book V 457b–466d. In this famous passage, Plato's Socrates advocates the end of family; women "belong in common to all the men" but admits that "considerable controversy might arise over whether or not it is possible".

18 See *Republic*, Book VII 536b–540c.

19 As average CEO ages reduce (they are still over 50), concern has been expressed about whether the youngest can possibly be mature enough to manage large organisations growing rapidly. Obviously this is a particular concern in the tech industry. See Ante and Lublin, 2012.

20 For this typology of employees, see Chapter 11.

21 There were many lawsuits of stunning chutzpah in the banking industry after 2009. These included the Commerzbank/Dresdner Kleinwort Benson case, where over 80 bankers successfully claimed they were owed some £30m in contractual bonuses that were subsequently withdrawn after Dresdner's takeover by Commerzbank at the height of the crisis. Commerzbank claimed they were discretionary. The bankers won in the end.

6

Crisis – Point of Failure

cri·sis [krahy-sis]

noun, plural cri·ses [krahy-seez]

1. a stage in a sequence of events at which the trend of all future events, especially for better or for worse, is determined; turning point.
2. a condition of instability or danger, as in social, economic, political, or international affairs, leading to a decisive change.
3. a dramatic emotional or circumstantial upheaval in a person's life.
4. *Medicine/Medical.*
   a. the point in the course of a serious disease at which a decisive change occurs, leading either to recovery or to death.
   b. the change itself.
5. the point in a play or story at which hostile elements are most tensely opposed to each other.

SOONER OR LATER, all organisations suffer some form of crisis. For some, a crisis is a surprise, for others, just another disappointment. Some crises are inevitable given the growth of an issue, others are very avoidable. Some crises are industry-wide, others are unique to one organisation. Some crises are handled well and may even help build reputation for an organisation and its leadership. Others are mishandled, perhaps even to the point of organisational failure. Crises can increasingly create pariahs or even break them, or just reinforce prejudices against established pariahs. But they can also be the best thing that happened to an organisation by offering a high-profile way to see what the organisation is really made of. One way or another, when a crisis occurs you discover rapidly whether you are heading towards nemesis or nirvana.

In this chapter we will look at the nature of what the professionals call "issues" and "crises", provide a taxonomy of crisis and make some observations about how crisis management differs for pariahs, as well as how inept crisis management can cause an organisation to become a pariah in the first place. We will also connect the dots between these issues and what has happened in the genesis and hubris stages of organisation development.

Crisis Examples and Definition

We live in an age of intense concern over image and reputation management. We always did, of course: as animals we are wired for it[1]. But in a time where every day brings reputational challenges, what occurrences deserve to be termed crises? Let's look at a few examples:

+ A technology outage denies customers access to a critical service
+ Sexual misconduct by a senior executive is alleged in a newspaper
+ An accident with deaths and injuries dominates headlines
+ A political row about taxation occurs on Twitter
+ An NGO starts a campaign around a well-established issue against a large company
+ A product launch goes wrong amid much derision
+ Financial results underwhelm the market and there are calls for heads to roll
+ Rumours of a board-level row about executive pay are reported on a website devoted to industry comment.

Each of these examples has occurred in recent years (or even months). In each case, the organisation's attention is rapidly devoted to reacting to the crisis, internally and externally, and responding to press and social-media comment and questioning. There is no single established definition of what constitutes a crisis, but if we are to respond effectively to a real crisis, it's probably worth knowing what would constitute one in our own organisation. Andrew Griffin comments drily that:

A crisis is an exceptional, unusual and severe situation. It is not something that happens every day, despite what the fraught communications department might sometimes think. So the definition should reflect this. At the moment of crisis declaration, it does not matter what has caused the situation; what matter are the severity of the situation, the potential impacts on the commercial, financial and reputational interests of the business and the need to manage it strategically.

(Griffin, 2014, p.155)

Griffin provides several real examples of crisis definition used by large organisations, which, for simplicity, I have conflated into a single generic definition here:

A crisis is an acute, exceptional occurrence which presents (or appears to present) a threat to the ongoing health of the organisation, including the wellbeing of its people, clients or wider stakeholders. It is triggered by an event, internal or external, and cannot be successfully managed using standard processes and protocols. The crisis ends when the situation is stable again and can be managed as part of the organisation's new normality.

Let's look at these features one by one:

- **Acute, exceptional occurrence** – "crisis" implies a degree of suddenness and urgency to deal with something outside routine experience. This differentiates crises from issues (see below) but also raises the challenge that organisations such as established pariahs which are highly experienced in managing serious crises may become inured to the cumulative damage of such incidents to their reputation. Crises may be frequent but they should not be regarded as normal. Organisations running in a reactive panic mode all the time can seldom approach crises effectively and calmly, or with a suitable recognition for the emotional impact of the crisis on others.

- **Presents (or appears to present) a threat to the health of the organisation** – a crisis which is no danger to anyone or anything isn't a crisis. It's just a panic. As we shall see, some organisations are much better than others at assessing risks cogently and differentiating between everyday noise and exceptional nascent threats. But we should take an appropriate view of what constitutes health in the context of the organisation. This is not just a matter of business continuity and operations (though those clearly are very important); it's also about overall reputation and longer-term licence to operate. It's about survival. There is almost always an element of fine judgement in declaring a crisis and correctly assessing how serious it is for the organisation. Experienced judgement is very helpful in the early stages to avoid false alarms or missed opportunities.

- **The wellbeing of its people, customers or wider stakeholders** – organisations that hold themselves accountable for the safety and wellbeing of their own people are certainly on the right track. Those that recognise their potential to impact on thousands of others are alive to a wider set of real risks and are less likely to be surprised by crises in the first place. If you don't think ahead about what an IT failure in your systems could do to third parties, you will find out the hard way after it occurs and the crisis magnifies. It's tempting not to take on legal responsibility and blame; it takes courage to think more widely and see one's role in the wider system. Clearly, no organisation can take responsibility for everyone's wellbeing, but it's sensible to acknowledge in the definition the accountability that society could place on you anyway ex post facto.

- **Triggered by an event, internal or external** – internal events are by definition easier to understand, monitor and perhaps avoid. Certainly in most organisations I have known there is more orientation towards internal triggers – such as an accident in a company plant or a behavioural lapse by personnel – than towards external triggers such as a change in public or political attitudes to tax avoidance,[2] unless the latter are clearly marked out as part of someone's job remit. Trigger events may be obvious and dramatic (we tend usually to notice explosions or headlines) but sometimes – indeed, often – they creep up on us as part of a wider set of issues. No organisation can predict all possible triggers, but the best ones are at least aware of issues and attitudes, and hence can prepare for and react to events more readily when they occur.

- **Cannot be successfully managed using standard processes and protocols** – organisations with inadequate processes or protocols will face a lot of crises[3], but it's outside "normality" that really serious crises create havoc. Here, years of experience and preparation for disaster pay off. The best-prepared organisations have well-developed crisis management processes and protocols that ensure the appropriate levels of senior leadership and specialist expertise are mobilised rapidly to respond in a crisis. However, what marks out a true crisis is its uniqueness and complexity, and even the most sophisticated will find from time to time that they are not following any recognised game plan. Having the basics covered well is like good first-aid training: you may not be able to treat the patient successfully, but as a trained first aider you can be calm, sensible and stop further harm being done until more specialist help arrives. Practice and experience in emergencies gives crisis-ready organisations patterns that they can recognise and react to, and conserves valuable leadership thinking time to focus on the most critical issues and decisions. The challenge is to recognise when a crisis has exceeded normal parameters and needs to be raised to a level at which others need to be involved; the tendency is to "cope" and forget to ask for help even within the organisation. Regular crisis drills and after-action reviews can help leaders recognise this tendency and identify the situations in which different responses are required.

- **Ends when the situation is stable again** – there may or may not be a precise moment when the crisis starts but there is almost *never* a precise moment when it ends. There is a natural tendency for tired, harassed executives to want to declare victory and move on, but there is a price to be paid if you do so too soon. As the crisis-management consultants tell their clients as they tire of news conferences and endless questions, "This is like wrestling a gorilla: you take a break when the gorilla takes a break."[4] In government and large organisations, the sign that the crisis is over is that the specialist governance arrangements put in place to handle the crisis end: COBRA[5] is disbanded, the Crisis Management Team ceases to meet, or at least the crisis is now managed at a lower level in the organisation by less senior leaders who can be solely focused on the minutiae of clearing up the problems. But it's a real possibility that this will be a matter of weeks or even months, not days or hours.

- **Managed as part of the new normality** – in a lot of crises the situation is managed to a close (with varying degrees of success and reputational damage – nemesis) and then life goes on again, often with limited change in the short term to how the organisation behaves. Rather like a patient with a minor injury, after a short period of first aid, the organisation rushes to re-establish its previous normality, managing around the damage in the expectation of rapid healing, and a few weeks or months later all is normal again. What happens in the most serious crisis situations is that the organisation has to change so much to cope with the crisis that it is never the same again. In these cases (BP Deepwater Horizon would be a classic case, as would Railtrack after the Hatfield train crash) it's obvious that the nemesis phase is really going to be long and the metamorphosis serious.[6] It's not an option for these organisations to retreat into pretending that all will go back to normal. In the most serious cases, the organisation is destroyed altogether by the crisis (as happened to Lehman Brothers, for example). Good crisis-management preparation based on a definition such as this would encourage leaders and staff to ponder these more extreme examples and not assume that they will be able to survive a major crisis as walking wounded. They may face the organisational equivalent of life-changing injuries, disability and death. Crises are really dangerous and, as I will show, are getting more common and more lethal.[7]

So we now have a working definition of a crisis, aimed at stimulating the right kind of crisis avoidance and long-term thinking.

Crisis Taxonomy

Just as there is no single established definition of crisis, so too there is no agreed way to analyse different types of crisis. A recent study performed by legal firm Freshfields (2012) to promote their professional services in crisis management analysed 78 publicly known crises in quoted companies to observe the impact on share price (see below for more on the findings). This study divided the crises into four types: behavioural (conduct); operational; corporate and finally informational (acknowledging the huge growth in

IT-related crises such as the theft of data, denial-of-service attacks or failures of digital products).[8]

I suggest that three headings can encompass most imaginable scenarios:

- **Behavioural** crises are those related to the reported conduct of employees, leaders and associates of an organisation, including illegal, unethical or forbidden behaviours.

- **Operational** crises (incorporating both the operational and informational groupings in the Freshfields study) are those involving a product, service, IT system or other core aspect of the organisation's delivery capability.

- **Financial** crises (akin to Freshfields' "corporate" group) are those where the principal issue is a financial impact, including failures to achieve performance targets as well accounting scandals, fines, frauds and legal threats.

In each of these areas I am going to suggest there are **internal** and **external** variants. In the internal variants, the crisis solely involves the organisation itself and can be regarded as more under its control and certainly its responsibility. In the external version, at least some of the responsibility lies outside the organisation.

Behavioural Crises

Behavioural crises are certainly problematic for established pariahs, as they reinforce their detractors' negative stereotyping of them as "bad people". However, there is less shock value (and hence less crisis) for detractors when an established pariah has certain types of behavioural crisis than when more trusted organisations do so. For example, who now is really surprised or shocked that a major bank reveals yet more conduct issues? But within established companies the shock may in fact be much greater than on the outside. Expectations of ethical behaviour are actually just as high as in other organisations. It is the NGOs and others who conflate their existential opposition with an expectation of poor behaviour. That said, once a reputation has been earned (deservedly or otherwise) for repeated behavioural issues, it's incredibly hard to lose. And of course there have been many established pariahs with profoundly unethical cultures doing terrible, illegal and/or unethical things. Nothing in this book should ever be seen as denying that obvious fact.

For unestablished pariahs, a behavioural crisis may be more upsetting and challenging to both their self-image and their reputation if these have been hitherto pristine. The key question that emerges rapidly in every behavioural case is: is this a one-off case or is this typical of the organisation's culture and values? Press and publics alike can be forgiving of individual failings, even sympathetic, if there is a good reason for the lapse, but there is evidence that repeated crises have serious impact on the overall reputation of the organisation. Curiously, this may have no impact at all on people's preparedness to transact with the organisation as a customer, even if the relationship overall is scarred. I recently talked to a senior member of the House of Lords who cheerfully described all bankers to me as "a bunch of crooks". But he still had a Barclays bank account and declared himself well satisfied with how he was treated by the bank. His opposition was to the established industry, as well as to some of the egregious and much-publicised problems and failings the bank had experienced in recent years.

Lord X, as I will call him, was reflecting a widespread issue for the banks: people need them as a utility, they don't think any one of them is much better than any other, and they often quite enjoy being disgusted with them as organisations. For the noble Lord, there was no cognitive dissonance in holding these opinions simultaneously, nor need there be. But it shows that the banks should take no solace from their low customer turnover rates.

Behavioural crises are always treated as internal – that is, they are caused by people within the organisation. But of course, the organisation is not a bubble. The real scandal is usually that the behavioural issues are part of a country or industry norm (for example, LIBOR fixing was not solely a Barclays issue, let alone a solely British one), the roots of which may be deep. Rooting out and solving the real causes of behavioural crises (as opposed to treating the symptoms with some prominent sackings) is hard work and marks out those who are serious about metamorphosis and catharsis, not just a corporate respray.

Operational Crises

Worse than behavioural crises for established pariahs are operational crises, as these puncture the claim that they are the "most responsible/capable" actors in what may be a pariah industry. BP's image as a potentially responsible actor in the industry was demolished with the Deepwater Horizon rig. Because these reputations are so important, huge efforts and resources are put into maintaining them. As we noted above, a series of behavioural crises had not yet driven away Lord X from Barclays' doors, for the bank – I am glad to say – had not let him down personally by messing up his financial affairs. Customers are rather less forgiving of serious operational failures. One of the worst yet recorded occurred in June 2012 to RBS/NatWest systems: a routine system update to payment processing software caused a domino effect of problems, including back-logs of payments to and from customer accounts. The resulting issues for customers were highly publicised and, despite a sensible crisis response plan, the bank was hit hard with press reports about irate, inconvenienced customers. This particular crisis also included a sting in the tail: a false rumour that the IT failure was due to an outsourcer in India (when it actually emanated from Edinburgh); perhaps another case of truth being the first casualty of war.

Operational crises are deeply painful because they are so obviously connected with the core competence of the organisation in question. We tend to take the view that "at the very least" the phone company can supply us with a working 3G connection, not feeble attempts at humorous tweets; that the supermarket will stock meat that is what it says it is (and not something else that has been introduced to the supply chain); or that the hospital will do its best to make us well, not kill us. If and when they fail, something has gone wrong at the heart of our trusted relationship with them and we respond with unfeigned anger, often of childish intensity, at the failure of the brand. Although many operational crises are entirely internal, there are increasing examples of externalities outside of the organisation's control contributing to operational failures. For example, a power failure in a data centre in India might take down a critical website such as Facebook, if they did not take the time and trouble to anticipate such an issue and create an infrastructure capable of handling redundancy.

Although there was immense sympathy for the many companies unable to operate after the 9/11 attacks, there had in fact been plenty of warnings from previous events, including the first World Trade Centre bombing years before, that critical financial services firms needed fall-back systems, hot data backups and other features that would make them less exposed to a single point of failure. Ten years after the attack, the website *Continuity Insights* noted:

> Many companies were lulled into a false sense of security because they utilized multiple communications vendors or had dual power and communications feeds into their building. However, many of these vendors used the same underground infrastructure or power lines.
>
> In other words, companies may have done a good job of eliminating single points of failure (SPOFs) within the walls of their own building, but all they did was move the SPOF to some external entity.[9]

In a world of global trade and just-in-time manufacturing, dozens of organisations have discovered that someone else's operational crisis becomes theirs – and in turn, their customers' – even though it is not in their control. Identifying these external risks to execution – whether these are Chinese hackers, hurricanes, Japanese chip manufacturers or the next SARS outbreak – is critical to planning ahead. Those who fail to deliver on customer promises and who cannot blame such externalities are not likely to avoid pariah status, at least for a while. Angry and empowered customers now rush to Twitter to complain and reveal even quite minor lapses[10], turning them into potential crises for the brand. There have been several stories in recent years about Ryanair passengers occupying planes in mutinous moods because they have not landed at their destinations, or not taken off for hours.[11] Ryanair's reportedly cavalier approach to customer care, communication and provision of food and drink means that these stories are posted in national news media.

Financial Crises

For private-sector organisations, particularly those that trade on their commercial competence, worst of all are financial crises, which tend to weaken support from investors who may otherwise remain sanguine about temporary behavioural or operational crises. At their worst, these crises are fatal for the organisation. Why so? Not because they represent inept bookkeeping but because they are usually indicative of some deeper underlying malaise which is not being honestly communicated. A trading scandal that sank Barings bank first surfaced as a financial crisis. Accounting scandals did for Enron (and Andersen), WorldCom and many others, including most recently Kids Company. Behind all of these were various forms of leadership failure, behavioural lapses and other cultural or even strategic issues. But as the old adage goes, you only run out of cash once. If trust dries up, that becomes a financial problem very quickly, as Bear Stearns and Lehman Brothers discovered in 2008. If that trust deficit had spread just a little bit wider than it did in the subsequent weeks and months, a much worse catastrophe might have occurred than actually did.

Shell's reserves crisis of 2004 was also essentially a financial crisis. For complex reasons which are still debated, the company was forced to reveal that it had not been accounting consistently for reserves according to the required rules of the SEC. As a result, restatements had to be made which eventually knocked some 25 per cent off the booked reserves[12] on the balance sheet and led to the demise of three senior leaders including then-CEO Phil Watts, a £17 million fine from the FSA, a $120 million fine to the SEC and a $450 million payment to US shareholders. The share price impact was perhaps less dramatic than the shame this incident brought onto the company. I was heavily involved in the years of recovery. Shell's reserves crisis, like most financial crises, was not just an accounting glitch; it revealed issues which had been troubling the company for years. But the high-handed way Shell had managed its relationships with the City and Wall Street for years beforehand intensified the pressures, and for some period the company realised it was relatively friendless.

The issue for established pariahs is that they leave themselves exposed if they disappoint (negatively surprise) one of the key constituencies that are usually supportive to them. Their Faustian bargain is to accept that it's OK to have lots of people hate them, as long as they can keep the bankers and traders positive. When that bargain unravels, it's not pretty.

Crisis Impacts

As the crisis occurs, the negative impacts start to hit home. These days, organisations can expect overwhelming and often highly negative press and social-media comment to hit them at the same time as they are frantically trying to deal with an operational crisis they may not fully understand. The Freshfields study above looked at the share price impact of crises on the day of announcement, and again after two days, five days, six months and one year after the crisis "broke". The team discovered that behavioural crises caused the greatest initial drop in stock price but that it was operational crises which caused the greatest hits in the long term – still down 15 per cent after six months. Serious crisis fallout hits the boardroom. Even as the organisations concerned are still dealing with the crisis, senior leadership may be leaving. Freshfields noted that some 10 per cent (87 out of 899) of the directors of companies involved in scandals left within six months. Of these, 39 explicitly linked their departure to the crisis (4 per cent), but we can reasonably assume that at least some of the rest were linked to related restructuring, and that others left tainted by the crises later on.

Intrinsic vs Extrinsic

The Freshfields study also analyses crises as either intrinsic or extrinsic. Intrinsic crises are those that appear to be caused by things within the organisation's control (such as a network outage for a phone company). Extrinsic crises are outside the organisation's control (such as a government expropriation of company assets). In the short term, the study notes that extrinsic crises are more suddenly destructive of value than intrinsic ones, but this picture is reversed over a longer timeframe.[13] In other words, although organisations may be blamed for not spotting external "predictable surprises", they are certainly blamed for those which should have been under their own control.

Crisis Impact by Stakeholder Group

So we can see that crises are bad news for investors and, by extension, for the leaders of the organisation. But who else suffers in a crisis and at what stage of the crisis does this occur?

Table 5: Stakeholder Impacts by Crisis Type

CRISIS TYPE	MAIN INITIAL IMPACT	SUBSEQUENT IMPACT
Behavioural	Employees, Investors	Employees, Investors, Partners
Operational	Customers, Employees, Partners	Partners, Investors, Employees
Financial	Investors	Investors, Employees, Customers, Partners

Employees have a lot to lose – perhaps the most. Only in one type of crisis (financial) are they potentially not impacted in the first place and, unfortunately, the subsequent impact with financial crises can all too often be the termination of employment for innocent people with no responsibility for the problem, as costs are desperately cut or businesses exited. There are predictable and measurable slumps in employee engagement after a major behavioural crisis, and employees are often among the first to experience hostile reactions via press, customers, family and friends. They are also likely to be involved in work to change their behaviour afterwards, even if they had nothing to do with the behaviour in question beforehand. This work can be discouraging and unmotivating if poorly managed. Operational crises can be devastating for employees' sense of pride in a well-run organisation, but paradoxically can be very engaging, exhilarating, even enjoyable for those directly involved if they feel they are being successful at containing the crisis. Usually, the more powerless and uninvolved with the crisis they are, the worse employees feel about it, as again they tend to have to absorb reputational flak without having the knowledge with which to countermand criticisms.

Customers lose out in crises too. In behavioural crises they are subsequently impacted by the reputational fallout of association with a tainted brand. Drivers thought twice about filling up at BP service stations after the Deepwater Horizon disaster, not only because of their own misgivings about the company, but also because they were not keen to let others see them associating with a toxic brand of a seemingly "irresponsible" company.[14]

Investors are badly impacted by crises – sooner or later, because crises are literally and metaphorically costly. Although behavioural crises are the ones which have the most negative initial impact on share prices, operational crises have a more profound impact on revenue (74 per cent of the Freshfields sample). Across all cases, the number of firms that experience falls in their share price of 30 per cent or more rises from 3 per cent on day one to 21 per cent after one year.

Partners have mixed fortunes in crises: they may face significant losses, but also can benefit from opportunities if they are agile and relevant. Some, like Freshfields, want us to rely on them as a source of lucrative (for them) emergency advice and support during a crisis. Other professional service firms, particularly management consultants and auditors, will also be keen to "help" (as well as protect their own reputations if they have been closely involved with the organisation – recalling the fate of auditor Arthur Andersen, which perished alongside its client Enron in 2002). Suppliers at a more nuts-and-bolts level tend to suffer, as cash flows may tighten, ordering may stop and the ability to engage or commit the organisation grinds to a halt. In the longer term, true partners (in joint ventures, for example) may shy away from involvement with tainted organisations.

Given so much pain and loss, it's notable that we don't take crisis aversion, or at least crisis management (aka crisis reaction), more seriously. It wasn't much taught in business schools until quite recently, and still tends to be taught as a "how to cope when it happens" course rather than as a holistic approach to avoiding crisis. Why is this? Surely there should be massive incentives to get organisations better prepared for both avoiding crises in the first place and dealing with them when they do occur? There are several possible reasons for this anomaly. Partly, it's just that the nature of most activities, particularly in business, requires an optimistic bias and a focus on delivering a vision. Spending time and effort planning for when your product breaks or your executives misbehave is still counterintuitive to most of us. We'd rather put our efforts into making something work. And I think that's just as true for the NHS or other aspects of public service. The exception might perhaps be something like local authority adoption services, which have learned through multiple bad experiences that they will get blamed if things go wrong, and plan and act accordingly "by the book".

But the other, less palatable reason why organisations leave themselves open to the risks of crisis is that leaders may have less to lose than other stakeholders. Of course that is not how they see it, but the central problem of agency theory remains: the managers of the organisation may well be operating in their own interest. Of course leaders stand to lose a lot in a crisis. There is no evidence that Bob Diamond, Phil Watts, Tony Hayward or Fred Goodwin wanted the torrents of abuse they faced as their reputations were ruined by uncontrolled and uncontrollable crises on their watch. In all cases they would, I think, believe they had acted in the interests of their organisations, had tried to do the right things, but had been unfortunate victims of circumstance. Therein lies the problem we described in the previous chapter. Hubristic leaders, or to be more precise, narcissists, are usually far from self-aware. Leaders and organisations with hubristic tendencies don't value the downside risks as they do the upside opportunities. In short, they have an optimistic bias, which in at least some cases may be exacerbated by the reward systems they work in.

Are Crises on the Increase?

I believe we are facing an unprecedented avalanche of crises because of four related factors:

- **Globalisation** – we have legitimate interests not just in the local news and scandal of our own village or town, but in international affairs. A ruptured oil pipe in Canada is no longer a minor issue of concern to a few people in northern Alberta; it's a factor in the geopolitics of where pipelines go and an evidence point for NGOs wanting to find fault with an oil company.

- **Transparency** – we expect to be able to see what's going on, everywhere, all the time. If something happens, we expect to be able to find out the truth about it soon after a rumour surfaces. If we don't, conspiracy theories rapidly surface.

- **Technology** – we have the capability to gather data ourselves (pictures of floods, Arab Spring) and share our views on Twitter and Facebook. News (true or not) can massively propagate in minutes or even seconds that would in the past have taken hours or days to report. News is no longer owned and controlled just by the professionals in the newspapers, radio and television. Expectations have shifted; we expect high-quality, live video of what is going on. We expect polished spokespeople who can explain what is happening and why. We digest our news faster. Also, organisations are collecting and using vast amounts of data about us, with as-yet-unexplored knock-on effects into privacy and reputation.

- **Democracy** – we have strong democratic expectations about our right to information and access. We don't accept deference any more to authority figures from the Establishment telling us not to worry or that things are safe. We expect to take part in the crisis if we want to, as commentators, activists and even as actors.[15]

If I am correct, then the onward march of these factors may inure us to crises. If crises are present wherever we look, and if our own organisations are suffering them as well, perhaps it will become easier to ignore them. However, my worry is that we will, in fact, become not less but more sensitised to crises by their ubiquity. We hardly notice one bee, but a swarm gets our attention. It's notoriously difficult to forecast accurately what future social trends will be. However, I am concerned that in a world of constant organisational crises, trust will degrade to a point that will have serious consequences for our inter-actions. What economists call frictional costs will rise – we will have to audit, check and vet to an ever greater degree our business partners, employees or investments. And our individual trust levels could well suffer too. If my organisation and yours cannot trust each other, then why should I trust you?

Crises vs "Issues"

The professionals in crisis PR and response like to distinguish between crises and "issues". Issues are the long-term questions and problems in an industry that are either well established or emerging, but not necessarily at some flash point of crisis. Well-managed organisations, so the thinking goes, monitor issues and attempt to influence thinking across multiple stakeholders in the organisation's interests. In a perfect world, a well-managed issue never becomes a crisis. A good example of an issue would be oil spills in the Niger delta. A significant amount of crude oil is spilled in Nigeria, as a result of accidents, leaks and carelessness. Shell's Nigerian joint venture,[16] as one of the leading operators in the country, is frequently criticised by Greenpeace, Friends of the Earth and also local activist groups such as MEND (Move-ment for the Emancipation of the Niger Delta) for being responsible for these spills, because the oil comes from Shell fields. However, there are complex reasons why spills occur. As well as operational failings, there are significant numbers of spills due to sabotage and theft.

This situation has gone on for many years. Arguably it has been conven-ient for Shell not to force the issue on spills: most are small and cause limited problems. Tackling the pervasive, systematic theft of oil, which occurs at scales which involve corruption to the highest levels of government, is much more difficult. And it is not always clear what Shell's appropriate role should be in the politics of a country where the unfair division of oil wealth is an ongoing challenge.[17] So Shell observes an issue like Nigeria oil spills, with both line leaders and specialist issues management professionals involved, over a long time. Eventually a crisis occurs related to the issue. Perhaps a pipeline is sabotaged to allow locals to steal oil and then explodes, killing dozens (this has happened on several occasions). Or European workers are captured by MEND guerrillas protesting at the damage being done to their communities.

At this point, one could argue the issues management piece has been a waste of time. Certainly on the surface it can look bad – Freshfields report that 25 per cent of companies had "months" of notice before a crisis broke in the media. But Shell would argue that there is a world of difference between monitoring and not monitoring an issue, even if a crisis does subsequently occur. I suspect that is what was happening in some of the cases Freshfields alludes to. Firstly, even if the crisis is not averted altogether, it may be less serious (e.g. in these cases perhaps rapid reaction can be achieved to shut off the pipeline flows). But more importantly, the relationships have been established with the relevant parties so dialogue and joined-up action can take place, whether that is with the security forces, local people, perhaps even MEND itself. And it's this connection with the wider system that is so important. At its worst, it makes the organisation less surprised and more capable of reacting to the crisis. At its best, it can aid effective metamorphosis and catharsis, and the avoidance of recurrence. It is in the nature of issues, even more than crises, to be "unmanageable". But as complexity increases, it will become more and more important for organisations to have dedicated groups (internal and external) who can help identify, monitor and influence issues in their own interest.

Pariah Crises

Which crises form pariah reputations and why? Why do established pariahs get stuck in permanent crisis mode? Are there cases of pariahs redeemed by crisis? Crises force you to reveal your true character and ground out how you've been treating the world in preparation for the current event. Relationships your organisation has with its customers, regulators, financiers and the press, all become highly significant as the crisis takes hold. There is no precise moment at which one becomes a pariah. But certainly, the slow drip of crises building on each other has a growing impact on reputation, which is trackable.

A critical issue is the capacity of the potential pariah organisation to cause harm to people, either physical (including killing them or injuring their health) or mental (as the press have sometimes damaged people with unjustified persecution). So clearly where there has been substantial negligence or a lack of care for people's health and basic wellbeing, no amount of slick corporate PR can save a reputation. This latter point is why so many of the recent pariah crises involve public-sector bodies, such as the NHS, social services or police. The trust gap between what we expect from such bodies and what has actually been delivered can sometimes be disturbingly wide. However, we should be cautious about falling into the trap of believing that just because an organisation is in an industry in which harm is possible, pariah status is inevitable. That is not the case; it's just that if you undertake such activity you need to be able to show that you have done all that you could have done to make those activities safe for your workforce, customers and others. Such risk assessment is considered a basic management skill in many industries now, and that skill needs to extend to the most senior ranks. Where such risks have been brazenly ignored and particularly where there are whistleblowers and 'smoking gun' evidence, it's unsurprising that external stakeholders are unsympathetic to those on the inside.

Crisis, Genesis and Hubris

Part of the theory behind the Pariah Lifecycle is that, given the genesis conditions of rapid growth, success/praise, brand prominence and weak governance, and with a hubristic culture in place, crisis is all but inevitable. In the genesis phase, future pariahs are building up their organisation and their collective reputations, not preparing for crisis and nemesis. In the hubris phase, it becomes increasingly impossible to discuss the potential for failure and crisis. The very nature of proper crisis preparation, when done well, is humbling: you realise very fast in any good drill how terrible the real thing would be, and your own organisational and personal vulnerabilities are ruthlessly revealed. Such preparations go against the nature of the narcissism at the centre of hubristic behaviour. When a crisis does occur to such an organisation, the whole way that the crisis plays out will reveal the flaws that have let it occur. The lack of humility, the arrogance and bravado of employees at all levels, the lack of planning, the lack of realism, the operational failings; all these become blatantly apparent. PR and press-management efforts are inevitably doomed at this stage: there is too much ill will to deal with, and too much schadenfreude in the distress of the deposed top dog.

Crisis as Redemption?

In some cases crises turn out to have redemptive qualities for organisations. This can happen in various ways:

- **Unification** – the crisis helps focus a fragmented company torn apart by infighting onto the real common enemy

- **Revelation** – the crisis finally allows the truth to be told and lets the organisation deal with a problem that had been growing for a while but had become undiscussable

- **Demonstration** – the efficient and effective way the organisation reacts to crisis demonstrates its character and quality more effectively than day-to-day operations could ever do.

But I am not convinced that these potential upsides outweigh the damage a major crisis causes.

In the first case – unification – there is no doubt that this dynamic does often occur in the early stages of many crises, and was certainly evident in the cases I have known best. The problem is that, although fighting against the outside world is a great dynamic in the short term for focusing the organisation's resources against the external critique, it can rapidly backfire once the crisis moves into nemesis mode (the subject of our next chapter). The dynamic is easily diverted into one where anyone questioning the accepted internal versions of the truth (which are almost invariably partially untruthful, either deliberately or otherwise) is vilified. This is how whistleblowers are usually treated both before, during and often long after crises. The best hope is that the unifying force is a determination to look hard and honestly at what has occurred, admit personal and collective responsibility for blame and punishment, and seek to change and gain real forgiveness through the process of catharsis (see Chapter 9).

In the second case – revelation – crises do indeed tend to blow the covers off things that may have been skilfully hidden for years or even decades. Although this may be a relief to some inside the organisation who may have been pressing for fuller openness in the past, it's usually a horrible shock to most, and the realisation that even a few people knew is invariably destructive to trust and internal cohesion at the point when it is perhaps most required. So although it's usually good to get the truth out, it would be better not to do it at the moment of crisis.

In the third suggestion above – demonstration – the way that the organisation responds becomes its own answer to its detractors. There is no doubt that where organisations are able to respond rapidly and effectively to crisis, provide honest information and deal with complex problems with integrity, there can be highly positive feedback. The PR industry cites the examples of Virgin Trains' handling of the crash at Grayrigg in Cumbria in 2007 and Tesco's handling of the horsemeat scandal of 2013 as exemplars of how to "do it right". And as this book was being completed, BHP Billiton were receiving praise for their handling of a huge and deadly dam collapse in a joint venture in Brazil. I am not so sure: certainly these are good examples of how to leave press and critics with little to quibble about on PR execution, but in all these cases there remained serious questions about how these organisations became involved in systems that had the power to harm their customers, and whether they asked the right questions or operated in a way that could have avoided harm to others. Certainly none of the companies would want to have suffered the crisis in the first place.

The simple point is this: crises are bad things. We risk confusing the benefits of effective metamorphosis and catharsis with the destructive impact of crisis at our peril. Sadly, some organisations have become addicted to the adrenaline of crisis and almost seek out trouble to prove to themselves how tough and enduring they are. This seems very ill advised. Crises occur because organisations have, in some measure, failed. In the future, we can expect stakeholders to be carefully monitoring crises (number, type and quantity) as a proxy for management capability.

RECOMMENDATIONS

6. Assume It Will Happen

Crises are particularly painful for those who don't think they will ever have one. On the whole, the best advice for any large, complex organisation is to assume that:

A) Even your organisation will succumb – a crisis serious enough to make you a pariah can and will happen to you sooner or later.

B) The types of possible crisis are predictable – it will be financial, behavioural or operational, or some combination thereof.

C) So you can prepare – there are some ways you can prepare even without knowing the specifics.

D) Planning's a good idea because you won't have time to do much once it's real – although you may get some notice, you may get very little or none at all.

E) You will need a plan that can go at any time – the crisis will not occur at a time or place of your choosing.

Therefore, a smart organisation, even if it believes it has installed good anti-pariah defences, will have thought ahead about how it might react under certain scenarios. It will have formed plans and will have assigned 24/7 resources and plans ready to react to a crisis. Finally, it will train its leaders and relevant specialists so they can concentrate on the unique aspects of the crisis, rather than be excessively shocked that they are even experiencing one at all.

7. Prepare and Practise for Crises

Organisations that practise crisis drills perform significantly better than those that don't when the real thing occurs. Much good material has been written on preparing for crisis and conducting crisis drills.[18] The one lesson that is very hard to impart but quite critical to success is allied to item 13 in our recommendation list below (maintaining healthy paranoia). If you engage frequently and thoughtfully in crisis preparations and drills that involve the entire leadership team, you will engender a learning culture that is a) aware of how painful and unpleasant a real crisis might be and b) has heightened awareness about some of the sources and how hard it can be to react fast enough in real time. So the organisation gets two benefits: the practical, analytic, prophylactic benefit of understanding the weaknesses which the organisation has (and the associated opportunity to fix them); and the cultural benefit of understanding how humbling a crisis would feel, how out of control leaders might become, and the systemic learning as organisations realise they are in interdependent worlds, where the weakest link that may undo them may not be directly under their control.

So I am an advocate of including a wide range of people in crisis simulations, not just the PR and spin doctors, or those responsible for health and safety or operational continuity. Include the regular leadership of the line. Include HR and IT. Include Finance. Sooner or later in a real crisis they would be involved, and certainly affected. And it would also be great if regulators or other "neutral" facilitators could convene more regular exercises (as are done in London for multi-agency disaster response planning) to simulate systemic issues. In preparation for the London Olympics in 2012, the banks were forced to take part in such exercises, which were incredibly insightful in terms of revealing some of the danger spots for the whole system in the face of determined external threats. But relatively few of us took part in the exercise, and although the lessons learned were shared and acted on, I wonder whether an opportunity was not missed to enable a wider form of systemic learning.

The final reason why crisis planning and simulation is a good idea is that it can be a powerful opportunity to view leaders under pressure and how they react. Those who lack humility tend to reveal themselves quite quickly in these conditions, as do those who are reckless or bad judges of people or don't understand their industry. Over time these simulations could become a powerful and differentiating part of an organisational culture. On several occasions, I attempted to get Shell to treat its leadership conference for the top 300 as such an exercise, but with no success! But the idea remains intriguing to me. Would an organisation that was prepared to try this out not learn at a faster rate – about itself and its people – than its competitors? Would it not survive longer? Or would it become, over time, smug and overconfident, and even more prone to pariahdom?

8. Develop a Broad and Supportive Coalition

Earlier we introduced the concept of reputational entrepreneurs, those who will tell our story for us to others, and set the tone for external debates about our reputation. Long before a crisis occurs, we should be clear who we think these people should be. If we don't establish them and look after them before crisis descends, it's likely to be impossible to generate them afterwards. Here are a few of the groups we should focus on (in no particular order of precedence):

I. **Customers and clients** – if they hate your products, feel cheated or ignored, or are simply ashamed to be associated with your organisation's antics, you will know about it. What is shocking is how slow executives have been (compared with, say, politicians, who are also dependent on the good opinion of their clientele) to embrace social media and connect directly with those who use their products or services.[19] In the future, failure to maintain close connection will be an unacceptable risk.

II. **Employees** – it seems painfully obvious that we should take the time to cultivate a deep emotional relationship of loyalty and mutual respect with our employees. Yet all too often we encourage a transactional mentality, or allow unions or others to dominate direct communication. When a crisis strikes, we often neglect employees, although they are well placed to be authoritative and effective communicators on behalf of the organisation to other influencers.[20]

III. **Politicians** – like it or not, politicians who know and understand your organisation and its culture will be incredibly helpful if and when things go wrong. Of course they will have to be careful and you must not embarrass them, but no organisation has too many friends in government.[21]

IV. **Media and commentariat** – this group is still so crucial that, outside of the government relations area, this is where most organisational effort and professional resource is expended. Haughty, distant and aloof is not the way to go here; give access and be transparent, honest and open to criticism and debate. This is not to condone some of the awful fawning that has gone on to newspaper proprietors in the past; leave that to the politicians. But to develop relationships with journalists who know your organisation, understand it and can speak knowledgeably to its merits is only sensible.[22] But it is still all too rare: people seem to think that consorting with the enemy outside of some communication transaction is bad form.

V. **Wider social publics** – organisations are still in the early days of managing relationships with individuals and groups on Facebook, Twitter and other platforms. Generally these relationships are dominated by product brands. Much is written on the subject.[23] But more can and should be done to ensure that those who know and understand the organisation, whether out of interest, concern or as customers or owners, can maintain an open level of dialogue at the appropriate level. And social media can be a tremendous early warning system on growing problems.

VI. **Regulators and other special publics** – I hardly need to add anything here. Of course, there has to be some balance between the arm's length relationship in which there is no mutual trust and respect, and a revolving door where there is no proper restraint on the regulated. In between is a gulf of understanding where both sides can do their jobs effectively within a framework. Where the special publics include NGOs or others dedicated against the organisation, I would still suggest that any relationship is better than no relationship.

VII. **The City (investors)** – investors deserve respect and don't always get it. In turn, they need to understand the pressures on the organisation and not pretend it is solely a financial entity with no other purpose than profit.

If all of the groups above were truly well disposed towards your organisation, I think it's pretty clear the credibility of the scandal would be lower (i.e. at the very least people would be more surprised by a crisis of reputation and more prepared to hear what you were doing about it, or treat it as an aberration rather than a smoking gun).

9. Communicate by Listening not SHOUTING

This is really just an extension of the previous suggestion. If you are always in dialogue and can monitor and manage issues effectively, you are much less likely to be surprised by crises. The best way to understand your stakeholders is not to shout at them until they understand you properly. It's to listen to them. And I don't mean the sort of shallow listening we all indulge in where we smile, nod and wait for the other person to stop talking.

> Inquiry is as much an attitude as it is a specific behaviour.

> (Schein, 2009, p.69)

Real listening is a deep skill. Most of us can't do it well – or not consistently, at any rate. And some people can't do it at all. Because of the critical importance of real listening to successful leadership, many organisations are now beginning to teach executives earlier in their careers the skills to do it better, and in the future I think we may start to see listening skill as one of the shibboleths for determining who is and is not worthy of senior leadership roles. Those who are naturally skilled at listening on an individual level can add a lot of value to organisations. They don't have to be the most senior leaders to do this (although that certainly helps), but they do have to have a deep sense of respect for other people. Organisational listening in the modern age can become pretty sophisticated. We have discussed briefly above how use of social media is now revolutionising to an undreamt of degree the level of intimacy and understanding that organisations can have with their customers. Or presumably that's the government's excuse for reading all my email…

Actually, I am not comfortable with the idea that companies have thought through any better than governments what the downside risks are for their unwarranted snooping on us. One of the features of generative listening is that the other person a) knows you are there, listening and b) has given permission to you to hear what they are saying (and thinking). So we will likely see a flood of pariah crises in coming years whose essential features are that the consumer or customer or client feels their rights to privacy or choice have been violated by a big business, or that their data has not been protected as it should. Whatever the legal position turns out to be (and no doubt there will be some sophisticated arguments on both sides), we don't yet know what the views of mass consumers will be. Perhaps the generations that come after us, the digital natives brought up on a life lived in public, online, will see things differently than those of us for whom "private" is a default setting and "none of your business" applies to almost everyone except their most trusted friends. This is one of the hardest future challenges for large organisations. The mixed-up moral demographics of a multi-generational, multi-ethnic, multi-national world are tricky to navigate, to say the least. But if our organisations can genuinely listen, really react to different points of view, and question their own purity of motives and outcome, perhaps we may see some avoid the bear traps ahead.

Notes

1   See Lieberman, 2013. It appears that in terms of functional MRI studies, physical pain and the social pain of, for example, rejection appear essentially identical. Our brain spends a vast amount of its resources on thinking about how others will assess our actions and react in turn; we are evolved from species which spent their whole lives in social groupings (as chimpanzees, gorillas and other apes still do) and we are primed to want to avoid rejection by the group.

2   Starbucks and Amazon – US headquartered companies – were blindsided by the rapid shift in UK attitudes to tax avoidance after the recession hit in 2009, and found themselves on the wrong side of a massive campaign opposing their (legal) efforts to minimise taxation in the EU. The specialists who might have monitored such political issues were in Seattle, far from the relevant action. HMRC were not complaining, so they assumed all was well. Both brands sustained significant reputational impact even though convenience and service delivery maintained customer growth.

3   This can be a successful strategy in some contexts – some would argue that Internet companies such as Google and Facebook have operated in this way for years. But as these companies become larger and more essential to the successful functioning of our lives, they are discovering that they need processes to handle these crises just like an oil company does.

4   Quoted in Regester and Larkin, 2008.

5   COBRA stands for Cabinet Office Briefing Room A. This is the room in which critical personnel can be brought together in an ad hoc committee to steer major crisis responses involving multiple government and private-sector bodies.

6   Railtrack was in effect taken into public ownership as Network Rail (and is a rare case of a reformed established pariah).

7   For example, Burson-Marsteller has formed a Crisis Club which reports on increasing volumes and types of organisational threats such as new market entrants and cyber terrorism. See http://burson-marsteller.s3.amazonaws. com/wp-content/uploads/2015/10/15110706/BM-Crisis-Club-Report-2015. pdf

8   The Freshfields studies appeared well before the incidents that impacted Sony Pictures in 2015, when their entire systems were hacked, films stolen and embarrassing emails leaked. But such tech-enabled crises are clearly becoming more common. Eventually such events will cease to be seen as special cases, and attention will turn to the way that leaders have (or have not) prepared to protect the organisation's and customers' data. At the time of writing, a major crisis was engulfing UK telco Talk Talk with much criticism of CEO Dido Harding's response as customers realised their data had not been adequately encrypted.

9   Article: 10 Years On: Lessons From 9/11, http://www.continuityinsights.com/ articles/2011/09/10-years-lessons-9/11

10 Customers during major recent outages have not been slow to get onto social media websites to express their views. A typical tweet from a recent Vodafone Australia outage read: "We can (allegedly) place man on the moon in 1969 yet in 2014 we can't even make a phone call #vodafail".

11 http://www.dailymail.co.uk/news/article-2564683/ Ryanair-passengers-Stansted-Airport-forced-call-police-refused-food-water-right-leave-aircraft-11-HOUR-delay.html

12 As so often, behind the lurid headlines was a more nuanced set of issues. Shell's bookings were wrong in that they did not scrupulously follow the (rather conservative) SEC guidelines required globally. A combination of Shell's weak pipeline of new projects, inconsistent global reserves accounting policies and overconfidence in their own cleverness (and dislike of the US making the rules for the world) all conspired in the crisis. The hubris, of course, lay in believing that the rules should not apply to them.

13 As Freshfields put it: "Over the longer term, the market is more lenient on companies that have been struck by an extrinsic crisis. They inflict a cut in share price of over 50 per cent on the first day and are more likely to harm the share price in the first week. But after a year only a quarter of firms that experience an extrinsic crisis continue to suffer a drop in share price of 70 per cent. Intrinsic crises account for two-thirds of firms that experience a fall in share price of 30 per cent or more after 13 weeks. After six months this rises to more than three-quarters (78 per cent), with share prices still down 70 per cent one year after the event became public. The upshot is that unpredictable crises have the greatest upfront shock value, while problems that go to the heart of the company's operations deliver a longer-term negative impact."

14 Wang, Lee and Polonsky, 2015 linked decline in BP gasoline sales to the intensity of the negative news reports on the crisis.

15 The Arab Spring uprisings in 2010–11 famously started after the self-immolation of Mohammed Bouaziz in Tunisia sparked a chain reaction of protest and regime change across North Africa. The role of Facebook and Twitter in organising protests, spreading news outside the control of the regimes concerned, and enthusing fellow activists was an accelerant, if not a critical factor, in the success of these movements. A survey conducted by the Dubai School of Government in 2011 found that between 32 per cent and 51 per cent of respondents felt that "Social Media played a role in empowering me to influence change in my community/country", and 9 out of 10 Egyptians and Tunisians used Facebook to organise protests and disruptions. During the riots of 2011 in England, Twitter provided protesters, looters, police and citizens alike with the most accurate picture of what was happening live in a fluid situation.

16 Shell operates onshore in Nigeria in a joint venture called SPDC (Shell Petroleum Development Company of Nigeria Ltd). Shell only owns 30 per cent of the venture, but is the operator (a common industry practice to spread risks and capital costs but focus accountability and risk management).

17 At the time of writing, former Nigerian Oil Minister and former Shell

executive Diezani Alison-Madueke was reported to have been one of five people arrested (but not charged) in London by the UK National Crime Agency as part of an investigation into bribery and money laundering. The case related to some $20bn of missing oil revenues from her time in office. See Diezani Alison-Madueke: Behind the "reformer" of the Nigerian oil industry's arrest (http://www.independent.co.uk/news/world/africa/reformer-of-nigerian-oil-industry-diezani-alison-madueke-arrested-on-bribery-charges-a6685146.html). There is no claim Shell is involved in this corruption, but it's embarrassing – at best – to have former executives involved in such cases.

18 See Coombs, 2007 for a particularly useful bibliography.

19 A 2012 CEO.com study noted that only 8.1 per cent of Fortune 100 CEOs (Fortune 500 CEOs: 3.8 per cent) were on Twitter, although 34.3 per cent of the general public were on the platform. For Facebook, the numbers were: Fortune 100 CEOs: 12.1 per cent; Fortune 500 CEOs: 7.6 per cent; US public: 50.5 per cent. The statistics imply yet another dimension of life where the busy, over-stimulated and over-scheduled lives of the elite no longer relate to the reality most of the public experiences. The exception is LinkedIn, where CEO participation rates were pretty much that of the general population, at about 25 per cent.

20 See Riddell, 2013.

21 Politicians are also very connected by Twitter. According to Tweetminster.co.uk/mps in 2015, there were 409 UK MPs on Twitter (62.9 per cent of the total). So they also have to be treated as a critical social media and commentariat audience for any crisis.

22 See Coombs and Holladay, 2006.

23 For example, see Kietzman et al., 2005.

7

Nemesis – Downfall

nem·e·sis [nem-*uh*-sis]

noun, plural nem·e·ses [nem-*uh*-seez]

1. something that a person cannot conquer, achieve, etc.: *The performance test proved to be my nemesis.*
2. an opponent or rival whom a person cannot best or overcome.
3. *(initial capital letter) Classical Mythology.* the goddess of divine retribution.
4. an agent or act of retribution or punishment.

IN THIS CHAPTER we will examine the concept of nemesis and what happens during the nemesis phase that follows a hubris-induced crisis. We will see that nemesis is an important symbolic part of the process to signal the end of the crisis and to enable a real metamorphosis and catharsis to occur.

Nemesis and the Model

We hardly lack for examples of nemesis. The failure of Lehman Brothers. The demise of Enron and their auditor, Andersen. The collapse of the Royal Bank of Scotland (RBS) or the charity Kids Company. The closure of the *News of the World*. All of these organisational failures were surrounded by shame, blame and reputational ruin for leaders, financial ruin for investors and staff.

A really good nemesis has the following features as part of a narrative from which we can learn:

- **Justice** – for something to be nemesis, rather than just bad luck, there has to be a sense that the negative outcome was deserved. In our model, we will suggest that the cause is in the hubristic behaviour, or even starts in the genesis, of the organisation.

- **Closure** – the best nemeses create closure over the crisis period, either by ending the organisation's life entirely, or by providing a symbolic closure (a resignation, a contrite apology, a visible change in structure, process or behaviour).

- **Symbolism and learning** – proper nemesis provides a symbolic learning point for others; look what has happened and why.

My argument in this book is that as social beings we need narratives and symbols of storytelling to help us make sense of the world. Children's stories teach us that baddies come to bad ends or at the very least experience a change of heart and become goodies after all. I think it's significant that many believe that insufficient nemesis has taken place[1] for the events of the great financial crisis of 2008–9, poisoning the basis for trusting relationships between taxpayers, shareholders, consumers, politicians and bankers. So even if nemesis doesn't lead to outright organisational failure, it does lead to severe organisational damage and it's in our failure to understand and value nemesis that we miss the chance for the organisational learning that could help us escape the pariah lifecycle. Organisations must therefore realise that without visible nemesis, crises won't end, and there can be no legitimate start to metamorphosis and catharsis.

Origins

The Greek word νέμεσις (nemesis) is related to the verb νεμειν (nemein), meaning to "give what is due". In Liddell and Scott's dictionary, the entry reflects the religious overtones of the entry on hubris:

> Distribution of what is due; but in usage always retribution, esp. righteous anger aroused by injustice…

Nemesis with a capital N is the personification of such divine retribution. Rarely visualised in Greek art and never put on stage in any of the extant plays we have or know of, Nemesis is all the scarier for being so shadowy.

We should avoid calling Nemesis the goddess of revenge.[2] Revenge as we know it is a very different concept; nemesis is not just a settling of personal scores. Rather, nemesis implies the rebalancing of the universe to where it should be, as though a tectonic plate has shifted and caused the earthquake to release the pressure.

In our own reactions to crises, I am going to argue that we have a deep-seated, felt need for nemesis to occur, particularly to pariahs, and that its repeated absence is a problem in terms of unresolved emotions around guilt, punishment and justice, and hence licence to operate. Without some visible nemesis there can be no meaningful metamorphosis, and hence no catharsis and forgiveness. Nemesis was said to be the goddess who lured Narcissus to the pool in which he became transfixed by his own reflection in a pool. Narcissus, a beautiful youth, had scorned the nymph, Echo, who duly cursed him to fall in love with his own reflection instead.[3] It is not for nothing that David Owen's model of hubris (see Chapter 5 above) takes so many of its elements from Narcissistic Personality Disorder, perhaps. Too many leaders (and indeed whole organisations) fall into the trap of loving what Ovid called "an imagined body which contains no substance." Ancient Greek Nemesis disliked people having excessive amounts of happiness or natural gifts. Something of a natural socialist, she ensured the rebalancing of the world through her interventions. But to the unfortunate victim, her actions could seem random and unfair, and the source of their own sin and hubris often remained opaque to them. In this respect I believe there are deep parallels with modern reality. Organisations and their leaders rarely feel they deserve their downfalls – unlike their opponents, who tend to feel that they got their comeuppance.

When Shell admitted defeat and pulled out of drilling in Alaska in 2014, the official press release was part of the new CEO's first presentation on results and strategy:[4]

> The recent Ninth Circuit Court decision against the Department of the Interior raises substantial obstacles to Shell's plans for drilling in offshore Alaska. As a result, Shell has decided to stop its exploration programme for Alaska in 2014. "This is a disappointing outcome, but the lack of a clear path forward means that I am not prepared to commit further resources for drilling in Alaska in 2014," van Beurden said. "We will look to relevant agencies and the Court to resolve their open legal issues as quickly as possible."

Greenpeace, which had been campaigning vigorously against Shell as part of its opposition to drilling in the Arctic, was delighted[5]:

> Today's news caps a miserable decade in the Arctic for Shell. This included a [sic] accident prone drilling effort in 2012 that would have been laughable if it hadn't been so dangerous. In the space of a few weeks we saw two grounded oil rigs, engine fires, crumpled spill response equipment and air pollution fines. These failures led the US interior secretary to complain that Shell "screwed up" – hardly the kind of language we're used to from serving politicians. In 2013 the company saw no alternative but to suspend its plans in the Arctic. In 2014, following the court ruling, Shell will yet again be spending money for nothing.

Although Shell privately recognised at least some of the shortcomings that Greenpeace mentioned, it would have been unlikely to mention them in the new CEO's first major public outing; he needed to keep the door open to further drilling, as well as minding his legal liabilities and the morale of his troops. Nevertheless, it's always instructive – as we shall see – to note whether or not organisations are able to admit the full truth and do so promptly. If Shell had persisted in an official line that pretended that all was basically well, but for some trifling local legal difficulties, it would have been doing so in the face of several very public engineering and safety failures. Far better to admit that performance had fallen below its own high standards, surely? No investor, engineer or friend of the company believed this was purely a financial decision, though that did provide the cover required for eventual exit when, in late 2015, high oil prices drove van Beurden and Shell to abandon Alaska altogether.

A new breed of more radical transparency will be required to save pariahs from themselves. Shell has in effect given up convincing stakeholders that it can be a credible operator in Arctic oil extraction, whereas Greenpeace has been emboldened to win the hearts and minds of the next generation before they form a fond bond with the Pecten brand.[6]

A Separate Step

Nemesis does seem to team up neatly with hubris, giving a satisfying schadenfreude[7] to the moment of downfall when the crisis occurs. In our model it's tempting to conflate nemesis with crisis, as the two often come almost simultaneously. As soon as disaster strikes, the knives are out for the organisation and the leaders responsible.

But my argument is that nemesis is a necessary and subtly separate step in the process we are describing. Without it, the crisis has no precise point of ending, and hence a true and honest metamorphosis cannot occur.

This is why we have traditionally required the resignations of senior leaders when they are (or might plausibly be) responsible or accountable for crises in their organisations. We even call these metaphorical sacrifices "scalps". Why would that be, if not to recognise that this is a form of organised expiation, a formalised ritual to avoid vigilante justice and provide a symbolic victim for the (real or metaphorical) crowd? It's basically a modern version of ostracism.[8] So it's worth calling out nemesis as a distinct phase. Let's look at a notable example and see how nemesis did (or did not) facilitate the next phase of change. We can also point out a few areas where incomplete or unrecognised nemesis causes problems which ultimately lead to failure and a "repeat cycle".

Incomplete Nemesis

One of the more notable examples of incomplete nemesis in recent years seems to have occurred in the banks, and it was partly observing this reaction that led me to form the view of the importance of nemesis as a phase in the cycle. The problem was personified in what happened (or depending on your point of view, didn't happen) to Bob Diamond, the colourful President of Barclays Capital during the financial crisis of 2008–9, who later became the CEO of Barclays Group at the time of the LIBOR scandal of 2012. Diamond was forced to resign in July 2012, a matter of days before appearing at the Treasury Select Committee to give evidence about LIBOR.[9]

At one level, this resignation, this "scalp", should have been the token of nemesis required for the scandal to have closed. The symbolic act of the UK's best-known banking CEO having to give up the job he "loved", then questioned in a hostile fashion by MPs in a public forum, seemed to many to provide the perfect riposte to the apparent hubris of his comments to the same committee eighteen months before when he had infamously suggested that the "time for remorse was over". The problem with Bob Diamond's nemesis was, and remains, that it remains incomplete from the point of view of the British public. Had Diamond and others shown more convincing contrition and perhaps some greater pay restraint in 2010–11, there might have been a sense of closure and hence a true fresh start. Had he been thrown into prison for some crime, that would have given a different form of catharsis. But as things stand, no-one feels satisfied. Diamond committed no crimes[10] but was nevertheless ruthlessly ousted by his own regulator. As we noted above, society finds non-legal ways to exact punishment, particularly on reputations.

Diamond's successor as CEO at Barclays, Antony Jenkins, was initially well received by most constituencies, though he rapidly found himself struggling with the same issues that bedevilled Diamond. Stylistically less brash, he found it much easier to get a reasoned hearing than his predecessor, and gained considerable support for his broad and systemic attempts to shift the values and culture of the bank. As he wrestled with conduct issues new and old, rows about bonuses, and the viability of the investment bank in a world in which the government had decided it didn't want a UK champion universal bank, Jenkins must have felt he had inherited more curses than blessings. Without a clear new strategy, the bank tired of the ever-increasing number of scandals and concerns, from FX rate and gold-price manipulation to more recent challenges of "dark pool" trading. Eventually Jenkins too was ousted in 2015, though at least in the conventional form of being fired by his own board. Jes Staley, his successor, comes from JP Morgan, where the complexities of managing multiple banking businesses are also high on the agenda.

Diamond, meanwhile, disappeared the day after his appearance at the Treasury Select Committee to New York, to lick his wounds, teach, ride the subway like a regular Joe (if the *New York Times* is to be believed) and reluctantly lie low. He has returned to public view via his African investment vehicle, Atlas Mara, but said little about what happened in and around the time of his leadership of Barclays. His uncharacteristic silence and the unique circumstances of his leaving Barclays mean we simply don't have a narrative ending that satisfies either his supporters or his enemies. To me, that's a great shame and emphasises that an incomplete nemesis is a barrier.

Is Nemesis Sufficiently Bad?

But perhaps there is still not enough downside to becoming a pariah? Some feel too many pariah organisations do indeed survive, even if gravely wounded. Their view is that we ought to consider stronger state-sponsored penalties than we see today to discourage pariahdom. These might include increased taxes, punitive regulation, and the punishment and social shaming of their leaders.[11] In Chapter 1 we raised the notion that ostracism – the Athenian democratic process of exiling those in disfavour – might be due for a comeback. Well, the technology surely exists if we want to do it. Just imagine the joys of running a competition via social media to define who should be exiled. As in ancient Athens, the selection of candidates would become a viciously political process. If we took these discussions seriously (as Athenians must have done), would we really vote to exile people? Perhaps we would. In fact, I fear we already have and that the rule of the mob on these issues of popularity and personal accountability is now out of control. It's just a matter of time before something far worse than exile occurs.

Even without ostracism, the social exile of Nemesis is pretty awful. It's bad enough when bad things happen to you, but when others say you deserve it and have brought it on yourself, it hurts even more. The nemeses of pariah organisations and leaders are increasingly public, humiliating and vicious. The public shaming,[12] loss of leadership, reputational damage, share price impact and hits to morale of a major nemesis event are tough to bear, and it's understandable that people work hard to avoid them. However, in this chapter we have seen that a real nemesis – unless totally destructive of an organisation or a leader – is rarely complete enough to satisfy the organisation's enemies. Where a skilful nemesis can be achieved, with suitable amounts of time, apology, real remorse and clear learning, there can be both a metamorphosis and, most importantly, a societal catharsis, forgiveness and a proper renewal.

RECOMMENDATION

10. Redefine Nemesis as Organisational Learning

There is a lot written on surviving crises, and certainly as the number of crises increases the volume of experience and useful ideas for others to learn from increases too. Rather than add to that literature, which generally revolves around how you can quieten critics and get back to the script as soon as possible, I would like to remind readers that the crisis and the nemesis, although of course a threat, are in some sense inevitable, and *deserved*. That doesn't mean we should take injustices lying down or fail to fight for the reputation of the organisation, or do all we can to ensure our organisation survives. But it does mean we have to balance that fight for survival or justice with starting a process of organisational learning that will be profoundly uncomfortable. So the first aim of the organisation should be to **understand** what has occurred, not to deny facts.

When oil companies have accidents, there are established protocols for investigation and learning from these incidents. The intent is not to blame people (the lawyers come later and more than take care of that side of things). It is to get at the heart of the matter and prevent further accidents. It's a great, great shame that this process, which is highly valued by engineers and should be emulated by everyone seeking to run a continuously improving organisation, is not always extended beyond the narrow confines of the technical cause of accidents.[13]

Time and again, the real cause of accidents and, indeed, of crises more generally turns out to be the systemic and human factor issues. Occasionally a part fails or there is a previously undetected design flaw, but mainly the problem is that people at various levels made mistakes. These may have been technical in nature, but more often they are mistakes of judgement (e.g. deferring maintenance to save money, rushing a job to hit a deadline, failing to confront a performance issue or a staffing shortage). The latter are, of course, leadership issues and are invariably heavily influenced by the wider corporate culture.

After the horrific 2005 BP Texas City disaster, in which 15 people died, it became apparent that the immediate culpability for these deaths should not just lie with the line supervisors or even the plant management, but with the wider BP leadership and culture. The final report of what became known in the industry as the Baker Panel recognised that this was not just an isolated incident:

> The Texas City disaster was caused by organizational and safety deficiencies at all levels of the BP Corporation. Warning signs of a possible disaster were present for several years, but company officials did not intervene effectively to prevent it.[14]

The report was much read by all of us at Shell, keen to learn whether we were as exposed to the same risks. In 2009, Andrew Hopkins, an Australian sociologist, published a fascinating book on the disaster called *Failure to Learn*. His view was that the root cause problem of the accident, as well as BP's cost pressures and other management failures, was a deep-seated failure to learn from previous incidents and accidents across their own system (as well as in other companies).

> The culture of BP, and of Texas City in particular, was a culture of blindness to major risk.[15]

Given our responsibilities for the overall culture and organisational health of Shell, my colleagues and I were much haunted by this book and its thoughtful insights into the deep failings of the BP culture under Lord Browne's much-vaunted leadership. Especially when, a year later, Deepwater Horizon occurred, killing another 11 people and then almost destroying the company in the ensuing environmental catastrophe and political firestorm. It wasn't as if we were so sure at Shell that such awful things could not occur in our organisation. Quite the contrary. They could, all too easily. Shell was incredibly careful not to say anything critical after either disaster: it's too close to home and your instincts are to help, support and learn, not kick your competitor while they are down. One day it can and will be you, but in the meantime you do everything in your power to avoid that fate. But I do think we were perhaps – at least at that time – ahead of BP on two critical areas. One of these was that our culture valued learning in general. Shell's HQs physically include its learning centres, which are open to and used by employees throughout the globe. So it's not unknown for someone coming to attend a course to ride up in the same elevator as the CEO. That's symbolic. At BP, this couldn't happen: the HQ and top leadership are focused in a small block in leafy St James's Square in London, opposite the London Library where this book was written. This was great for allowing John Browne, the CEO, to keep a close eye on emerging rivals, but not for keeping senior leaders humble and well connected with the people up and down the company. You don't build a learning culture overnight, and Shell has worked for many decades to create its current set of traditions and capabilities in this area. Those are hard things to replicate. Secondly, Shell moved much more aggressively than BP in the last 20 years to create global organisations in both health and safety and technical disciplines such as drilling. This created stronger capability to move best practice around the world. BP, on the other hand, was much lauded in the market for treating each asset as a business unit, and handing overall control of everything to the general management of each unit. It wasn't until after the Deepwater Horizon tragedy that BP created a powerful safety directorate with a global remit.

The best wider investigations after the initial reports get at the heart of these issues, often with surprising speed and insight. The *National Commission on the BP Deepwater Horizon Oil Spill and Offshore Drilling* reported in January 2011, only nine months after the accident. Its report was pretty insightful and balanced given the febrile time at which it was written. That report looked at not just the accident but also had views on lessons learned for industry, government and energy policy. No such equivalent external, unbiased investigations are made into most crises, so there tend to remain afterwards various versions of even the hard facts, and hence two problems occur.

First, the organisation never fully analyses what caused the crisis, especially where the cause is not within organisational boundaries but is part of a more systemic set of issues. The failures of Lehman Brothers and RBS are classic examples of the genre. Second, because there is no full analysis, and because lawyers and others tend to get in the way of even the most straightforward admissions of responsibility, there is often no forgiveness. So in the future we should ask ourselves which forms of investigation have provided the most timely, accurate, fair and helpful analyses of events, and which have provided slow, partial, inaccurate, unfair and largely useless ones – and then have more of the former. For my money, the value to the industry of the Presidential Commission's report was pretty high, and I hope that the Salz report was similarly of genuine use well beyond Barclays' walls. A small, focused investigation, led by an impartial but competent figure, assisted by independent experts and with a suitable staff, can get behind even the most complex of issues and events in a matter of weeks and months. Of course, there are issues on how to balance the output of these investigations so that they are neither a whitewash nor a paradise for tort lawyers to pick over until the company concerned is bankrupted. But these concerns can be overcome. Certainly the Salz experience at Barclays was a helpful one, and I think without the hard external challenge and home truths of that investigation we would have perhaps not achieved as much as we did in the ensuing change programmes.

In the future, the role of public inquiries (though preferably not only by MPs with their political agendas) might be developed and accelerated to provide speedy but fair ways to process evidence and data and give some opportunity for the first draft of history to be based on facts not fiction, assign some real responsibility and achieve some cross-sectoral learning and advice for policymakers. The Salz Review might be a useful benchmark for speedy delivery: it was first conceived in July 2012,[16] staffed up by October 2012 and reported in April 2013 after just six months, having taken evidence from over 600 stakeholders inside and outside Barclays, as well as considering huge quantities of written data. However, the recent experiences with the Iraq Inquiry (which at the time of writing was scheduled to report in the summer of 2016, seven years after it started) and the Independent Inquiry into Child Sexual Abuse (two chairs have resigned and it has now been reconstituted as a statutory inquiry) suggest that we shouldn't expect speedy public inquiries. The recent penchant for allowing those criticised in such reports right of response before publication appears to have made it nigh on impossible to deliver prompt but fair outcomes. This is highly regrettable and should surely be the subject of urgent review.

None of this is to suggest there isn't a place for purely internal investigations or normal regulatory inspections and reports when these are held or required. I am just pointing out what stimulates relevant organisational learning: in my experience a great deal hangs on the attitude and intent of the leaders who commission inquiries, as well as the determination of the inquiry team to share the truth. Such reviews and learning will inevitably have to take place at the same time as the outside world is hurling abuse, demanding scalps, and pushing for action and answers on plans for change. Nemesis will never stand alone for long as a distinct part of the cycle: it is already underway as soon as crisis hits, and rarely over before metamorphosis starts. If we can get better at reviewing complex events more quickly and effectively, utilising the pace and transparency of modern technology to full effect, perhaps we can get to a place where more people learn what those at the top of the complex organisations (and certainly the established pariahs) know already. Because they (we) know that the trite blame game of the tabloid newspapers is not a fair or adequate way to describe what has happened, and yet they must take accountability for their decisions and actions in context. And if we all reflect for a moment, we all know that unless the nemesis is just and deserved, it isn't a nemesis at all. Equally, if nemesis is seen to be avoided, there is no hope of the catharsis and forgiveness that our societies need for trust to flourish.

Notes

1   The Burson-Marsteller Corporate Perception Indicator 2015 suggests that 55 per cent of the general public in the developed world agree with the statement "Corporations generally were not humbled by the economic crisis that began in 2008 and they do not act more responsibly than they did before." 52 per cent of C-suite executives agree! The figures for the developing world are not much more optimistic: 41 per cent of the public and 47 per cent of C-suite executives. See Burson-Marsteller Corporate Perception Indicator at http://www.slideshare.net/BMGlobalNews/ the-bursonmarstellercnbc-corporate-perception-indicator

2   In Greek tragedy, perhaps the best example of revenge is the relentless, implacable hunting down of Orestes in *Eumenides*, the final play of Aeschylus's Oresteian trilogy. Only through the intervention of Athena herself are the Erinyes (the Furies) reluctantly placated from taking blood for blood; Orestes has killed his mother Clytemnestra and must die in turn, they claim. As with so many blood feuds, it takes a spectacular external intervention to halt the exchange of violence. Although one might argue that the Furies are Orestes' nemesis, this is a more personal form of justice than nemesis elsewhere in the Greek theology.

3   See Ovid, *Metamorphoses* III.400ff.

4   New Shell CEO Ben van Beurden sets agenda for sharper performance and rigorous capital discipline: http://www.shell.com/global/aboutshell/media/ news-and-media-releases/2014/2014-results-announcement-media-release1. html

5   Shell's Arctic Albatross: http://www.greenpeace.org.uk/blog/climate/ shells-arctic-albatross-20140130

6   Greenpeace in 2014 successfully pressured Lego into severing a 50-year partnership with Shell, even though this partnership has nothing to do with Arctic drilling but is focused around Ferrari and motorsport. Greenpeace were not going after beloved brand Lego directly, but cleverly leveraged/ attacked the connection to pariah brand Shell and their attacks on Arctic drilling. The tactics by which this campaign succeeded in making life too hot for Lego to handle was described by Elena Polisano in the *Guardian*: http://www.theguardian.com/voluntary-sector-network/2014/oct/10/ greenpeace-lego-shell-climate-change-arctic-oil

7   The Greek word ἐπιχαιρεκακέιν (epichairekakein – to rejoice in another's misfortunes) would perhaps be more appropriate in this book, but the German term is better known. In the ancient world, although Aristotle notes that the emotion is bad in itself, and had no "mean" between two vices, rejoicing at

one's enemies' misfortunes was often seen as a reasonable and moral thing to do. It may be significant that Twitter and other social media have allowed such a morality to reassert itself at scale.

8   See Chapter 1.

9   At the time of writing – partly for legal reasons – no reliable, neutral and well-informed public account of all the internal and external aspects of Barclays' LIBOR crisis has been published. Readers can piece together the main events from the transcripts of the select committee hearings, associated news reports and in particular Salz, 2013, section 6.55 ff.

10 An even more dramatic version of this incomplete nemesis has occurred at News International, where after being acquitted of charges of conspiracy to hack phones, conspiracy to corrupt public officials and conspiracy to pervert the course of justice in 2013, Rebekah Brooks was reinstated to her senior role in 2015 despite widespread negative commentary.

11 Though as we noted in Chapter 2, pariahs already receive most of these punishments already in the form of "windfall" taxes on disfavoured industries, legal actions against negligent or criminal actions and the role of the press as the judges of who gets vilified.

12 Ronson, 2015 delves into the new issues of how rapidly reputations are being destroyed online, particularly on Twitter. Ronson focuses on individuals, but the conclusions he draws regarding the care we need to have over online bullying could apply to organisations as well.

13 Syed, 2015 points out the difference between different industries and their capacity for open loop learning (and hence improvement, as has been the case in aviation safety via multiple systems of reporting, communication, codification and training), vs the closed loops where no-one even will admit that something has gone wrong, and where unfalsifiable narratives are allowed to drive practice.

14 See U.S. Chemical Safety and Hazard Investigation Board, 2007, Executive Summary 1.2.1.

15 See Hopkins, 2009, p.139.

16 As a matter of disclosure, I should note that I helped draft the original terms of reference for the review, and was also involved in helping Anthony Salz appoint his supporting team of consultants, as well as leading on Barclays' side to marshal our responses to data requests regarding HR matters after the independent review team was in place.

8

Metamorphosis – Change

met·a·mor·pho·sis [met-*uh*-mawr-f*uh*-sis]

noun, plural met·a·mor·pho·ses [met-*uh*-mawr-f*uh*-seez]

1. *Biology* – a profound change in form from one stage to the next in the life history of an organism, as from the caterpillar to the pupa and from the pupa to the adult butterfly. Compare complete metamorphosis.
2. a complete change of form, structure, or substance, as transformation by magic or witchcraft.
3. any complete change in appearance, character, circumstances, etc.
4. a form resulting from any such change.
5. *Pathology.*
   a. a type of alteration or degeneration in which tissues are changed: *fatty metamorphosis of the liver.*
   b. the resultant form.

NEMESIS IS NOT the end of the story for a pariah organisation. Morale is usually now at a nadir, and exhausted staff and leaders are pleading for the crisis to be over, to let them rest, regroup and come to terms with what has happened. Unless you have experienced such a trauma, it's hard to explain how emotionally and physically draining such moments are. There is an immediate expectation that something will change. The question is: what? Thus does the metamorphosis stage of the Pariah Lifecycle begin. It is at this point that there is a fork in the road. The path chosen by leadership now will determine whether the organisation can escape reliving the cycle of hubris–crisis–nemesis or is doomed to repeat it. In this chapter we will take a look at the difference between a false metamorphosis and a real one. We will see that although many organisations and leaders claim that they are undergoing a metamorphosis, very few indeed actually try seriously to do this. And as a result, although quite a lot of superficial changes occur, very few make a fundamental switch. Finally, we will observe that the consulting industry, with its promises of "transformation" has debased the terminology of fundamental change and hence made it harder for organisations to avoid future problems.

Metamorphosis and Histolysis as Metaphors

In English, the word "metamorphosis" retains in one of its primary senses the shades of quasi-supernatural shifts, akin to magic. But the meaning I want to focus on is the hard science of metamorphosis as we learn it in biology, as caterpillar truly (and if not magically, then at least to our continued wonderment) turns into butterfly. This latter process may be instructive for us in considering metamorphosis as a metaphor in our model.

A true metamorphosis (such as that of caterpillar to pupa to butterfly) is a massive genetic investment. Instead of developing another, larger, skin to accommodate the rapidly growing and voracious caterpillar body, a special pupa skin is created. Within this pupa, most of the existing body is demolished by the very chemicals that usually digest the caterpillar's food intake. This extraordinary process, known as *histolysis*, enables the raw material of the caterpillar to be efficiently reconstructed into a completely different body, that of the butterfly that struggles out of the pupa days later. Histolysis provides us with another powerful potential metaphor to serve within our metaphor of organisational metamorphosis: the new and changed thing emerges from the matter that constructed the old one, but only by thoroughly deconstructing it first.

Relatively few species undergo such a dramatic change of body. There are substantial risks in being vulnerable during the changes and many individuals do not survive the change of state. But for those that do, there is the developmental advantage of being able to operate in a completely different environment, at a different speed, and in a way that enables the all-important transfer of DNA to propagate the next generation. As we will see, there are some potential lessons here for organisations in taking risks for survival. Five areas seem particularly relevant:

- **Time** – true metamorphosis takes an investment in time, effort and energy, when it might be more attractive to keep eating, breeding or otherwise doing what is normal around you. In organisations, we have noted that the pressure to react to crisis and avoid nemesis severely restricts the amount of time available for reflection and renewal, just when it is most needed.

- **Focus** – during metamorphosis, an organism's focus goes inwards. This has risks: threats from predators may increase, while opportunities may be missed to eat, move or otherwise interact with the environment. For organisations, there is an understandable worry about focusing on self at a time when customers, regulators and the public are keen to see responsiveness and may wish to be involved in changes.

- **Creative destruction** – the organism literally destroys itself in order to rebuild as something radically different. This also seems like a highly risky strategy that might not pay off if something occurs in the external environment at this critical moment (e.g. a change of weather). For organisations, there are some parallels with modern change theories[1] which advocate having to give up a great deal in order to reconstruct as something better.

- **Radical structural change** – the organism is building itself for the future world it will live in, not the past. It is not important for a butterfly to maintain a caterpillar's jaws or for a frog to have a tadpole's tail. So too must organisations look forward without sentimentality for the past and construct themselves for the world they will actually be in after nemesis, not for the world they were in before, or wish they were in.

- **Behavioural change** – a butterfly behaves very differently from a caterpillar. It flits and flutters; it doesn't wriggle. It drinks nectar; it doesn't munch leaves. Changing organisational behaviour is notoriously difficult but, if it's essential to survival and thriving in the new world, it must occur.

The point I am making here may seem trite to some. But I want to highlight how loosely and carelessly we use a term that has a precious, deep and important meaning. It's relatively recently that we have hijacked the word "metamorphosis" to refer to changes which, to an unbiased eye, lack the fundamental and dramatic shifts the word should entail. No wonder we are so often disappointed – the word promises so much that is really hard to deliver. But we should hang on to what the term really *should* mean, and be honest with ourselves whether our own organisations really deserve to use the word so loosely, when at best we are watching normal changes associated with growth, perhaps a shedding of the (brand) skin, or a seasonal shift in colouration. The number of organisations that have really and truly undergone a corporate metamorphosis aligned with my definition and criteria is very small indeed. In this chapter, then, we will see how frequently claims of organisational metamorphosis are overblown, and how rarely pariahs are able to take the time and energy required for a true metamorphosis to take place.

False Metamorphosis

The first path of change post-nemesis is the easier one, so it's no surprise that it's the road most travelled. I am not going to suggest that these changes are not real or that they are not meaningful shifts in organisational development. But I am going to suggest they are insufficient for real metamorphosis, and that for pariah organisations they tend to doom them to repeat the cycle and move towards the next crisis. What happens in a false metamorphosis? A typical cycle goes like this:

As a reaction to the events of crisis and nemesis, visible changes are made in the organisation and widely publicised. Communications, PR and legal experts lead the response efforts. Leaders are changed out, perhaps from the board on down. Changes are made to rules, processes or products. Brands may be changed. Lessons have been learned from the crisis, it is claimed. Some form of internally controlled investigation occurs, but is cursory or limited in scope. The organisation cooperates with statutory or external enquiries (such as accident investigators or regulators) but seeks to position the causes as "industry wide". It is communicated that change will occur, perhaps over a lengthy period of time. There is perhaps some talk of going back to basics or reminding the organisation of its origins and history. The importance of certain stakeholder groups is reasserted (customers, the public, voters, shareholders). Never again will they be let down like this, it is claimed. The new leaders are interviewed in the press, often now with some sympathy for their plight in cleaning up the mess. The press starts to get bored with the story. Although suspicions may remain that nothing has yet actually changed, the benefit of the doubt is usually given to new leadership. There is a settling-in period. Initial results can be good; the stock price recovers from the low base set during the crisis. Employee engagement and belief in the organisation perhaps improves. There is talk of restoring pride in the organisation. Soon, surprisingly soon, the crisis is confined to organisational folk memory, or may even be forgotten altogether. The organisational culture continues to hold the same values it did before. The crisis is said to have been overplayed. The organisation starts to reassert itself.

Until it all happens again. The problem is that, in animal terms, the organisation has remained a caterpillar. Perhaps it is smaller, or larger, or a different colour, or can eat different kinds of leaves. But it's just not a butterfly.

Let's look at a few examples of what false metamorphosis looks like. If it's an oil company, it's a bit safer, a bit more aware of opinion, a bit more cautious about what it invests in or how it manages its third-party stakeholders. But it hasn't stopped digging up oil and gas as its core business. It hasn't given up its asset base (well, not unless it has had to sell it to pay the fines and legal bills). Its leaders are largely the same ones as before and they are still largely home-grown lifers who have always worked in the company. If it's an NHS organisation such as a Trust, there will be new rules and policies and processes and training.[2] Perhaps whistleblowing is less discouraged. But the essential challenges of trying to provide everyone with every kind of care remain: the fundamental issues of how to pay a growing bill with fewer taxpayers remains untouched. And it is still anathema for insiders to speak up or disagree with official points of view or question authority when things are going wrong.[3] And if it's a bank? Here in the UK we will get to see whether such a metamorphosis can and will occur in the coming years. The fundamental structural separation of retail banking from investment banking (as originally enforced by the Glass-Steagall Banking Act in the USA in 1933) was rejected by the Vickers[4] report, but the pressures on universal banks are clearly going to be to split structurally and to end the implicit guarantees and the cheaper cost of capital for the investment banks. Whether these changes will drive sufficient changes into the rewards, culture and behaviour of bankers and bank executives remains to be seen.

However, the sort of discontinuities that would be required to make pariahs truly acceptable to all stakeholders are rather harder to imagine. An oil company that was acceptable to Greenpeace would not only not seek to exploit oil and gas in the Arctic, it would be winding down its operations and moving its capital towards renewable energy research and exploitation. And in doing so it would probably become a pariah to the City (because it would be unclear where the returns on the capital would accrue), and to its old friends in the governments of the major resource holders, whose tax base might be threatened. Its own employees would also have to be won over. What would be their future job security if the technologies they specialise in are made irrelevant? The challenges would be tremendous. An NHS trust that was really able to talk about its failures, its mistakes and the clay feet of its medical staff as well as its administrators would be quite a thing too. It might become pariah rather rapidly to the powerful doctors' establishment (and their union, the BMA) by admitting that they made mistakes,[5] even though there is ample evidence that such honesty doesn't just improve patient care but also *reduces* legal liabilities. It would probably annoy the other unions too: it might reveal that not all nurses are saintly, or always hard-working or helpful. And it would almost inevitably upset politicians by telling the truth about funding and how it really works and the tough choices that have had to be made and why. Similarly, a bank acceptable to Positive Money (who oppose the right of the banks to "create money" via debt) or even to the New Economics Foundation[6] (a left-wing think tank) would be an extraordinary thing. It would have to advocate a system in which its own interests were subordinated to those of the state it operated in, to eschew the ability of the banks to create debt, indeed to question the entire system of money as we know it. Hardly an enticing prospect for existing investors or management, even if one believes the intellectual and political arguments behind the schemes in question.

So it's not surprising that so few pariahs ever make it out of the loop. The status quo is not only more comfortable than the alternatives, it's usually a lot less dangerous; and to keep some groups in opposition is a small price to pay compared with the monumental task of persuading the other interest groups to advocate changes which might appear hugely detrimental. Histolysis is vanishingly rare in nature for a reason.

True Metamorphosis

So what would a true metamorphosis look like, should such a thing occur? The second path is truly the road less travelled. There are marked similarities with false metamorphosis, but also some notable differences. Firstly, in a true metamorphosis there is **less of a rush to pretend all is well**. The organisation and remaining leaders **take serious time to investigate at multiple levels what has occurred**.[7] Deep organisational learning and reflection is usually time consuming and difficult, and consumes organisational resources that might easily be repurposed elsewhere. During such a learning period, there is widespread involvement of operational-line people at all levels, as well as functional experts from legal, HR, IT and others in the investigation process. **The investigation values getting at the truth more than pointing the finger of blame**.[8] There is a systemic understanding of what has gone wrong which gives due regard to both technical and cultural failings, and does not hide accountabilities to reduce legal exposures. There is an openness to the need for truly fundamental changes to the wider system beyond the immediate accountability of the organisation itself.

Changes within the organisation itself are made only once it's really clear how to make the process better, not as a knee-jerk response. **The changes benefit multiple stakeholders; they are not just ways to paper over the cracks or avoid future blame or liabilities.**[9] Proposed changes are widely supported beyond the organisation itself. There is an understanding of the need for change that transcends the limited interests of any one organisation or interest group. **Leaders take the time to think hard about what the crisis means for their own leadership and behaviour, and about the values that are actually at work in the organisation.**[10] There is a preparedness to rethink purpose and values in a major way. The process through which values are created is itself participative and involves a wide range of stakeholders, not just an elite group.

Others from outside the system[11] are engaged and involved in the process of understanding and critique so that there is an established understanding of what has happened that crosses organisational boundaries, and allows what is constructed next to have better support. Once the new norms are established, actions are seen to align with them, and **rewards, incentives and ways of working are comprehensively changed to support the new world.**[12] **Leaders are changed out, perhaps in considerable numbers**, but these changes are carried out with respect and dignity, and with an understanding of how to maintain continuity where this is still important. **The past of the organisation is not unnecessarily trashed or vilified**; it is investigated and held up against the new realities of the world and society in which the organisation operates. **The success of the new organisation is measured by some different metrics**, which go beyond operational and cost and include perceptions and reputational metrics. **Leaders in the new organisation are developed**[13] in ways which explicitly take account of the new requirements, and are intolerant of hubristic behaviour or low emotional intelligence (EQ).

A Counsel of Perfection?

It would be extremely easy to dismiss such a description as a flight of fancy on my part. So feel free. However, I believe it is indeed possible to achieve a change of this type where there is enlightened and courageous leadership. The courage has to come not just from within the organisation affected by crisis. It has to come from around the entire system in which the crisis has occurred. It is no good lambasting oil companies for staying in the fossil fuels business but not introducing meaningful carbon pricing as a matter of public policy, or providing due credit when they get things right. Nor can one expect the tobacco, gambling or drinks industries to reduce their sales activities when government provides so much covert support for a lucrative source of tax revenues. But let there be no doubt, the courage has to come from the heart of the organisations at the centre of the problem. It took white as well as black South Africans to change the country from the apartheid system. It is taking men as well as women to shift gender politics in the boardrooms of the FTSE. There is much to be gained for those rulers who are brave enough to admit their part in the system, tell their truth and open up a dialogue of possibility. It is within the confines of the broader set of rules and assumptions that changes take place. Very few organisations are in a position to change the rules around themselves to the degree required for a true metamorphosis to be on the cards.

There are exceptions, particularly in unique industries, practical monopolies or industries in their start-up phases. We have yet to discover whether Google will become a fully fledged established pariah in the future (see Chapter 10), but in the past it was able successfully to reinvent itself through several distinct stages of growth and development. So perhaps the very paradigm of what it means to be a successful company will start to require more capability for real metamorphosis and less reiteration with slight changes. Many technology companies do seem to have achieved something like a metamorphosis, if only because of economic necessity or out of the ashes of real failure. The relative lack of regulation and government interference in the industry, the short histories and cultural memories of the organisations, and the expectations of the other players in the industry (including risk-taking investors) are all key factors in this being possible. As a company such as Google grows larger, it may lose the flexibility it once had to change its business model and how it responded to challenges. Certainly, the pain of major changes, such as those undergone by IBM, indicate that as organisations become larger and less nimble, more interconnected with the interests and needs of others in the wider business eco-system, and more conservative in their own outlook, this impedes the kinds of really meaningful change that are required for survival.[14]

So leaders of organisations who want to take real metamorphosis seriously as an option after a crisis and nemesis need to have substantial convening power across the range of organisations and agencies involved in their old (and new) systems. This is a tough ask of leaders, who are themselves often new to the level of leadership they have been thrust into, and may lack the wider strategic experience that will give them the context and contacts required. Small wonder that we struggle to think of many successful examples.

Role of Government as Conveners

Of course, in a democracy one of the claims that can reasonably be made about an elected government is that it has a mandate to leverage just such a convening power across the actors in an industry. Given that the licence to operate an organisation is granted, in effect, by the people of the country in which it exists, it is only reasonable that the representatives of the people via their legislators should re-form the rules and shape of industries where they feel these have failed.

We have certainly seen real-life examples of this. In the USA we recently saw just such a mandate used (albeit with great reluctance by Congress) in the bailouts of the banks and the auto industry under the TARP[15] legislation of 2008. The initial fears about how much the bailouts would cost, how long companies would effectively be in government control and whether the interference would work seem to have proved inaccurate[16]. The Congressional Budget Office reported in 2012 the total cost to taxpayers of loans totalling over $400 billion was "only" $24 billion, rather less than the cost of the savings and loans crisis of the Reagan era. Many nevertheless believe that this was an opportunity missed to radically restructure the banking industry and make it safer, not just to provide a temporary balance sheet boost to a broken business model. Others stress that it should never have been the government's business to own and run banks (or insurers or auto companies), and that the swift and largely successful exit is the only good news about this entire episode. Clearly, political beliefs and principles alter the lens of perception here considerably, even looking at the same fact base.

Similarly, the UK's Parliamentary Commission on Banking during 2013 could and should have taken the opportunity to ensure that the Banking Act of 2014 reshaped the industry towards a true metamorphosis. In both cases, it proved very difficult to achieve a broad consensus on what a successfully reformed industry would look like, although there was scope (in theory) for a wide range of options ranging from outright nationalisation through to rescinding many of the Gramm-Leach-Billey[17] changes to the Glass-Steagall legislation. What is obvious is how hard it is to go against ingrained interests, imagine a different world and react while in the crisis. And how few people really understand that the process whereby really great innovation takes place across industries (that is healthy for all stakeholders) is not imposed from above, but is emergent from a process of deep listening and a new understanding. Too often we see lawmakers mistaking their role in these situations. Their job is not to sit as judge and jury on behalf of their electors in bringing errant organisational actors to heel, however satisfying that may be. In fact, all that such political posing achieves is to deepen the problem.[18] What the electorate needs is not showboating for the TV cameras; it is solutions to the underlying issues. These are rarely found in select committees, where hostile questioning and abuse of parliamentary privilege is becoming increasingly entertaining, but decreasingly useful and insightful. What government *can* do usefully is enable the discussion, the exchange of views (including some difficult ones, which organisations need to hear). Such a conversation becomes the container from which new insights and ideas emerge. In doing that, they may also have to take actions to remove power and control from industry incumbents – that's legitimate. But they are not there to serve up big heaped servings of revenge for those who think the system has screwed them in the past.

The Story of Saturn

The difference between a false and a true metamorphosis is fundamentally a function of the quality and vision of the leadership available to the organisations in the system. Where there are suitably courageous and thoughtful leaders, it is possible for extraordinary changes to occur in even entrenched positions. I had the great privilege to meet and work with Skip LeFauve at General Motors in the late 1990s. GM was then, as now, sadly, seen as something of a corporate zombie trading on former glories: too big to fail, but struggling to compete fairly with the product quality that the Japanese car companies, in particular Toyota, had achieved during the 1970s and 1980s in producing reliable vehicles that customers actually wanted. GM had a strong union culture, entrenched in its Michigan base in and around Detroit. LeFauve, a lifelong GM exec, realised that the company could never build and sell successful small cars to compete with the Japanese on the back of this cultural tradition.

His leadership of the revolutionary change process that subsequently occurred is rightly legendary and led to the creation of an utterly new company called Saturn, which at least for a while was a beacon of hope to those who believed America could win in this sector as well as in trucks or other categories.

continued

The critical elements of the Saturn story are simple, yet incredible to anyone who grew up in the entrenched politics of the US auto industry. Management and the United Auto Workers (UAW) union representatives worked together to run the project. They spent the first months and indeed years on a learning journey, simply understanding what other companies were doing well. They learned how to rethink utterly not just modern manufacturing techniques, but the whole supply chain from design to dealership. They located their factory in a southern state (Tennessee) that had never previously seen a car factory, and hence had no traditions of the skilled labour required, but also fewer preconceptions and biases on how things should be done. Saturn was, I know, a very special achievement. I was impressed with it when I was 29 years old. I am much more impressed now.

Skip was central to this achievement, but it's very telling how modest he was – until his untimely death in 2003 – about his own role. He believed in achieving things as a team, and the central role of learning and self-development for everyone. Bonuses were not payable at Saturn unless everyone (bar none) in the organisation completed their training hours. Leaders were required to teach in Saturn's state-of-the-art learning centre.

I could go on. The point is that this didn't come about because LeFauve had read some modish consulting manual. It came about because he was smart enough to create a project through which leaders and unions could learn together what mattered to customers, about processes and process improvement, about how to learn, about manufacturing and technology, in a safe way together that built relationships and trust.

GM was – unsurprisingly – unable to learn from Saturn, and eventually wrecked its own creation; GM's overall near-death TARP experience in 2009 allowed them finally to kill off the Saturn brand, but in reality a long series of decisions had picked apart Saturn's unique position and autonomy before that coup de grâce.[19] Let that be a lesson to all of us on how hard it is to achieve lasting catharsis when a big organisation is really, deeply, structurally sick.

RECOMMENDATION

11. Avoid False Metamorphosis

Central to this book is not just the idea that pariahs exist, but that they can be cured. And central to the cure, after achieving a full appreciation of what has actually occurred and the organisation's responsibility in the crisis, is avoiding a false metamorphosis. The central irony of the contemporary pariah lifecycle is that the pressure on speed, cost and action that causes crises in the first place is also the cause of many false metamorphoses, so most organisations are doomed to repeat the loop again. Although the media and commentariat talk a good game about "giving X (insert CEO or Chairman name here) time to sort things out" the very language of that commentary reveals that a) giving time is abnormal and b) such time will run out, probably rapidly. Pretty soon, even if the board is happy with progress against an agreed plan, investors may become impatient. And even if investors are happy, the "teenage scribblers" of the business press can be mischievous as they try to fill their columns with something for their readers to chew on. So the first tenet of the true metamorphosis is to acknowledge the time that such an ambitious plan will take. Antony Jenkins was suitably forthright on this when he took over at Barclays in 2012. He was smart to be quoted on this subject frequently in interviews:

> "In my view it will take several years – probably five to ten – to rebuild trust in Barclays."

> "In my view leadership sets the culture in big organisations and culture drives organisational performance. If you want a different sort of organisational performance, a more ethical business, you're going to have to change culture. Culture takes time to change and it comes back to leadership. If you take a long term perspective you'll build the right culture," he said.[20]

But despite these clear warnings that this was a multi-year process, within six months Jenkins was being criticised as the next wave of scandals (this time lawsuits over "dark pool" trading) emerged. It's never hard for the journalists to find a quote at such times, no matter how little the individual knows about the subject at hand:

> "He's lost some credibility," said Colin McLean, founder and CEO of SVM Asset Management Ltd. in Edinburgh, which oversees about $830 million and holds Barclays shares. "He hasn't achieved the cultural change he's talked about. A lot of activities will come under scrutiny."[21]

Mr McLean was simply complaining that the shares he had bought were not performing better, which he's entitled to do. And he was very entitled to be angry that Barclays were being cited in another lawsuit about alleged behaviour that occurred well after the LIBOR scandal broke. But given the clear notice Jenkins had given, the criticism that the culture change hasn't been achieved was utterly premature and unfair. You don't declare victory or defeat on such matters in a matter of months. Nevertheless, Jenkins was fired rather unceremoniously in 2015 with the culture change incomplete as the investment bank's performance slumped. It remains to be seen what the new regime will do and whether the changes Jenkins began on values, culture and behaviour will be developed or dumped. New CEO Jes Staley wrote encouragingly in his first letter to staff before he joined in October 2015:

> We must therefore complete the cultural transformation of the Group. There can be no retreat from becoming a values driven organisation which conducts itself with integrity at all times. My ambition is to restore Barclays to its rightful[22] standing – successful, admired and well regarded by all.[23]

A real commitment to honesty in a large organisation means nasty things in the woodshed will keep emerging for years to come. The press cannot accept this, perhaps because the cultures of their own organisations are so poor they are hardened into cynicism about the prospects for others. Here's the *Financial Times*:

> The forex scandal has already led Mark Carney, governor of the Bank of England and head of the Financial Stability Board, to conclude: "The succession of scandals means it is simply untenable now to argue that the problem is one of a few bad apples – the issue is with the barrels in which they are stored." This is a pretty damning indictment of the clean-up efforts being trumpeted by Barclays and other banks.[24]

I cite this uncomfortable, close-to-home example to make the point. You need real balls to do this work. You have to take on lots of vested interests. Your own board and perhaps some of your own leadership may doubt whether the result you need to achieve can be delivered within the timescales required. So you really have to believe, and also to mobilise the whole organisation to support you. Based on what I have experienced, here are a few pointers to authentic metamorphosis:

Go deep on understanding the root causes – as we have said above, you need to do a thorough and disinterested analysis of what has occurred, and your plans on what to do may well need to involve a wide range of internal and external parts of the system. No part of the organisation system can be regarded as sacrosanct here. Follow where the logic and the data take you, forensically. Be prepared to accept that really major shifts may be required in how the business is run, and activities, people and assets that are seen as iconic by others may have to be given up for the greater good and the longer term. Get outside help if you need it, but also leverage the people within your organisation so they understand the analysis and own the conclusions. Act with pace and urgency.

Marshall your coalition – leadership of the change won't just come from the top. And some people at the top will – not necessarily through any fault of their own – be your biggest problem. By definition, those who have been at the heart of the organisation that needs to change may not be capable of understanding or leading the shifts in behaviour and attitude required. At Barclays we recruited over 1,000 internal values champions, whom we trained first on the values and what we wanted from leaders in the future. It was these people, many of whom were not hugely senior, who drove the first and perhaps most emotional part of the change process, where we explained to our peers and employees what the purpose and values were all about. Later on, values workshops and onboarding became slicker and more sophisticated, but it was the energy of the willing volunteers from all parts of the bank that struck me as the most powerful sign that the CEO had real support for what he was doing. It's not that the ExCo or other top leaders were not capable of leading the change, or making changes themselves. But for many reasons it's smart not to wait for them and to get a wider range of the willing involved right from the off.

Get on with it – yes, it's a journey of a thousand miles, but get on with the first steps. Pace and urgency are required, although there is of course a paradox that the highest feverish pace cannot be sustained forever. Ideally those early steps will have symbolism, and nothing speaks louder to the inside and outside worlds than the choices made on people. Initially this can be very difficult, if not impossible to pull off. Even the redoubtable Margaret Thatcher found her first cabinet full of Heath-ites and "wets" (as she would have put it), and even after ten years she still had issues with loyalty. Nevertheless, a bold

CEO signals changes via such choices as soon as possible, and ensures that although everyone is dealt with respectfully, it's clear that you have to get on the bus if you want to stay.[25]

Change things visibly – changing out people, especially leaders, is one visible thing you can do, but there are others. Changing the physical environment symbolically is the second most potent way I know of supporting cultural change. If you want an open, transparent culture, the buildings have to support that. Getting senior people out of offices and into more open workspaces has symbolism, but be careful that you are not doing things that get in the way of work being done. Go easy on changes to logos and brands unless these are very much part of the change. At Barclays the decision was taken to put the RISES (Respect, Integrity, Service, Excellence, Stewardship) values on massive perspex screens in the HQ of the lobby. This made them impossible to miss (and hence a natural talking point for thousands of visitors with their hosts – a cunning plan) but also gave natural ammunition to detractors: a transparent sign with "INTEGRITY" on it is something of a hostage to fortune, albeit one we felt was worth taking on as a challenge to ourselves.

Lay out this year's plan – modern organisational life does not move in neat five-year plans. So even while surviving this year's pressures and unexpected delights, you have to lay out clearly what progress you expect to make on the big shifts and how you propose to measure these. Some obvious things that can be done in the first year of a process include shifting all people processes to align with purpose and values. (Yes, HR will have to work their socks off, but what's the point of hiring people, promoting them or managing their performance and rewards on any other basis? If your current HR department can't face that pace, get some people in who can: those who really want to see the metamorphosis occur.) In year two you can adjust again. Also in year one, you can start to push in on how you define and develop leadership (HR *are* going to be earning their money and you need a great HRD and other senior HR specialists) and start to connect the dots between these abstractions and the realities of your performance. I am a big fan of using larger top-leadership groups (at Shell we had a top 50 and a top 200, at Barclays a top 150) which can take CEO input directly and bypass the inevitable difficulties in translation of operating via the ExCo.

Don't let the industry hold you back – one of the depressing aspects of making serious, deep-seated changes in the context of a whole-industry perspective is that you can easily be dragged back into the norms of what your competitors are doing. Other industry participants are quickly alerted when one of their number makes a shift towards a more radical position outside the cosy club that allows everyone to defend the indefensible by alluding to "industry norms". So don't expect cheers of encouragement from your peers or the industry regulator as you shift your base. You just have to remain steadfast and clear in your vision and leverage the supportive coalition (see Recommendation 8, above) who do "get it" to spread the word on why your intention and execution are the right ideas.

Keep going – year one won't be enough. As we noted above, some of the commentators and opposition will rapidly write off a change that hasn't demonstrably shifted the outcomes of a 140,000-person organisation: well, ignore them and keep going. Of course, you do need to maintain the dialogue with the outside world, including the critics; but I think the key thing is to maintain the pressure on them to make positive suggestions. If they deny that things need to change, ask why they believe that. If they think that you are changing the wrong things or in the wrong way, engage in the debate. We are far too passive about avoiding constructive debates with critics which could be genuinely helpful. At the same time, you will have to keep on renewing the change programme each few months, or at least every year to remain relevant to the changing market conditions. This is a challenge, as you have to get the balance right between, on the one hand, maintaining consistent language for some things (purpose, values) which need to sound like they are deeply part of the history and DNA (forgive that word) of the organisation whilst, on the other, changing things such as the names of focus areas, change programmes or goals and targets, to suit the environment and external pressures. Barclays, if it chooses to stick to its guns, may not change the purpose or values for years or even decades. But the Transform programme that Jenkins launched in 2013 didn't last much beyond 2014, after which most of the main recommendations from the Salz Report had been implemented. Such challenges are often likened to surfers needing to catch a new wave: it's the same sea but each wave only takes you so far towards the beach.

Notes

1   In particular, we should note the similarity between some of the techniques I am advocating and those suggested by Otto Scharmer, Peter Senge and others who have pioneered the ideas of presencing as a way to solve complex problems that affect multiple parts of society. In particular there are parallels between the type of effective and involving enquiry I suggest in the last chapter on nemesis, and what occurs in what Scharmer calls U Theory and the deeper listening that allows new solutions to emerge, as in a true metamorphosis. See Scharmer entries in bibliography.

2   The Francis Review into Whistleblowing processes in 2014 ironically provided no report of its findings or recommendations. https://www.gov.uk/government/groups/whistleblowing-in-the-nhs-independent-review

3   See Syed, 2015, Chapter 1 and passim for the cultural challenges of getting doctors and doctor-led cultures to accept and learn from failure.

4   The Independent Commission on Banking, chaired by John Vickers, looked at structural and related non-structural reforms to the UK banking industry in the light of the financial crisis. Its final report in September 2011 recommended ringfencing of retail from investment banks, as well as technical recommendations on capital and other matters. The ICB report presaged the recommendations made via the Parliamentary Commission on Banking Standards and subsequent legislation.

5   See Syed, 2015, Chapter 1. Matthew Syed explains how the crusade of Martin Bromiley, an airline pilot, to change medical cultures to be more capable of acknowledging errors, started after the tragic death of Bromiley's wife during a routine operation. We should acknowledge that much is already being done to change centuries' old cultures in the medical profession, and learn from their learning.

6   For more on Positive Money, see: http://positivemoney.org. For the NEF, see http://neweconomics.org

7   Despite what you might think, I am not beating the drum for the consulting industry here. The best investigations and analyses I have ever seen were conducted by people in the line who had been trained with the right skills to analyse multiple types of data and form helpful insights that their own organisation could actually use.

8   This reality alone places huge pressure on cultural norms in organisations that prefer to find scapegoats and sacrifice them, rather than acknowledge their own individual and collective failings. Therefore before such work can occur there has to be some credible form of amnesty to allow the work to occur safely. This can be via anonymity in evidence giving, or sensible use of third parties. The most courageous examples remain more open. Perhaps the best example ever was the Truth and Reconciliation Commission in South Africa, which provided a degree of legal protection to allow some terrible truths to be told. See http://www.justice.gov.za/trc/report/index.htm

9   It's extraordinary how many change programmes would fail this acid test: too often they are only advantageous to the current leadership and perhaps the financial or political owners.

10 This is the time when some leaders should go. Not laden with gold, nor in terrible shame. But it's often time for very different people to take on the next phase of leadership.

11 This is absolutely critical. If people who are essential to the whole system are not present, it's not just likely but certain that perspectives won't be considered effectively.

12 It's extremely rare that we see fundamental change rather than tweaks to reward systems that are well understood. This is not surprising given the vested interests in this topic from the boardroom to the shop floor. But if this aspect of the system remains untouched, how can we expect real change to occur?

13 There must be different criteria for selecting and developing leaders if we want to see different results.

14 It would be churlish not to note that IBM has indeed made a series of huge shifts in the last 30 years, and is still with us and still successful.

15 TARP: Troubled Asset Relief Program

16 http://www.cbo.gov/publication/43662

17 This US government act of 1999, also known as the Financial Services Modernisation Act, repealed aspects of the 1933 Glass-Steagall act that had prevented investment banks, securities firms, commercial banks and insurance companies from shared ownership. Many commentators felt that this act was an important causal factor in the 2008 crisis. Certainly the size and scale of "too big to fail" universal banks was and remains a complex and controversial problem for regulators on both sides of the Atlantic.

18 See Syed, 2015, Chapter 12 for a good discussion on why cultures of blame are ineffective in solving the underlying issues and create new harm.

19 http://www.forbes.com/2010/03/08/saturn-gm-innovation-leadership-managing-failure.html

20 Quoted in the *Independent*, 31 December 2013: Antony Jenkins admits "it could take 10 years to rebuild trust in Barclays". http://www.independent.co.uk/news/business/news/antony-jenkins-admits-it-could-take-10-years-to-rebuild-trust-in-barclays-9031350.html

21 From Bloomberg, 27 June 2014: Dark Days for the Man Who Would Save Barclays. http://www.bloomberg.com/news/2014-06-27/barclays-ceo-falters-in-culture-shift-as-suit-cites-fraud.html

22 I am not sure who drafted Staley's letter. I'd have preferred not to see words like this in it: it's far from clear that Barclays has a right to be successful, and must earn admiration and good regard.

23 Quoted in the *Financial Times*: https://next.ft.com/content/404b0d38-7d4d-11e5-a1fe-567b37f80b64

24 On the issue of bank conduct the consensus is more must be done – *Financial Times*, 1 December 2014. http://www.ft.com/intl/cms/s/0/3cabaad2-7977-11e4-9e81-00144feabdc0.html#axzz3LUSjhHsE

25 Nothing that Antony Jenkins said at Barclays resonated better with the outside world than the statement in his initial letter to staff that read: "I have no doubt that the overwhelming majority of you… will enthusiastically support this move. But there might be some who don't feel they can fully buy in to an approach which so squarely links performance to the upholding of our values. My message to those people is simple: Barclays is not the place for you. The rules have changed. You won't feel comfortable at Barclays and, to be frank, we won't feel comfortable with you as colleagues."

9

Catharsis – Cleansing and Redemption

ca·thar·sis [kuh-thahr-sis]
noun, plural ca·thar·ses [kuh-thahr-seez]
1. the purging of the emotions or relieving of emotional tensions, especially through certain kinds of art, as tragedy or music.
2. Medicine/Medical, purgation.
3. Psychiatry.
   a. psychotherapy that encourages or permits the discharge of pent-up, socially unacceptable affects.
   b. discharge of pent-up emotions so as to result in the alleviation of symptoms or the permanent relief of the condition.

THE CONCEPT OF catharsis, of a quasi-religious or ritual cleansing of the unclean, is a natural one to a human society of social beings. Beset as we are by opportunities to fail each other, to "sin" or otherwise let down the social grouping, it's important we maintain norms that allow some form of a reset button to be pressed, to make all right again. How we do this, why, and what we call it are a source of almost infinite variety. In this, the final chapter on the Pariah Lifecycle, we will see what can be learned from the Greeks and their conceptions of expiation and cleansing, and observe how in our model we can only achieve a similar level of social forgiveness if there has been (or is credibly going to be) a true metamorphosis.

Origins

The fundamental meaning of the Greek word καθάροις (catharsis) has its origins in the adjective καθαρός (catharos) meaning "physically clean, spotless"[1] and, by extension, pure (used, in ancient texts, of clothes and water but also of heaven and people). So a sense of religious purity has always been attached to the concept. Ritual purification was not a Homeric concept; it appears to have arrived from oriental societies and is associated with the expiation of blood guilt in particular[2], through the ceremonial use of blood to wash away blood, and then water to wash away blood. There remains something primally exciting about this idea, which must connect with mankind's earliest efforts to manage social conflict within the tribe. Catharsis, like nemesis, connects us with our darkest and most primitive selves, and a time before laws and justice as we now know and understand them. Catharsis speaks to very deep needs in us to reconnect and rebuild broken trust, to deal with the pain of the past, to forgive but also to admit fault and seek redress outside and beyond a framework of judicial punishment. Catharsis thus has a principal meaning of cleansing from guilt or defilement; of purification. It also has related meanings associated with medical purging, pruning trees and thinning out the herd. So the sense of *cutting out the unhealthy* to preserve the healthy goes deep into the term.

Catharsis in the Model

In the Pariah Lifecycle Model, the positioning of "catharsis" could be described as hopeful, perhaps even pointless. Some won't see any possibility of redemption for the pariahs and their leadership, either because they don't need it (e.g. those who simply accept that there will be negative constituencies who need to be "lived with") or don't deserve it (those who don't accept that their enemies are capable of change). I am clearly in the hopeful camp. I think that there are reasonable grounds for seeing pariahs as capable of change and redemption. And in some cases, pariahs have managed this difficult state. I am the first to admit that this redemption is all too rare, and most pariahs who survive crisis and nemesis are too quick to take on a false metamorphosis, as we have reflected above. But where organisations and individuals are courageous enough to take on the hard work required, I believe catharsis can be achieved, and thus society can forgive and move on in a healthy way.

Why is Catharsis Rare?

As we have suggested elsewhere, there are all too few examples of effective catharsis we can use to amplify our model. Why might this be? Well, for one thing, although it's greatly to society's benefit for there to be organisational and personal catharsis and renewal, we don't always recognise it when it occurs. And worse, we often reward false metamorphosis instead. Doing the hard work of real metamorphosis takes time and effort, and requires giving up comfortable patterns of being. The reasons for this apparently perverse incentivisation are complex, but worth some discussion. Surely it would become obvious to critical groups over time that their needs were not being met by short-term quick fixes and false dawns? Would they not learn to prefer real, meaningful changes and metamorphoses? And would they not start to construct the very building blocks of these organisations – their ownership, governance, regulation, management, structure, processes and culture – in ways that made disappointment and negative surprise less likely? Yes and no, it turns out.

Private-sector Catharsis – Short-term-ism and Investors

Let's take the stock market and buy-side analysts (those who advise on purchasing stocks) as one set of important individuals who need to be impressed by changes in large private organisations. Without the support of the investors (and their proxies, the analysts) it takes a particularly courageous CEO and board to maintain the required level of long-term focus and tough-minded honesty required to get at what has occurred, and identify the deep root causes of previous issues in their organisation or sector. But numerous studies,[3] backed by the views of even more numerous commentators, attest that the stock market favours short-termism, ranging from the algorithmic mindlessness of flash trading (where speed of trading on technical movements in prices is what counts) through to the more thoughtful behaviour of fund managers (who are supposed to understand the long-term plans and intentions of management, and make well-informed decisions about where to invest our pension funds and so forth). The deficiencies of each class of investor in a public company are well-documented elsewhere,[4] but clearly investors remain as imperfect as a class in their competence and capabilities as any other group we have discussed in this book. This is because they are all *people,* or at least programmed by people, and hence are prone to the inevitable lapses and failures common to all homo sapiens, of any gender. And of course they may be performing in ways that are exactly as they intend, but immoral, unethical or greedy.

Much ink and angst is expended on why the public limited company in particular creates such apparently perverse incentives,[5] even in its most intelligent and reasoned experts, and even more on the ethical dilemmas that such design challenges create. The problem, of course, is that the managers are incentivised to do what the owners want (which is usually to do whatever will boost the share price over some short-ish timescale of months). The owners themselves turn out to be either ephemeral or impersonal, with the same set of agency theory problems applying to them as to those they are supposed to "own". The results of this system have been far from disastrous from the point of view of investors overall, in that, on average, they have been able to make money from stock-market investment with returns with acceptable levels of risk over many decades. So although each major stock-market slump causes some navel gazing about the inherent difficulties of the system, few have come up with a better idea on how the large sums of capital required by companies can be acquired. And the next boom tends to mute such existential opposition to a minimum.

Privately Held Organisations

Where companies are privately held, there is generally a different dynamic that stresses a longer-term perspective on the returns to investors that is better aligned with the reality of the large capital and other investments required. Many companies are taken back into private ownership to avoid the short-term requirements for "results" in the public markets. It's not surprising that a consistent feature of successful long-term-minded companies is the presence of very strong CEOs and boards that can explain their point of view clearly to investors, and hence attract capital and investors who share their philosophy and timescale for returns. The doyen of such companies is Berkshire Hathaway, and the Sage of Omaha, Warren Buffett, famously stated that:

> If you aren't willing to own a stock for ten years, don't even think
> about owning it for ten minutes.

It has become modish to decry the capitalist pressures of Wall Street, while still living in a society that benefits greatly from the capital markets and the free flow of capital investment towards best returns. We should not forget that the great virtue of the current capitalist system is that when it works it can be fast and efficient in ways no central government plan can be, and that its incentives work to drive capital where it is needed. The reality is that these pressures are amoral and apolitical. In a free capital market, if an investor builds a powerful and influential position in a stock, and then chooses to exert activist pressures on sleepy boards and lazy managers, that is not a bad thing in itself (though it's usually bad for the sleepy boards and lazy managers concerned). However, we can only observe that achieving double-digit growth in profits or returns on capital is rarely a sustainable objective over the longer term (many years); and that once such investors have achieved their objectives they – understandably – sell, perhaps having irretrievably changed the nature of the organisation and its other constituencies in the process. Such are the rights of ownership.

The problem – as exemplified so well by the banks in the recent crises – is that many of these downside risks are socialised, whereas the upside opportunities for wealth and "performance" are not. As a given sector is shaken up, what tends to happen is that the gains are heavily focused on a few (perhaps worthy) investors, and increasingly the executives whose rewards have been "aligned" with their interests. Given how hard it is to get managers actually to do what investors want, rather than what they like or feel able to do, this is actually no mean feat when and where it occurs. But too often these periods of massive growth and improvement seem[6] to be followed by periods of social destruction (whose costs are not fully borne by investors) as underperforming assets (factories, companies, even whole towns in some cases) are disposed of. It is one of the wonders of the modern age that democracies continue to allow large companies (private and public) to benefit from tax breaks and other forms of publicly funded expenditure when in setup mode, but don't successfully get them to contribute to the other end of the investment. Oil and gas companies are pretty honourable exceptions to these criticisms, but then they actually think ahead and plan for the end of their assets in ways few other industries do. Beset by complex legislation and regulation, they make poor targets for those looking for quick bucks in asset stripping. Perhaps there are some lessons to be learned for other industries there about what to require from organisations in their relative infancy about their end of life plans for assets, even for workforce talent.

What's all this got to do with catharsis? When organisations become pariahs, the danger is that they close ranks to exclude and marginalise the groups that find them unacceptable. This makes a proper catharsis and regaining of reputation and trust across society nigh on impossible. It also has the detrimental effect of associating those who direct capital and company ownership (which, we must remember, for public companies means people acting on behalf of second and third ranks of investors back to us normal folks trying to invest for our pensions) with the pariah behaviours. It's a subtle ploy, but it works well for most parties. The management and executive leaders of the organisation gain the sense of having powerful allies, who are then more obliged to back them in other areas where their interests might be better served by reserving judgement. The opposers, as we have noted before, have their own agendas served by suggesting that the bad actions of the pariah organisation are supported by shadowy institutional or private owners.

So, what we need to see is reform of the institutional investors, so they cannot take the attitude that the behaviour of the companies they collectively own and control is beyond their focused concern for financial growth and their own bonus. That no such reform is on the agenda of any government is surely one of the root causes of the dearth of catharsis and the growth in credibility of those who criticise capitalism and the financial 'system' as the root of societal evil. We ignore this problem at our peril.

Public-sector Catharsis

We have noted throughout this book that the issues are as applicable to public- and third-sector organisations as to private-sector companies; it's just that the mechanisms of control are different, and hence the way these organisations fail is different too. In the UK public sector, there are several contributory factors to the difficulty of catharsis, but also some powerful mechanisms to enable it which might be sources of learning and redemption for the private sector.

The factors that impede public-sector catharsis are:

+ **Confusion of political and administrative accountabilities** – in public life, when things go wrong, the first person who bears the brunt of accountability and feels the pain is the person we voted in to supervise the process. It's the minister who has to resign, not the permanent secretary, and the civil service likes it that way. As Sir Humphrey Appleby, the fictional permanent secretary at Jim Hacker's Ministry of Administrative Affairs puts it in an early episode of the BBC TV comedy, *Yes Minister*: "Minister, the traditional allocation of executive responsibilities has always been so determined as to liberate the ministerial incumbent from the administrative minutiae by devolving the managerial functions to those whose experience and qualifications have better formed them for the performance of such humble offices, thereby releasing their political overlords for the more onerous duties and profound deliberations which are the inevitable concomitant of their exalted position." All very amusing, but there's been surprisingly little progress in the ensuing 35 years since that was written. Clearly it's not career enhancing to bungle an IT implementation or a failure at the Passport Office, but it's (quite rightly) still the responsible minister who feels the heat in the Commons or the select committee. During the last 10-to-15 years, there has been an increase in the profile of senior civil servants, who are also now routinely grilled at select committees as well, but the confusion in the minds of press and public over who is really responsible for mistakes and incompetence remains. The civil service can always blame their political masters for a mis-judged policy, over-ambitious timescale or lack of funding or resources. And the politicians can blame their own organisation for being inadequate, as most famously did the bluntly spoken Home Secretary John Reid when, on joining the Home Office in 2006, he described his entire Immigration Directorate as "not fit for purpose".[7]

• **Absence of consequences** – this fundamental confusion of accountability at the top, wherein it remains tough to pinpoint individual accountabilities, means that, despite a lot of huffing and puffing, few top players lose their jobs or have to exit their profession as a result of scandals. Of course, no-one wants to be in the press for the wrong reasons, and I am not suggesting that Whitehall is indifferent to the embarrassment of crises; far from it. But where private sector and public sector meet, it's clear the private sector faces some immediate consequences that are absent on the other side. A good example of this was the fate of G4S's CEO Nick Buckles after the 2012 Olympic security fiasco.[8] Buckles was fired by his board within months of a series of inept performances in front of the Home Affairs Select Committee. Keith Vaz, the chairman, goaded Buckles at the end of his first visit with words that betrayed little respect for the actual processes of corporate governance: "In the end it is a matter for you to decide what you do about your future." But this was bluster: it was a matter for G4S's board. Despite justifiable anger at the company's ineptitude in a public contract, it wasn't Vaz's job to sack him; and it was arguably an abuse of his position to seek to do so. Do we see similar vigilance over those who are employed by the public purse? Of course, there are issues in the British system; it would not be appropriate for political masters to decide who stays and goes, but increasingly it's not been seen as appropriate just to move disgraced civil servants to other departments, as appeared to happen to Sir Richard Mottram when he was moved sideways from his role as Permanent Secretary at the Department of Transport to the Department of Work and Pensions after the series of scandals involving Railtrack that cost his Minister, Stephen Byers, his job in 2002.[9]

+ **Incompetence** – this is an increasingly popular word with organisational detractors. Of course, for incompetence to be an issue, it has to be clear what competence would actually look like. If we take the three types of crisis as a guide as to where incompetence might occur, it's obvious that public servants are increasingly under pressure because of operational, rather than financial or behavioural, issues. It's our rising expectations in terms of service delivery, and the associated pressures these place on public-sector capabilities in IT project management, data processing and people management, when the bar on these areas is rising rapidly in the private-sector domain, that create a lot of the sense of ineptitude. And it's the repeat of debacles that makes the mud stick, here just as much as in the private sector. In Chapter 1, we discussed the catalogue of prolonged failures that comprised the Mid-Staffs NHS scandal. We could easily have looked at the endless chain of crises enveloping social workers or child protection, or any number of others where the defining feature of the scandal has been not just poor governance but also incompetence and failures at the most basic operational level. Such incompetence is bound to breed where there are cultures which don't confront performance problems at any level, where procedural exactitude or political correctness become proxies for delivery and output, and where turning up at all becomes a nice-to-have rather than an assumption (the public sector still tolerates absence rates twice that of the private sector).

♦ **Lack of trust** – it's not surprising that when these factors are so common, and scandals and crises are becoming rife, trust begins to fail widely.[10] But whereas in the private sector organisations can, should and do fail completely and are either replaced or not by the world according to need,[11] in the public sector, wounded organisations can and do limp on for years or even decades. You can vote for a different party, but as in our system this creates no changes in the people managing and delivering services, there is no guarantee whether much will change when you do. I was once told by a senior civil servant that the Prime Minister had told his minister that "everyone knows your department is crap, and has always been crap." And even if you can establish that such an unhelpful claim is broadly true, can you get any support for change? Reformers sometimes wonder who to vote for in a country where the public sector has become the majority.

Each of these public-sector catharsis blockers has its private-sector comparators; I am certainly not going to pretend that the public sector has a monopoly on incompetence or poor consequence management. But these seem to be quite acute in the public-sector crises of recent years, and they are the sorts of issues that are brought up repeatedly by frustrated voters and commentators. So the problem of catharsis failure is deep and wide. It's closely linked to the collapse of mutual trust that we observed in Part One. Repeated failures, whether by the banks, health service, oil companies, pharma companies or your local council, lead to cynicism. That cynicism is the enemy of progress, of change. Because at the heart of catharsis lie forgiveness and a preparedness to trust again. If you have been hurt or damaged (or, thanks to the press, think you have, or have read about others who have) then it's harder to trust again. And in an age where authentic responses are becoming rarer than hen's teeth, we see very few credible apologies or resignations on matters of honour, or any of the mechanisms that used to provide an outlet for hurt feelings.

Examples of Catharsis

So if catharsis is becoming harder, should we despair? If it's unachievable, then the project to describe the cycle remains useful analytically, but its only useful action points will be in the first half of the cycle, avoiding crisis. That doesn't seem a satisfactory conclusion. Surely there are some examples in which organisations have achieved successful catharsis and regenerated well. In the previous chapter, I touched on the story of Saturn Corporation, the GM spinoff that reinvented the entire US small-car auto industry model in a way that successfully delighted customers and regained trust from millions of consumers who had given up on the big US automakers. I do think that Saturn offers really useful lessons on the depth, cost and timescale of real metamorphosis. But I am not sure it's a story of catharsis, ultimately, because of the organisation's eventual failure.

In the rest of this chapter, we will consider the catharsis of two other organisations: Railtrack/Network Rail and McDonald's. Both are controversial, but I hope they can illustrate the challenges of not only achieving catharsis but maintaining it.

Railtrack and Network Rail

Railtrack was created as part of the controversial privatisation of British Rail in 1994. Its job was to own and manage most of the critical underlying hardware of the UK rail system, the track, signals, tunnels, bridges and most of the stations across the system nationally. On these tracks would run trains (usually owned by other third-party leasing companies) operated by yet other companies, the train operating companies (TOCs) that passengers would, in the main, interact with. Railtrack would, in theory, charge market "rents" to TOCs and others to travel on its tracks and use its stations, and thereby gain a return on the (massive) fixed asset values tied up in them, thus paying for maintenance, renewal and enabling excess profits to be distributed to investors via dividends.[12] Even if you *are* a fan of rail privatisation, you have to admit there are compelling arguments that splitting accountabilities structurally like this was one of the causal factors in Railtrack's ultimate demise.

Devastating criticisms of Railtrack emerged from a series of fatal accident inquiries around the turn of the twenty-first century. A signalling failure had led to the Southall disaster outside Paddington station in 1997, in which six people died. Then in 1999, 31 died at Ladbroke Grove in a massive collision, also near Paddington and also traced to a signal passed at danger (SPAD). It became apparent in both accidents that lessons learned from significant British Rail fatal crashes in the 1980s and 1990s had not been heeded, and that key automated infrastructure train-protection systems that could have prevented the crashes had not been prioritised due to cost concerns. Railtrack meanwhile had been paying its senior executives handsomely and rewarding its investors with equally handsome dividends. The press, always sceptical of the rail privatisation idea, now managed to make this commercial success look like blood money. Railtrack's senior management were frequently berated on BBC Radio 4's influential *Today* programme and the company began to achieve pariah status as it lurched from crisis to crisis.

Further accidents at Hatfield in 2000 (four dead) and later at Potters Bar in 2002 (seven dead) cemented Railtrack's reputation for incompetence. By the time of the latter incident, Stephen Byers, the Secretary of State, had put the organisation into forced administration, one of the most extreme examples we have ever seen of the state exerting its right to end the existence of a public corporation (see Chapter 1). This was arguably an act of necessity, but also required considerable courage given the implications for the public purse (it was in effect, renationalising Railtrack).

The reason for the administration was, at least nominally, the imminent insolvency of the company in the face of its own mismanagement and the exceptional £750m costs associated with the Hatfield disaster, after which much of the UK rail network was reduced to a crawl while rail inspections took place, necessitating hefty refunds to the TOCs and their passengers for the massive delays they suffered. The press, of course, had had their usual field day throughout this process. This administration was an unprecedented event, a complete breakdown of trust and an admission of systemic failure of the highest order. It was, in other words, a total nemesis, but also a structural true metamorphosis. The manner and nature of the administration – which was essentially the government in the form of Byers refusing further state guarantees and funding, then forcing the legal remedy onto a private-sector company – remain controversial, and Railtrack's senior leadership continued to believe that had the government stuck by them, the difficult period would have been overcome. Byers became the subject of shareholder lawsuits as the outraged shareholders discovered they were no longer controlling a FTSE 100 company but had been effectively nationalised. But what happened next turned out to be an unlikely catharsis.

Network Rail was created as a company limited by guarantee,[13] which meant, amongst other things, that it did not have to pay the dividends that had proved so controversial for its predecessor. This important change signalled to the public that the government "got it" about their disquiet in letting a private company take the lead responsibility for safety on the network. It also enabled very large sums of subsidy to be provided in the ensuing Blair–Brown boom years of public spending. Had such investment been possible for Railtrack, no doubt it could have made different choices (though it might have simply diverted these investments to owners as the banks later were accused of doing with quantitative easing). In many ways, Network Rail did all the same things that Railtrack's[14] main infrastructure company had done before. But now it was a company firmly under the control, not just the influence, of the government and run by engineers (Railtrack had been controlled by its investors and run by accountants). Network Rail rapidly set about assessing its difficult legacy of broken and under-maintained assets, securing the funding and running the projects to fix them. Over the ensuing decade, a remarkable improvement occurred on the network. Reliability, punctuality[15] and safety[16] all improved dramatically.

The following table[17] illustrates the dramatic nature of the improvement.

Table 6

PERIOD	DEATHS	INJURIES
1985–1994 (British Rail)	75[18]	1,452
1995–2004 (Railtrack to '02)	77[19]	890
2005–2014 (Network Rail)	8[20]	105[21]

There are lots of reasons why Network Rail has been able to outperform its predecessor organisations (in a fair world, we must note that British Rail was no better at safety than Railtrack, didn't even track its on-time performance or reliability as the TOCs do, and wasn't exactly famous for its cuisine, either).

However, we see the hallmarks of a successful catharsis:

1. There was a **clear and identifiable break with the past**, with a change in structure and brand. It was obvious to everyone that Network Rail was meaningfully different from Railtrack, and it soon had different leaders too, even though the assets and most of the operating personnel remained the same.

2. There was a **thoughtful period of reflection that involved all players in the system**. Changing the behaviour of unionised train drivers (who were used to passing signals at danger without consequence) was as important to achieving safety as investing in automatic systems to stop trains.

3. A **detailed plan** was introduced, politically supported and properly funded, to achieve transformation.

4. **Trust returned**, partly in the form of increased passenger numbers using a more reliable and safer network, but also in the form of support for increased public funding.

5. In the long term, **proper funding** enabled assets to be planned, built and maintained appropriately.

6. **Leadership improved**. Out went the purely financial businessmen of the City and in came competent engineers who could understand the long-term nature of the renewal required and construct the plans to undertake that revision in a measured way. There was meaningful work done on cultural and behavioural change, involving the whole workforce.

Network Rail – on this telling – is one of the unsung success stories of the public sector in the last 50 years. Perhaps it was only able to achieve what it has on the back of the multiple tragedies and politicised arguments that beset Railtrack. But perhaps also we should give credit where it's due to the many men and women who worked so hard to regain our trust and help us feel proud of our railways again. Of course, its recovery story is a fragile one. Another major accident, the perception that quasi-public servants are overpaid, a behavioural scandal – any of these could occur and tarnish what has been achieved. And true to form, no sooner had I started writing about Network Rail in 2014 than a series of project-related operational problems occurred, apparently related to over-ambitious planning and some poor execution. But by now we should realise this is true for all organisations, whether they have been pariah or not. Achieving catharsis sets a new, higher but less cynical baseline for future relationships of trust to be built. It is still up to the organisation to live up to its new promises and avoid future crises.

McDonald's

Our second candidate for catharsis is the fast-food restaurant chain McDonald's.[22] McDonald's cheerfully ticked most of the boxes in our pariah genesis phase. One of the most successful brands ever seen, the company grew rapidly throughout the second half of the twentieth century. The story of how businessman Ray Kroc grew the company from a small franchise operation into a global behemoth is an American legend. Kroc bought the rights to franchise the McDonald brothers' successful California burger joint across the USA. By 1958 there were 34 restaurants. In 1959 alone, Kroc opened a further 68 locations – an extraordinary achievement. By 1968, McDonald's had undergone a successful IPO and was opening its thousandth restaurant. The mixture of owner-operated (franchise) and company restaurants was a success, mixing the innovation of franchisers (who invented some of the best-known items on the menu) with the discipline and brand control of the corporate centre. By 1974, it was time for international expansion, as the domestic market was becoming saturated. McDonald's opened its first restaurant in the UK, and since that time it has depended on its successful international operations to drive corporate growth.

McDonald's now has over 35,000 restaurants in 118 countries, serving 70 million customers a day. 2013 revenues were over $28 billion for the company and the underlying franchised sales were $70 billion.

In other words, there has scarcely ever been a better example of an organisation creating the genesis conditions for subsequent hubris and crises.

McDonald's Culture

So is this what actually occurred? The McDonald's culture – at least as I experienced it in the Oak Brook, IL headquarters in the late 1990s – is unique. Hubristic is not the first word one would pick from the air, however. McDonald's is too down to earth and pragmatic for that to be what hits you. It's not a place where senior leaders have generally been parachuted in from top universities and business schools. The business is relatively simple in concept; winning at it is about ensuring millions of people are served a product they enjoy, cheaply and quickly, by friendly and competent people. What gets you promoted up the chain is not your education or cleverness, but your ability to deliver on that promise, to delight customers and grow the business.

McDonald's was a rather closed society, preferring to promote from within. The culture was therefore somewhat "cult-ish" in the devotion to the brand[23], but no more extreme in that respect than any retail or consumer company. Lower down the organisation, McDonald's required everyone to conform to strict rules and requirements about everything from how to cook a burger to the architecture of its franchisee restaurants. This strength was potentially a great weakness: if the organisation's activities were the wrong ones, then the bad actions would be faithfully amplified across millions of transactions, globally. As McDonald's had effectively created a highly efficient distribution system not just for burgers and fries, but also for culture, ideas and practices which could dramatically influence how the world farms sustainably, it became more and more important that its leaders could think beyond the short-term need to grow sales in a given region of the map.

At higher levels, there was more pressure to remain innovative, introducing new products (many failed, a few became winners) and updating and improving cooking and hygiene techniques. McDonald's is particularly fine at developing its people – few organisations can match its capacity for taking an entry-level workforce and teaching them not only how to prepare food safely and run a restaurant, but also how to motivate and manage such a workforce. Others may laugh at Hamburger University, but it remains a visible commitment to learning that many other serious companies wanted to emulate.

McDonald's the Pariah

Nevertheless, McDonald's has encountered serious issues and opposition over its lifetime, and it's in how it has ultimately reacted to those that I think it can be regarded as a candidate for at least partial catharsis. The main arguments against the company were often existential opposition to the entire fast-food industry of which it was the most visible proponent. For some,

McDonald's represented not a refreshing change from other food options but a relentless, heavily branded, unhealthy piece of American empire building. It's still pretty rare for Americans to recognise that McDonald's can be seen as pariah, so ubiquitous and comforting is its presence in the country's psyche. But to Europeans, who had not grown up bombarded with comforting images of the brand and its products, there were major concerns that went beyond cultural hegemony. These revolved around three areas: the food itself, the expansion of the chain, and the company's business practices and supply chain.

Let's look at each of these in turn and note how the company has reacted:

Food and Menu

McDonald's has been attacked for the last 30 years or more for its menu. The concerns range from issues of animal welfare to the growing disquiet over the impact of sugar, salt and fat in our diet, to portion control. It would take too long to list all the issues here, but most were rehearsed in Morgan Spurlock's infamous 2004 film, *Supersize Me*. In its simplest form, the accusation against McDonald's is that the company colluded in activities which were hugely damaging to the health and wellbeing of its own customers (over time), and took no responsibility for the ensuing impacts on public health, in particular the epidemic of obesity that has seemingly followed its progress round the world. Also it was ethically troubling to many to purchase food products that, in order to lower prices, had been factory-farmed, genetically modified or sourced other than via fair trade.

McDonald's reaction to these protests was initially one more of deny/ignore than engage. But over time, it was realised in Oak Brook that there was a meaningful shift in public opinion on these issues. People wanted to consume their food, but wanted to feel good about doing it and to be able to defend their choices to their friends.

Some changes were relatively cosmetic: to offer salads is one thing; to do so alongside the core menu of salty, fatty alternatives is another. But once these options were firmly established, and with adequate information available to customers about nutritional information, it was far harder for detractors to claim that McDonald's was being secretive about its menu and how bad it was for you. McDonald's could legitimately claim now that it was for customers to balance their intake, and that it was at least theoretically possible to eat healthily in their restaurants. This latter claim has become less spurious since the focus on cafe products as the chain competes with the likes of Starbucks.[24]

Food sourcing also improved dramatically: in the UK in 2014, McDonald's sourcing for all meat (beef, pork, chicken) was local, sustainably sourced and from farms which have some reasonable guarantees of animal welfare. Eating at McDonald's is ethically a better bet from this point of view than eating at any number of restaurants that are using unsustainable fish species or sourcing their meat less carefully. McDonald's was utterly untouched by the horsemeat scandal of 2013. The milk used in all products is British and organic milk is used in tea, coffee, milk bottles and porridge. Eggs are free-range. Their chips (fries) are made largely from UK-grown potatoes and cooked in non-hydrogenated vegetable oil. In short, McDonald's is able to compete, even at a low price point, with the quality and sourcing provenance one might associate with a much smaller or higher-end provider. So good are these bona fides, they leave McDonald's detractors with no meaningful avenue of attack other than to decry meat eating in general, and the company is now (2015) advertising to consumers directly to educate them about the truth of what they are eating and dispel urban myths about what is really in their food.

Being able to execute on such a shift in sourcing (because things were not at all so rosy decades ago) has been a long-term challenge for the organisation. And a future full of challenges lies ahead, replete with the expectation of increasing pressures on the core products, and the branding association that gets kids "hooked" on the brand.[25]

Expansion

The arguments against expansion are tricky for McDonald's. It's actually hard for them to grow the core business much in its historic markets. In fact, City analysts and investors fret that there is little or no further growth to be had from their existing business model once they have saturated the world's population centres. At some level of density each restaurant is merely cannibalising another restaurant's potential clientele, although it is arguable exactly how close together restaurants have to be before this effect is truly pronounced. Alternative strategies that have been tried to increase share of wallet include the disastrous attempts in the late '90s to sell more expensive burgers, opening up to new times of day (breakfasts, coffee etc.) and another failed attempt to extend the core capability of the organisation into running different types of restaurants.[26]

At the other end of the spectrum, there is the argument that there are still billions of people on the planet who are becoming wealthy enough to consume the company's products, and that by competing effectively with other food options for time-starved urbanites McDonald's can grow further. But as it does so, concerns rise about the expansion of waistlines that appear to track the company's burgeoning revenues.

I am not sure McDonald's has an utterly effective answer for this, any more than any for-profit enterprise has. The simple reality is that the planet as we know it cannot afford to turn all its current and projected future inhabitants into people with the living habits of Americans: they consume too much energy, eat and drink too much of the wrong things, and have a number of prevalent and unsustainable habits. McDonald's is on the cutting edge of the ensuing debates about American cultural imperialism. And it will take more than just a bit of local menu innovation to deal with these challenges.

But by becoming more diverse, by inviting in and providing for customer groups previously unserved (including wealthy, skinny, health-conscious people), McDonald's has achieved a form of catharsis that can inspire us even as we seek the wider solutions to the growth challenges of the capitalist debate.

Business Practices and Supply Chain

McDonald's is a vast employer of people in what are politely termed "entry-level" roles. These are jobs for which one requires limited education or other skills, and the company trains people from scratch to work in the restaurants, cooking and serving food, cleaning the facility, and then invests in training managers at every level. The company resents the criticism that it merely provides "McJobs" at "minimum wage", but inevitably such a big employer for whom so many have worked – at least for a while – is under constant surveillance.

A key crisis for McDonald's was the so-called McLibel trial, a complex

UK libel action against two activists from an organisation called London Greenpeace. The trial took 10 years and made McDonald's look like a bully. The original accusations in the defendants' leaflets (which had had only a small audience) were repeated to a global audience. These included some lurid complaints from some of the 160 witnesses about how they had been treated, including issues over forced overtime and actions against those who tried to organise into unions. McLibel was not unlike Shell's contemporary experience with the other Greenpeace, in that the big company was probably correct on most points, but lost the war of public opinion. Since that turning point, it's notable that the company took action on just about every single area that the McLibel defendants complained about in their leaflets.

The outstanding performance of McDonald's is really in its capacity to manage its massive supply chain. One of the company's top leaders was able to point out that by making the menu changes described above (the increase in salads and healthy options) they had to source more than just shredded lettuce for the Big Mac.

> We probably sell more lettuce, more milk, more salads, more apples than any restaurant business in the world.

> Walt Riker, VP Corporate Media Relations, McDonald's, 2010

McDonald's is perhaps as open as any company about its supply-chain practices and provides much educational material (which of course we could dismiss as propaganda) on the challenges it faces, and how it is positioning its leadership on these issues. On the website in late 2014 one could see[27] how McDonald's leaders are trying to make programmatic progress against priorities of three E's (ethics, environmental responsibility and economic viability) for critical areas such as raw materials (including packaging – where the aim is to become sustainable in all areas), fish, beef, coffee and palm oil. McDonald's stopped sourcing beef from deforested Amazon areas in 1989 (in response to the early campaigns that the McLibel trial emulated).

It's hard to think of a company that has done more to listen to and respond to its critics, whilst still focusing itself on its customers. At the scale of operations of a truly global company, it's hard to think of a better candidate than McDonald's for having achieved catharsis. Despite all this, there are many who cannot bring themselves to consider McDonald's as an acceptable business. A legacy in which past behaviour was not trustworthy, or where the truth was suppressed, makes life very difficult for a long time. It's probably impossible to make every group permanently happy. But there's no doubt McDonald's has been highly effective – much more so than Shell or Barclays – in making themselves organisationally acceptable again to a vast group of stakeholders, including customers and investors.

Washing Away the Stains

Catharsis as a process requires some form of sacrifice, a source of the symbolic blood to be washed away. Something has to be given up on both sides of the argument and that giving up has to be marked in some way.

In the cases we have looked at, the organisation itself and in particular its leaders are to a great extent these sacrificial victims moving towards their opponents (or even, as with Bob Diamond, losing their jobs to appease them). But also we must recognise the role played in the story by other symbolic victims, such as whistleblower employees, courageous activists, regulators and even governments who oppose hubristic activity. The French philosopher René Girard notes that there is a universality to such experiences across human history; we are in effect repeating a necessary story as part of a natural process:

> the death of a single victim serves to appease the anger of some god or spirit. A lone individual, who may or may not have been guilty of some past crime, is offered up to a ferocious monster or demon in order to appease him, and he ends up killing that monster as he is killed by him.[28]

It does seem reasonable to recognise that, as social beings, we cannot restore balance and faith in our mutual trust, either at an individual or a group level, without resorting to at least symbolic acts of purification and forgiveness. Perhaps what we have neglected too much now are the arts of seeking and giving forgiveness, of repentance. Where we have seen such processes, in South Africa, Northern Ireland and elsewhere, they have the curious and almost magical property of changing both parties. Here is an excerpt from the Provisional IRA's statement from July 2005, announcing it would finally lay down its arms:

> We appreciate the honest and forthright way in which the consultation process was carried out and the depth and content of the submissions.

We are proud of the comradely way in which this truly historic discussion was conducted.

Nine years later, when the Reverend Ian Paisley, the Unionist leader, died in 2014, Martin McGuinness was able to say this about the man who had once been his arch-nemesis, but became his fellow leader in the new assembly: "We were once opponents, but today I've lost a friend." And as anyone who grew up in the shadow of the "Troubles" will tell you, that was a pretty extraordinary statement. We should never stop believing that anything is possible and that it's worth the effort to achieve catharsis. Yes, it takes a long time, and it's painful and difficult. But it's worth it.

RECOMMENDATIONS

12. Ask for Forgiveness – Candour and Catharsis

Alongside a solidly constructed change programme aimed at the "right" underlying issues, attention needs to be paid to the fundamental characteristic that differentiates authentic metamorphosis from its common cousin. One area that needs more consideration is whether apology is actually necessary, let alone sufficient, for catharsis.

A good deal has been written by my friends the PR and communications experts on apologising.[29] They generally agree that:

◆ Apologising is a high stakes game for the CEO and the organisation given the potential loss of face and liability at issue.

◆ It has nevertheless become more common – even fashionable – for leaders to apologise on behalf of their organisations.

◆ Fear of the possible legal risks created is lessening, and there are increasing moves to enable apologies to replace legal processes (for example, a lot of medical malpractice suits might never reach court if the doctors would just admit the errors and apologise).

◆ Insincere and half-baked apologies do more harm than good.

It seems to me we complicate these things too much. The point about an organisation that is going through a sincere, authentic metamorphosis and wants to get out of pariah territory is that the rest of the world (or significant groups within that world) don't trust it, and don't think it understands the role it has played in causing its crises. Given the personhood generously allowed by the law to organisations, it doesn't seem too steep a requirement to ask those persons to enter debates with those who are angry at them, and to understand some of the same rules of engagement that we all follow in interpersonal conflicts:

- Being defensive is normal and we all have to learn to stand our ground and explain what we did and our motivations for doing it. No-one reasonable thinks organisations should just cave into their critics.[30]

- Skilled negotiators recognise that a lack of preparedness to apologise is damaging to trust and respect over time. The first thing that a sincere apology does is acknowledge care for the other person's state of upset, even if the apologiser does not think it's warranted. By skilful enquiry, an apologiser can figure out what the (perceived) facts are and what their own behaviour has contributed to the situation of upset. For maximum points, they will be able to diagnose this failure with minimum prompting, and identify how they are going to make amends and how they are going to change to avoid a repeat performance

- Equally, insincere or superficial apologies are trust destroyers, as they betoken a lack of respect for the other person's feelings or status.

Managing inter-organisational relationships is not so different from long-term marriages. What we are trying to avoid here are divorces from stakeholders. **Pariahs are organisational divorcees, as well as exiles, with all the psychological problems that go with those states.**

One of the finest writers on predicting divorce is the American professor John Gottman.[31] Through scrupulous video analysis over many years of the actual interactions of real couples, Gottman has assembled a compelling body of understanding, which he claims can give him up to 91 per cent accurate prediction rates for which couples will subsequently divorce. The six key signs, which might perhaps be emulated by organisations in their dealings with their own critics as well as friends, are:

Harsh start up – negative, accusatory or contempt-filled beginnings to conversations usually betoken the tone of the whole conversation to come and doom it accordingly.

Four horsemen – criticism, contempt, defensiveness and stonewalling are all profoundly damaging to the relationship because, in different ways, they make communication and change impossible. Contempt is the worst of the lot.

Flooding – a natural defence mechanism to criticism and attack is to stonewall as one is flooded with emotions (fear, anger, anxiety) that also preclude engagement and generative discussion.

Body language – alongside flooding, your body's natural reactions to the conflict can also preclude rational debate, hearing what is actually said (as opposed to what you think was said) and raise the fight-or-flight reflex to the fore. Our dinosaur brains are running the show, not our frontal cortexes.

Failed repair attempts – one of the saddest items on Gottman's list is that when one person reaches out to apologise and it's rejected or ignored, that is a predictor of failure. This is because trust and respect have been lost to an extent that such repairs are no longer wanted, valued or felt to be worthwhile.

Bad memories – if the overriding memory of the past is poor, then this is also a bad sign for the couple.

I've seen leaders who represent pariah organisations exhibit just about every one of these six signs in their interactions with not only critical external agencies but also their own peers, when they felt that they were being questioned or criticised. So before, during and after our attempts to "fix" our own organisation, we might usefully think about the nature of our relationships with our stakeholders and what we can do to improve them based on some of these data. One of the most powerful things that strike me about this parallelism is that one person cannot fix a marriage without help or support from the other side; and conversely, I guess one organisation cannot be wholly accountable for the state of a poor stakeholder relationship. But it's striking how often one reads that senior leaders and their functional sidekicks treat press reporters, financial analysts, regulators, politicians or even customers and clients with disdain, hauteur or even downright contempt. And yet there is absolutely no way that one can exist without interacting with these critical stakeholders in the ecosystem.

We discussed above the vital importance of introducing the right leadership characteristics into the organisation, and here is another reason why that is so important: without a mature appreciation for how interpersonal dynamics work, without the skill to listen deeply, without a mastery of their own emotional needs, how can we possibly expect our leaders to represent us effectively? And if they don't do so, how can we expect others to mirror that, either within the organisation or outside it? To that extent, it lies in every organisation's gift to achieve its own catharsis. But this must be sincerely based on mature enquiry, not on shallow charisma. It's a big ask and it's small wonder so few manage it.

13. Maintain Healthy Paranoia

The overall lesson of this book should be that it's possible and worthwhile to try to avoid pariahdom, and that even if you are a pariah you can do many things to recover your position of trust in the world. Nevertheless, I am going to advocate that alongside hard work and humility, those seeking to create a long-term success for their organisations will also cultivate a degree of what I'll call "healthy paranoia". No-one should be too certain that they can assess all the risks they face, manage all the relationships, avoid all uncertainties. All you can do is let others know that your values and motives are good, your purpose worthwhile, and that you care about more than just your own success or survival. Then, when crises occur (and they will occur) you will have the reputation and the entrepreneurs to defend and support you through the attacks. And you will learn from what happens, and get better. Meanwhile, smart organisations are also strategically paranoid, much as Andy Grove, CEO of Intel, suggested in his book:[32]

> The person who is the star of a previous era is often the last one to adapt to change, the last one to yield to logic of a strategic inflection point and tends to fall harder than most.

And this is the real point. Becoming successful takes tremendous hard work, smart judgement and a lot of luck. But *remaining* successful requires organisations to compete with themselves, to work out what is going to kill their business model or is going to be politically toxic to them, and get ahead of that. Continuous improvement is not comfortable. You never get to rest on your laurels as you are always worrying about the future and whether you are going to survive. It's not a good mix with hubris.

The organisations that get this right in the future will be ones that really get back to believing in the importance of the whole beyond the part and, in particular, avoid falling for the wiles of self-oriented leaders. To do this will be to sail against the wind of contemporary popular culture, with its emphasis on instant success, insecure self-puffery and blinged-up lifestyles. If that sounds rather dour, it needn't. Such cultures don't have to be dull, worthy or lacking in fun. They exist already – we just need to help them emerge. To that end, we should remember how effective the ordinary workforce can be in keeping organisations out of trouble. If we stop treating people as troublesome, conservative costs and let them help leaders work out how the organisation could work better, and if we show them respect and give them some reasonable degree of security and clarity of direction, there are still massive, untapped resources in most organisations that never get a proper say in how to run the place.

So ultimately I believe that we are not all doomed to work for pariah organisations. But it is up to all of us to do something about it. It's no good moaning at the press or Twitter for being unfair (though they are), or lambasting boards and CEOs for acting in their own self-interest (though they will). We need to have the workforce – not just "organised labour" as we have known it, but the entire body of those who do the work of the organisation – get a grip on its own collective reputation and survival. I think we can do that through a number of methods, including:

- Deeper interest by boards in the views and engagement of employees in the organisation as part of their duties to understand and manage risk (without relying too much on engagement surveys alone)

- Training and involving employees in performance improvement, particularly LEAN and other process analysis and improvement methods, as well as generally improving the quality of economic literacy in the workforce so it understands how the organisation makes and spends its money, and therefore what constitutes "waste"

- Developing new, ongoing forms of organisational "audit" (but NOT performed by existing financial audit companies) that give a more honest perspective on items of concern that are visible to workers and leaders at all levels

- Getting people-driven risks much higher up the list of things that can and do sink the organisation, and hence considered formally by leadership and governance at all levels

- Opening up as many of these processes as possible to external challenge and scrutiny.

Notes

1 All dictionary definitions from Liddell and Scott.

2 See Burkert, 1992.

3 A 2011 speech by Andy Haldane, a senior figure at the Bank of England, summarises some of the arguments, including the excessive and irrational discounting applied to future earnings. http://www.bankofengland.co.uk/publications/Documents/speeches/2011/speech495.pdf

4 Lewis, 2014 focuses on the world of flash trading, where algorithms, not human input, dictates trades worth billions a day.

5 Such angst has a long history. It has become modish to quote the famous Scottish political economist Adam Smith as being "opposed" to joint stock companies. See Smith, 1776, V.i. More recent challenges have been made on ethical grounds. See for example the evidence of Professor Roger Steare to the Banking Standards Board in 2014, where he suggests that it is only through individual accountability that better ethical behaviour will emerge. http://www.bankingstandardsboard.org.uk/assets/docs/responses/roger-steare.pdf

6 For example, the controversial purchase in 2000 of British carmaker MG Rover by the Phoenix Consortium, a group of four businessmen who were paid over £40m in pay and pension contributions even as the company was going bust with the loss of 6,000 jobs in 2005. The Phoenix Four blamed the government and were never convicted of any criminal offence.

7 The comment was made in the light of a series of scandals regarding foreign prisoners which led to the resignation of Charles Clarke, Reid's predecessor. The scope of Reid's comments is impressively wide: "Our system is not fit for purpose. It is inadequate in terms of its scope, it is inadequate in terms of its information technology, leadership, management systems and processes," he said. Quoted in http://www.theguardian.com/politics/2006/may/23/immigrationpolicy.immigration1

8 G4S were contracted to provide trained security personnel for the London Olympics in 2012. In a very public failure, it became apparent weeks before the Games that G4S was not going to deliver and the Army had to step in. As this was a public contract, Buckles was duly hauled before the Home Affairs Select Committee to explain himself. See http://www.telegraph.co.uk/sport/olympics/9405503/Nick-Buckles-questioned-by-MPs-as-it-happened.html

9 There is no suggestion that Mottram was not very capable; indeed he went on to several more senior posts before his retirement in 2007. However, it's

hard to imagine a private-sector boss of equivalent rank surviving in the same parent organisation after such scandals on their watch. See http://en.wikipedia.org/wiki/Richard_Mottram

10 A recent report highlighted the plummeting levels of trust at the heart of the civil service between ministers and senior civil servants as the former increasingly forced the latter to face performance pressures and share the hotseat with them. http://www.bbc.co.uk/news/uk-politics-23978335

11 One of the big issues with private-sector pariah industries is that the industry and its players are often seen as too essential to fail. The normal rules of capitalism that would allow a company to fail don't seem to apply.

12 See Wolmar, 2001 for a critique of privatisation

13 Network Rail was subsequently classified as a public body on 1 September 2014. This made the government's complete control over it more transparent, and also added about £34bn to net public-sector debt that was previously "off the books" for presentational purposes.

14 Railtrack Group, the parent company, remained unaffected by the administration of Railtrack.

15 A trend graph showing the moving annual average improvement in a combined punctuality and reliability measure called PPM (Public Performance Measure) is at http://www.networkrail.co.uk/about/performance/.

16 Deaths and injuries in rail crashes are a somewhat crude statistic to measure safety across a network where so many factors can cause accidents, including vandalism, trespassing as well as driver or signaller error. Also one should note the dramatic improvements in survivability in these years as old wooden-framed rolling stock was replaced by all steel construction. However, given the huge increase in passenger miles ridden over this period, it's a remarkable achievement to have made the network as safe as it has been.

17 Source: http://en.wikipedia.org/wiki/List_of_rail_accidents_in_the_United_Kingdom

18 35 died at Clapham, the worst accident in this period.

19 31 died at Ladbroke Grove, the worst accident in this period.

20 Two teenage girls died crossing the line at Elsenham in Essex. All other deaths were single fatalities, mainly on level crossings. Two of these were in separate incidents on a short stretch of heritage steam railway not under Network Rail's accountability.

21 88 of these casualties were at the Virgin Grayrigg derailment in 2007, caused by faulty points. One person died in this incident.

22 I should declare my interest here. McDonald's was a major client of my employer, Towers Perrin, when I worked there in the late 1990s. I was involved in several projects for the firm, although I have not worked for them since 2000. In the course of these projects, I came to meet several of the top leaders of the company in that era.

23 Brand loyalty was total. When I consulted to McDonald's, meetings with the top leadership were invariably catered from the in-house restaurant, leading to the challenging task of eating a Big Mac and fries without getting it on their

ties being undertaken simultaneously by ten executives. A series of adverse health events, including the tragic sudden deaths of Jim Cantalupo and Charlie Bell, made some wonder whether a diet exclusively based on the company's products was a good idea, although no direct link was provable.

24 There are some parallels here to the ways that the tobacco industry handles criticism: the argument hangs on the assumption that individual, well-informed adults are in a position to assess risks for themselves and make decisions accordingly, and don't need a "nanny state" interfering in their transactions with those selling them things that give them pleasure.

25 See *Economist*, 17 June 2010: Good and hungry: More than menus need to be revamped if fast-food firms want to keep growing, http://www.economist.com/node/16380043

26 For example, McDonald's bought and expanded the Chipotle Grill chain in direct competition with its core restaurants.

27 http://www.aboutmcdonalds.com/content/dam/AboutMcDonalds/2.0/pdfs/McD_SixPriorityProducts.pdf

28 See Girard, 1977, p.87 in his discussion of Oedipus.

29 See Kellerman, 2006.

30 However, defending without listening fully to the accusations and considering the possibility of one's own behaviour is troublingly narcissistic behaviour.

31 See Gottman, 2014.

32 See Grove, 1996.

PART THREE –
DEALING WITH PARIAHS

10

Pariahs of the Future

If you don't think about the future, you cannot have one…

John Galsworthy, *Swan Song*

So there are things that matter and things that don't. Presidents
and recessions come and go. But the long processes that truly
change our lives are still there, and they are not always the things
that people are expecting or discussing.

George Friedman, *The Next 100 Years*

I N THIS FINAL part of the book, my intention is to give some answers to
the inevitable question "So What?" If the concept of pariahs and their lifecycle is to be of real value, we need to see what can be done to avoid further
additions to the roll of shame and set out some ideas on how to deal with
those already afflicted. This chapter concerns itself with predicting which
sorts of organisations and industries may be most at risk of heading into
pariahdom (and why). We will then make an overdue stop to consider the
employees (rather than the leaders) of the pariah organisation and how they
can contribute to the health or otherwise of the organisation and its future.

Future Risks

Precise prediction of the future is notoriously difficult, and I don't expect
to achieve much here other than to stimulate debate, perhaps denial, and
possibly even some outrage. Nevertheless it is worth pointing out that if the

number of pariahs is indeed growing at some non-linear rate, then it may be the case that the risk factors are not well understood or managed. Earlier, we noted the definition of a pariah organisation as follows:

A pariah organisation is well known, but is more infamous than famous. It has become – permanently or temporarily – stigmatised as unacceptable to many stakeholders in the society in which it operates because it has violated the norms of that society.

This definition in turn creates a set of potential risk factors which might be worth monitoring in non-pariah organisations:

1. Being well known creates risk
2. Stigma and unacceptability are more easily created in a connected world
3. Violations of norms are more likely in a more transparent world.

Let's look at each of these in turn.

Being Well Known Creates Risk

The modern obsession with brand and brand creation creates new risks for organisations, as we observed in Chapter 1. Being well known is essential (we are told), and individual and organisational fame are requisites. But the downside is of course that if something goes wrong, the brand and everything that goes with it are vulnerable. Those seeking to avoid infamy are reminded that obscurity, though no guarantee of moral rectitude, has its benefits.

Stigma and Unacceptability

The critical change brought about by the Internet, social media and modern news gathering (including citizen journalism) is that, when something negative occurs, that news will be everywhere, instantly, as we all jostle to show we were the first in the global village to hear the gossip. And the fastest way to attract notoriety is by criticising, not praising, the status quo. As well as speed, these changes have made it easy for like-minded groups to connect, share data (and their sense of moral outrage) and get organised about publicity, pressure and campaigning against something or somebody. There is a fragmentation of entities and sub-groups in audiences, which is making it harder to avoid focused, organised disenchantment. Where an issue gains traction with mainstream media as well, these effects can be highly magnifying. In the modern world, there is now a role for highly specialised organisations to whip up and focus online rage and get us to click for victory.

A good recent example is the organisation known as 38 Degrees[1] in the UK. The organisation is an online pressure group, named after the angle at which an avalanche allegedly occurs. The focus of their direct action is to use online petitions to focus attention and demands for action directly onto politicians and power holders. In this case the agenda is usually close to that of the *Guardian*, but such techniques have also been used successfully by the Tea Party Republicans in the USA. There is, of course, a significant risk in reducing the world to single issues where you have the buzz of power by clicking support, rather than taking part in the complex, dirty business of actually governing and managing a balance. Much easier to click on "Save our NHS" than to work out what that really means, how to raise the money and how to attain operational excellence.

Evgeny Morozov has memorably criticised this simplistic reductionism in his books:

> Perfection shouldn't be pursued for its own ends; democracy is a complex affair in which, in the absence of disappointments, there would never be any accomplishments.[2]

Much as I approve of Morozov's sentiments on this and many other topics, to criticise such things is to sound like a curmudgeon. The fact is that this is the way the world is going and, like it or not, this is going to be a world that creates – *has* to create – a lot of pariahs.

Violation of Norms

Given that more data than ever is available outside organisational walls about what is happening inside them (a trend which surely seems set to continue), it's going to get ever harder to keep things secret. So if there are errors or, worse, deliberate plots to cover things up or act against the interest of customers or other groups, this will increasingly become apparent. Coupled with the changes in communication noted above, this means that the likelihood of someone, somewhere, finding something to get bent out of shape about in your organisation has risen considerably. Indeed, the opportunity for outrage[3] to grow as it is mirrored, echoed and renewed is one of the defining characteristics of a modern media crisis. However hollow or contrived the emotions concerned may seem, there is now an enjoyment of being shocked and outraged that has caught on around the world. Assuming this globalisation of village gossip continues, it's going to be just a matter of time before your organisation violates someone else's norms, and that violation is amplified and communicated.

High-risk Candidates

Given these conditions, *all* organisations are at risk. Some people have asked me to identify which organisations might be most at risk. It's not easy, and to some extent we are talking about whether organisations are moving from or towards established pariah status. But let's start with some easy predictions and then move to some less obvious ones.

Energy Utilities

As we observed above, some organisations are rapidly moving into the pariah establishment. The UK's privatised energy utilities are a good example of this. Even though (or perhaps because) they are regulated, they have collectively achieved a reputation for being rapacious capitalists who pass on every wholesale price rise, yet never give their customers a break. High prices (relative to incomes) and poor customer service have been at the root of the issues for energy companies, despite an open and competitive market that was supposed to achieve the opposite. A mixture of xenophobia about foreign ownership of the companies, politicisation of the issues and occasional delivery failures when extreme weather threatens supply has provided the *Daily Mail* with a never-ending series of stories. If the supply of stories wanes at all, there is always some fresh outrage about executive pay to add to the mix.

This formula has now been in use for over twenty years. Who now remembers Cedric Brown, the original "fat cat" CEO at British Gas, whose pay package in 1996 caused a furore when his base pay soared from £275,000 to £475,000? Brown was eventually hounded from his job by the press and public outrage. These days his equivalent (Ian Conn, recruited from BP to run Centrica) has a base salary of £925,000 and considerably more bonus, LTIP and other share-related compensation opportunities. The issue for energy companies, as Conn is discovering, is that when you mix a mandatory service (we cannot reasonably all go off-grid) with global market pricing and a faltering domestic economy, as well as a corporate culture that commoditises its own product and its customers, you are sitting on political dynamite. The sane reality is that energy profits are probably not excessive given the high capital costs they have to sustain (interestingly the same is true of banks and oil companies), but to a largely innumerate and financially illiterate public ignorant of the cost of capital, stirred into frustrated anger by the press, such arguments are pointless. It will take an amazing shift by one of the industry incumbents to achieve any meaningful catharsis here.

Google

Slightly closer to the edge of fully fledged pariah status, and heading that way, is Google.[4] In some ways, Google deserves a chapter of its own, perhaps even a book, as it is coming to exemplify the difficulties of managing reputation and brand in a transparent world partly of its own creation. A few years ago, the idea (especially to left-leaning Californian techies) that the most successful of all dot com startups, with its company motto of "Don't Be Evil", could be seriously considered as perhaps exactly that – evil – would have been ridiculous. However, as the scope, breadth and depth of Google's mission to grab and categorise the world's data becomes more apparent, the challenges are becoming clear too.

In his book *In the Plex*, Steven Levy reveals how Google sees these challenges:

> Ill intentions, flimflammery, and greed had no role in the process. If temptation sounded its siren call, one could remain on the straight path by invoking Amit Patel's florid calligraphy on the whiteboards of the Googleplex: "Don't be evil." Page and Brin were good, and so must be the entity they founded.

(Levy, 2011, p.146)

The arguments around Google and its role in the world are closely allied with political points of view around openness, transparency and secrecy. On the one hand, the benefits of transparency are considerable: if I share my travel data with Google, then others can benefit as I do in turn from accurate information and insights.

But few of us are truly aware of quite what a Faustian bargain we are getting into. Do we really want a record of everywhere we have ever been, everything we have ever done and every picture ever taken of us to be recorded, catalogued and stored forever? How do we know such data is not being (or subsequently going to be) used against us?

Google's key position at the heart of the Internet industries makes it a natural target for dissenters, especially when it changes tack on issues dear to the geeks' hearts, such as the principle of "net neutrality" (the question of whether the Internet is designed to give equal priority to all packets of data travelling on it, or to allow for commercial interests to prioritise traffic that has paid for the privilege). When Google changed their policy on this issue, there was a furore:

> On August 13 – a Friday – protesters took to the Googleplex...
> [T]he highlight was a musical tribute to Google's perfidy by a singing
> group called the Raging Grannies. Yet the groups behind the event –
> including MoveOn, Free Press, and the Progressive Change Campaign
> Committee – represented true disenchantment by Google's former
> allies. And they carried a petition of displeasure with 300,000 signa-
> tures. Their signs read GOOGLE, DON'T BE EVIL.
>
> (Levy, 2011, p.384)

Despite these challenges (and those emerging around its global taxation arrangements), Google is much admired, usually at the very top of the lists for graduates, executives, peers and investors alike.[5] Of course, such ratings can be fickle, but there is no question Google has become a totemic talent machine, attractive to both new graduates eager to learn at the best, as well as to more seasoned engineers and executives wanting to upgrade their resumes and careers. Given the intense competition to join such a famous brand organisation, it's not surprising that those who do join consider themselves an elite, and that this very elitism breeds the beginnings of a dangerous arrogance if confidence and pride become excessive. Google is now facing a backlash in San Francisco for the impact it is having on everything from high house prices to bus routes and traffic congestion.[6] It's perhaps inevitable that such a large, fast-growing, successful and high-paying company will become involved with such local controversies, but one senses there is more to it than simple economic pressures or envy of success.

The big danger for Googlers has to be arrogance and hubris. Placed as they are in a position where they are thinking ahead of most people, encouraged to believe they are progressive, intelligent and (critically) morally correct, it's going to be hard for them to avoid seeing all opposition as misguided. Given the dominant engineering mindset in the company (where engineers are a clearly superior caste), there may be lessons to be learned from the oil companies, where similar dynamics occur. As we will see in Chapter 12, it's a hubris risk to create groups within the organisation who are seen as inherently superior or entitled. Stephen Levy, who spent hundreds of hours observing and interviewing Googlers, quotes a non-technical Googler as saying: "There is an absolutely crystal-clear hierarchy at Google. It's engineers and everyone else. And if you want to be here, you have to, at some level, appreciate it." (Levy, 2011, p.130)

Specifically, Google is going to have to use its own unique position in the information economy to listen to criticism of its own behaviour and act on it, or start to face more hard-edged opposition down the line that might seriously impact its business model. At present it operates a near-monopoly in search and associated advertising. It will be fascinating to see how such an impressive, aggressive and innovative company develops further and whether it can develop the leaders required for sustainable greatness over a long period.

Technology Startups

Just to be clear, I happen to have picked on Google here because of its current, particularly powerful position (and let's recall that hubris is a disease of power). I could just as easily have cited aspects of how Facebook behaves, and there are many signs that Facebook's attitude to its own customers and their privacy and civil liberties is even more troubling than Google's. And if we had gone back 15 years or so, we could say the same things about Microsoft or other tech giants, even of IBM in its Big Blue heyday. There is perhaps something about technology, engineering and finance companies that makes them particularly vulnerable to becoming pariahs. Perhaps it's the dominance of mathematicians and engineers, and the somewhat high tolerance that this can create in the corporate culture for "high IQ, low EQ" individuals. The organisational dynamics of these organisations have been amusingly described in Dilbert cartoons since 1989 by Scott Adams. Adams, an engineer himself, nails the central dilemma of these cultures: without the engineers and their brains and inventions, there would be nothing to sell, but without others to market and sell these inventions (and manage the company), would things really go so much better? Behind the satire lies the real engineers' belief: *they* are the clever ones who, if pushed, can do anything. The rest – finance, HR, marketing and any form of management – are relatively stupid and unskilled, yet frustratingly seem to have power over them. This (spoken or unspoken) belief is quite central to many startups, although the new generation of technologists, including Mark Zuckerberg at Facebook, has become more comfortable with developing "cross-trained" engineers as leaders who can manage functions such as marketing and sales, yet also command some degree of respect amongst an expert engineering fraternity.

As a result, we can suspect that many startups, including the few that will become spectacularly successful, will bump into unexpected challenges in which their technological smarts will suddenly and unexpectedly meet real-world opposition. Dave Eggers in his 2013 novel *The Circle* represents these challenges to a Google-like company. The Circle experiences occasional opposition from a senator who wants to "insist that the Senate's Antitrust Task Force begin an investigation into whether or not the Circle acts as a monopoly... The dominance of the Circle stifles competition and is dangerous to our way of free-market capitalism". Such objections and colourful language are very far from imaginary. Microsoft was accused in a well-publicised court case (ultimately settled with the US Department of Justice in 2004) of being a monopoly that abused its position to maximise its profits at the expense of customers and competitors. The legal process was lengthy, complex and expensive, with accusations of dirty tricks by Microsoft countered by personal attacks on Judge Penfold Jackson, who was accused on appeal of giving media interviews during the trial. Jackson in turn was not complimentary about Microsoft, as he reluctantly recused himself from the case. He said Microsoft executives had:

> proved, time and time again, to be inaccurate, misleading, evasive, and transparently false. ... Microsoft is a company with an institutional disdain for both the truth and for rules of law that lesser entities must respect. It is also a company whose senior management is not averse to offering specious testimony to support spurious defenses to claims of its wrongdoing.[7]

Although Microsoft was able to avoid being broken up (as originally ordered), there is no question that the case proved both distracting and damaging to the company's wider reputation and standing. Many felt the organisation went downhill after this point; certainly it lost any remaining sense of innocence, and the corporate culture was revealed to be one in which winning commercially was more important than ethical or societal concerns.

A consideration of the fate of tech behemoths past and present is important to understanding and estimating the risks for future startups. The difficult challenge, for tech in particular, is the very rapid pace at which the size, reach and complexity of a digital business can grow. Although modern entrepreneurs understand this (and aspire to such success), the fact remains that there are massive learning curves for their founders and leaders to undertake. It is naïve to pretend that great product, service and customer intimacy is sufficient; companies must learn about the politics of their industry, the different social morés of cultures far from their experience, as well as the considerable operational challenges of hiring, managing, housing and even feeding their rapidly growing workforces. It's a reasonable prediction that some at least of these fast-growth companies will not so much fail outright as businesses (though many – even most – will) but inadvertently become pariahs because they have not paid sufficient attention to avoiding hubris and learning from crises and nemesis moments. Those that avoid pariah crises will surely reap the benefits in terms of lower costs of operation, lower barriers to entry and a more grounded acceptance of their role in the world.

And as for Google, is it doomed? Google has to be seen as an organisation that has shown tremendous capacity to learn and develop rapidly as it has grown up, and this has so far enabled it to negotiate the very difficult issues of managing its business in China and Europe with considerable skill. It has very good, smart people and is increasingly politically savvy. A report in the *Washington Post*[8] indicated how Google has moved rapidly from spending nothing on political lobbying to become the second-highest spender on lobbying in Washington. It's probably no coincidence that this volte-face occurred just as the company faced stern criticism from Republicans, and the FTC was investigating its core search business for anti-competitive practices. The article points out how Google shifted in 2011 towards courting Republicans at the Heritage Foundation, a conservative think tank. This shift enabled both to campaign together successfully on anti-piracy legislation; it was a marriage of convenience that symbolised Google's pragmatic shift from a company of deeper political principle to one that has become so large it is more like a country, with "interests" that need to be defended in whatever way works:

> To critics, Google's investments have effectively shifted the national
> discussion away from Internet policy questions that could affect the
> company's business practices. Groups that might ordinarily challenge
> the policies and practices of a major corporation are holding their fire,
> those critics say.

Certainly Google has shown that if you have its level of wealth and connections, you can start to focus political effort on a point of view (in this case an increasingly libertarian, anti-regulation, Republican-friendly line notably at odds with their previous California-tech, Democrat positioning). Some will see such spending as inherently corrupt or corrupting, regardless of the content of the issues over which Google lobbies. Others would simply see it as evidence that Google is maturing into a grown-up company that has learned – at breakneck speed – how business gets done in Washington. Perhaps so; and certainly it's normal for big businesses to lobby for the conditions that suit them and their beliefs and objectives. But to many, it's a distinct change of gear for Google to have ramped up its spending and focus in this area from such a low base, to match Microsoft and others, and represents a change in moral focus for the company. What is not clear is how Google will successfully respond to existential challenges to their very mission. Surely no company, government or organisation of any kind has ever had such an ambitious raison d'être as "to organise the world's information and make it universally accessible and useful."

And there's the rub. There is just no way to be that ambitious without courting hubris. And the scale and scope of that ambition crashes through the first of the tests we laid out for established pariahs in Chapter 1 – because they matter and are dealing with non-trivial issues, they have real capacity to harm. And it's ultimately going to be society's view about that harm (vs. benefit) that dictates the extent to which Google becomes a proper established pariah, as opposed to a big multi-national with some tricky issues to resolve. The fate of Microsoft suggests that Google's greatest threat may remain a legal and reputational one from the US Government and its anti-trust statutes, originally used to reign in the original established pariahs of Standard Oil and its ilk. Certainly, the individual citizen seems to have little capacity to challenge its dominance, except by choosing competitor technologies for browsing, search, mapping and so forth. And unlike Microsoft, Google's products are often best in class, so there is a price to be paid there. Google's projects extend well beyond the web. It is perhaps through the driverless cars, or Google books, or another project as yet not envisioned, that a really deep pariah crisis will emerge for them that threatens their existence economically or undermines their values or reputation for technical capability. Time will tell. But in the meantime, the rest of the world will be watching – some to see them fail, but most to learn from how they don't. Given the track record and their learning ability, my money's on Google to avoid the established pariah big time for years to come, as long as they can remain humble despite their success.

Regulators

One might think that regulators ought to be immune to any serious risk of becoming pariahs. Controlled by government (and hence very indirectly responsive to democratic, or at least political, pressures) yet independent, at their best regulators are the champions of the consumer, the little guy and the employee against the vagaries of big business or institutional failure in the public sector. In any case, although an obvious and tempting pastime for the regulated, attacking regulators is both politically dangerous and difficult. Generally, it's left to other stakeholders (such as investors or even end consumers) to resist excessive regulation, usually via mild-mannered statements in public and back-room arm twisting.

Regulators are often vulnerable to claims that they are incompetent, whatever they do. They now face the threat of oscillating between being seen as the anti-business bogeymen, bogging down whole industries in red tape, and being positioned as weak failures who were in the pockets of big business all along. Pity the poor Financial Services Authority, which has experienced (and will continue to experience) both these polarities. On the one hand, the FSA was supposed to get out of the way and allow the City, the engine room of the British economy, to grow and thrive. But then it emerged that it had done that to an excessive degree and regulation had failed on two fronts.

Firstly, the rules that were to be imposed were not onerous enough to provide safety in the banking system; and secondly, they were inadequately policed and enforced. It also emerged that, despite considerable powers to influence or even veto senior appointments and pay arrangements, the regulator had not really intervened effectively in these critical areas either.

These failures, which were closely linked to the banking industry issues discussed in earlier chapters, were an acute embarrassment to successive UK governments (which had supported both the overall fiduciary regime and the appointments of the senior regulators over a period of many years). There was therefore no significant political capital to be made on either side of the House of Commons from damaging the regulator. So in traditional British fashion, formal investigations by MPs into the FSA's failings, with respect to the collapse of RBS, HBOS and others, were delayed until some time after the restructuring of the FSA into the Financial Conduct Authority and the Prudential Regulatory Authority that had been announced in 2010. This conveniently meant that no-one was left looking solely responsible for the massive systemic mess that had occurred on everyone's watch. Sir Hector Sants (with whom I had the pleasure of working at Barclays) was formally left holding the ball as CEO of the FSA when the music stopped, and everyone knew it. Adair Turner, who was the chairman from 2008 until the end, was adroit at criticising the system he had been in, but perhaps less keen to take career-ending personal responsibility. Who can blame him? No-one else was doing so, not the politicians who had encouraged the whole system and not the bankers who had benefited so magnificently from it.

Smoking wreckage and personal reputational damage on this scale are hard to ignore, even in the UK Establishment. We can only hope that the switch from the tripartite system to the twin peaks system will avoid not only the last crisis in the industry, but the next one. Although the FSA catastrophe is exceptionally bad, there are parallels and lessons for other regulators:

1. **Regulators risk taking the blame for the whole system when things go wrong** – even though we know that systems cannot be controlled by single actors within them, it's still tempting to pick on all the principals when things don't turn out as we hoped. Regulators are rarely the first against the wall, but in the long term they tend to bear a great deal of the responsibility for the failure of the whole system. This implies that regulators should develop wide-ranging

capabilities in understanding the extended system under regulation and insist on having the right powers to contain other actors. It is no good saying after the fact that you knew what was wrong but did not have the power to intervene; still worse to have the powers but to seem ignorant of what was really going on. And inexcusably deadly to lack the will to enforce what you are empowered to enforce.

2. **Regulatory leaders need sharp political as well as technical skills** – regulators need to be led by people who can combine the same degree of technically sophisticated understanding as those they regulate with an equivalent level of commercial and political savvy. This is a big ask, given the difficulty of developing such capabilities in leaders within most industries, but implies that a healthy degree of cross-fertilisation should occur between regulators and regulated. Of course, such exchanges risk the accusation of "regulatory capture", and there will always be cynics who accuse all who have worked in industry of being incapable of regulating without favouritism. Interestingly, I have never heard the contrary claim made, that those who have worked for regulators will damage the regulated when they move that way; instead, we are told that their expertise is being used to subvert regulation. My own experience is that knowledge, understanding and relationships across the divide are hugely helpful, and that the dreaded regulatory capture can be avoided if the culture of the regulator is effectively managed and led.

3. **Regulators need to get ahead of issues both locally and internationally** – regulators that are always reacting to the last crisis are doomed to being seen as ineffective. This isn't always fair; where regulators are indeed making an industry safer there may be no proof that their action has prevented a crisis.[9] However, most industry participants agree they would like to see more far-sighted and strategic thinking driving regulatory activity, acting in the best interests of the whole system, not merely assuaging blame for past crises.

4. **Talent cannot be inferior to that of the industry regulated** – you simply cannot expect a regulator to be successful in what are invariably technical environments without the right qualifications,

understanding and experience, as well as the right mindset. Ideally, the regulator should be seen as one of the strongest players in a system for high-quality thinking and expertise. Those who argue against public-sector pay levels matching industry should consider whether the costs of industry failure justify their claims. Although it would be facile to think that publicly funded regulators should ignore political realities or that everyone is motivated by money alone, it is equally facile to think that an organisation paying in the bottom quartile can consistently outperform its rivals in attracting and retaining the strongest minds in the industry.

Now that the norm of criticising regulators has been established, we can expect far more challenges to competence as the decisions and actions of regulators become more transparent. We can also expect regulators to be constantly on the wrong side of cycles of over and under regulation in their industries, either defending a failure to regulate (while under-resourced) or accused of strangling the industry with over-regulation (while over-resourced). If regulators want to avoid becoming some of the most significant pariahs outside the private sector, they will have to become politically adroit at influencing thinking and policy for years ahead, leading the very industries they police. This will be profoundly challenging, given the limitations observed above on leadership and talent, as well as the inevitable resource challenges. Hardest of all will be to demonstrate what success looks like in a measurable way, and to convince a wide variety of special interest groups, as well as the powerful and influential industry participants, that their multitudinous interests are being fairly balanced. It therefore seems highly likely that regulators, particularly those in established pariah industries, will face becoming pariahs in their own right.

The NHS

We saw in Chapter 1 how the NHS, although a deeply loved institution (or, perhaps more fairly, set of institutions), can deliver pariah-like outcomes despite its well-intentioned purpose. The NHS looks set to remain in a political tug of war, with all parties wanting to associate the brand and its "pro" values and popularity with their own party. Broadly speaking, political parties have two polarities to choose from, given the overwhelming support for the basic philosophy of the system. One polarity forces the issue of efficiency first, recognising the growing demand for health care in an ageing population against a potentially static or dwindling tax base. The pressures here will be to change operating models, privatise elements of the service, and ultimately to ration services and control access or reduce what the service promises, as a mechanism to control booming cost demand. The other polarity will emphasise effectiveness over efficiency, recognising the power of the original promise of the NHS to be "free at the point of care", and will seek to maintain or improve delivery quantity and quality, with commensurate impacts on cost, taxation and so forth. Of course, these polarities have always been present and always will be; and they have also always been intertwined. The arguments will continue. But if we look at NHS organisations against the risk factors above, we can see that the high profile of the NHS brand continues to create risk for individual public hospitals that is not such a factor in the private sector.

The other risk factors are also going to be higher in the future. Failures are more obvious, transparent and public in the NHS than in most industries, one might say, especially since the introduction of the much-maligned measurement and league tables of the last 20 years. And when things go wrong, the public mood has shifted from one that appreciates what it can get for nothing as being always a bargain, to one expecting the highest quality of sophisticated care and suspicious of cover ups, postcode lotteries or lazy excuses about resource constraints. Demand for strong governance will only increase as a result. We can expect the NHS brand to continue to struggle as the realities of running hugely complex, open organisations runs up against the idealistic promises of the 1940s. It's hard to imagine that there will not be further crises and scandals, but perhaps the NHS has done more than most organisations to attack excessive pride, arrogance and hubris in its senior medical and non-medical leadership. The combination of high competence and humility is stunningly powerful, and when it is absent in either the medical (e.g. Bristol) or non-medical (e.g. Mid-Staffs) sides then that seems to be where the big problems occur.

The dedication to purpose and patients (customers) is certainly second to none in most NHS organisations. There is much to learn from these institutions, but they must manage their pariah risks carefully.

NGOs and Charities

Perhaps the least-suspecting future pariahs sit in the "third sector" of voluntary, charity and non-governmental organisations. The risks these organisations run are worsened by their own (unwittingly hubristic) belief in their own purity of intent. Just as Google has learned that its own mission does not entitle it automatically to ignore laws and rights to privacy, so charities and NGOs will discover their lofty intent does not mean they cannot become pariahs in turn. As with other pariah candidates, it's the high-profile branding that will create the genesis conditions for pariahdom. The clever utilisation of advertising and social media that is so effective for grabbing the attention of donors, politicians and special publics creates a set of expectations that then have to be reliably fulfilled if the organisations are not going to create subsequent crises.

The key points of vulnerability for these organisations appear to be as follows:

1. **Execution failures** – an organisation that claims to be addressing a high-minded end but does not do so. For example, charities which are supposed to get aid to the starving but either the food is never delivered or is not distributed effectively or fairly.[10] Or an NGO that is supposed to act regardless of race and ethnicity in a war zone that proves to be biased to one side or another.

2. **Financial** – organisations that absorb too much cost in administration[11] or on relatively lavish rewards and perks for their own employees. Corruption, at all scales, including adapting execution to the wishes of major donors or governmental agencies in ways that are not open or fair, or simply using public money without appropriate safeguards.[12]

3. **Organisational values** – contraventions (or apparent contraventions) of the organisation's own stated values in how it is run, such as unfair labour practices, excessive pay for leaders, sexual harrassment or other bad behaviour by leadership. Collusion in corrupt practices or failure to stand up to opposition from individuals or regimes known to be hostile to the organisation and its aims.

4. **Contribution to the system** – a growing realisation that the organisation is not a helpful contributor to the system in question,

that it has become lazy, corrupt, unconstructive or just downright misguided in its thinking and approach.

All of these issues are really versions of the same one: lack of integrity. Because third-sector organisations trade on trust developed around a high-integrity position, they are particularly vulnerable to failures which make them seem insincere, even more than inept. This sector is also prone to its own kinds of arrogance and hubris. In this case, the hubris is born out of a smug self-righteousness that cannot listen to opposing points of view or acknowledge when it is in the wrong. Remember Greenpeace in the Shell Brent Spar campaign?[13] As large international NGOs grow in size, stature and clout, so does their ability to create hubris in their followers, employees and activists, increasing the risks of future crises. The other issue that NGOs have to watch out for is that they will be targeted directly by those they oppose. Where this is part of "dirty tricks", such activities typically rebound against the perpetrator (as Russia's heavy handedness in the treatment of the Greenpeace Arctic Sunrise protestors in 2013 backfired in the face of carefully orchestrated world opinion). But where other actors in the system can paint activists as extremists, whose arguments are weak or poorly constructed, they can degrade the impact of an NGO or pressure group quite rapidly. Oil companies are skilled at these tactics, whereby the noisiest protestors can often be marginalised from the real debates and discussions, while the rest are "managed".

In all these cases, the biggest challenge for the organisations concerned tends to be their own innocence and naïvité. Their leaders and staff are idealistic; they are hugely damaged by arguments against the existence of their organisation and appalled if they discover that it is not living up to its claims and objectives. All in all, I suspect there is more risk of pariah status than most third-sector organisations realise, simply because they think they are immune to it. They aren't.

Food and Drink Companies

In some discussions I have had, organisations such as Coca-Cola are seen as amongst the most likely candidates for pariah status – the "new tobacco" is how some refer to them. Certainly the growing medical evidence about the health disbenefits of sugary drinks and their role in obesity and other illnesses is troubling, and could leave Coke and its competitors fighting a long rearguard action against both the evidence and their own culpability, reminiscent of that fought by the cigarette industry for the last fifty years. Again, the pariah issues stem from the gap between a brand claim (Coke is presented as fun and associated with fun, positive images and feelings of happiness) and the reality of an increasingly fat, unfit, unhealthy lifestyle spreading from the US to the rest of the world in the tracks of its most globalised, famous brands.[14] If Coke is connected firmly in the perceptions of consumers and publics with this discontinuity, the damage to the brand and its franchise could surely be fatal.

Well, perhaps not. It seems a fair bet that a 127-year-old "iconic" brand that has consistently been at the top of brand value ratings charts will fight hard to retain its valuable positioning, and must enjoy strong support from a diverse base of supporters. So it proves, and Coke has been adept at managing potential sources of opposition, from Congress to the grocery store aisle. In fact, it seems most likely that there will be a long and potentially tedious war of attrition between public health officials and politicians on one side, and companies such as Coke on the other, with a somewhat confused public in the middle making its own decisions on what to consume. But it's not impossible to imagine that legislation, particularly in countries with publicly funded health-care systems, will increasingly grind away at the core product profitability of Coke and its ilk.

Whereas McDonald's (see Chapter 9) has been able to respond to critics with some astute changes to menu choices, restaurant formats and product sourcing and formulation, Coke is unlikely to reduce the sugar content of its flagship products – though it may alter some brands to suit changing tastes or launch alternatives. Sadly, the healthiest product Coke ever launched in the UK was a disaster. Attempts to diversify share of wallet by launching Dasani in 2004 as a water brand were famously catastrophic, and had to be abandoned in one of the all-time brand-launch failure case studies. No-one seriously objected to Coca-Cola launching a bottled water rather than another sugary carbonated beverage. But when the advertising campaign referred to the product as "bottled spunk" (odd enough in the US context, definitely a niche product in the UK), all didn't seem right. And when it was revealed that the "pure" water (sold alongside mineral spring waters in supermarkets) was in fact chemically modified tap water from Sidcup, the British press had a field day. To add insult to injury, Coke's reverse osmosis water-purification process proved ineffective, turning bromide in the input water into a potential carcinogen called bromate. The brand was pulled from the shelves and plans for a European launch were stymied.

Coke is not a bad company and it employs good, smart people. The questions they will face in the future are likely to be whether the fun and benefits of their products outweigh the (literally) growing weight of evidence against them, and whether their handling of issues outside their domestic US market can demonstrate sufficient nuanced subtlety.

Lawyers and Consultants

Professional services firms vary a great deal in their reputations, but both individually and collectively there have been some powerful indictments of their behaviour and impact. Despite their involvement in most of the pariah scandals to date, and a few of their own (Andersen–Enron remains the worst of these), the consulting firms, law firms and others remain adept at avoiding nemesis, and even crisis. How is this? Firstly, their brands are well known to specialist buyers, but not to the man in the street. CEOs know who McKinsey, Bain, Clifford Chance or Ernst & Young are. But the press know their readers often don't, or for various complex reasons associated with their own commercial requirements to work with such firms, choose not to abuse them. Or if they do, they focus on lower-end operational players such as Capita. So on brand, they are equivocal.

High growth is often a feature of professional services firms and certainly causes problems for them in terms of talent quality, training and leadership. So that genesis condition is often met. However, the nature of professional service work is that the client gets the glory and praise, not you. Although senior partners typically have robust egos and confidence beyond the norm, I suspect there is something in this latter dynamic that protects against much hubris. However cocky the consultants, they are easily fired and never see their names in the papers. Lawyers are occasionally given a degree of wider celebrity; the results are seldom good for them.

Professional services firms are also socially smart; they have to be, to sell their work into the complex political universes of their clients. They tend to spot trouble brewing and usually ensure that their own role is managed so that reputation remains intact. Occasionally things go badly wrong. McKinsey was badly shaken when one of its partners was jailed for insider trading. But it was clear that this was an isolated incident, a rogue, rather than a typical behaviour and the firm survived. What's interesting to me, as someone from this world, is how the reputation of the class, the industry, if you like, is much worse than that of almost any individual player within it. Consulting firms do well because we actually like the individuals we hire to work with us and trust the brand of their firm, even if we are sceptical overall about buying such services. Perhaps there are lessons there for pariah organisations: it may be best to divert flak onto an industry-wide basis rather than face it as an individual brand. Certainly this is felt to have been Barclays' great mistake in dealing with the LIBOR crisis. In that reading, all crises are turned into industry crises, but nemesis never attends individual firms. This seems to me a very unsatisfactory solution, one that can never deliver catharsis.

Out there are organisations and individuals who have been terribly served by professional services organisations, which have been paid millions for shoddy projects, bad advice and weak implementations. As well as suing in court, there is another critical agency for nemesis and catharsis in the professional services world and that is via the professional bodies, especially the chartered institutes. In extreme cases, solicitors or accountants can be struck off, fined or censured, though this usually only happens to small-fry firms and individuals – it's rare indeed to see one of the biggest firms and their partners humiliated in this way. Some have drawn from this parallel a need to do the same for bankers, though few who propose it understand that there is no longer a single profession to which the term can sensibly be applied. I think the final reason that we don't see professional services firms as long-term pariahs is because of their outstanding fleetness of foot. They are solution-oriented, but can use their position as advisors to avoid actual accountability. Not only are they not left holding the baby, they are usually busy telling you how to protect against nappy rash and prepare to raise a contented toddler. But perhaps a more charitable view says that they are speedy at metamorphosis, albeit perhaps rarely what we might term a true one!

Such adeptness, coupled with a wide network of influence in the worlds of business and politics, gives professional services firms enormous influence without needing hard power. But perhaps views will shift, and they need to be careful that the reality matches some of the hype as they become ever bigger and more global themselves.

Measuring Pariah Risk

It would be very helpful if we could measure pariah risk in some fashion to help us identify those who are going to be hit next. If we had such a tool, perhaps we could use it to "cool down" whole industries or firms before they got into real trouble. One of the key tasks for those of us in the industry surrounding boards and executive leadership in major organisations is now to work on how we can analyse, measure and manage pariah risk. An example of the inputs to such an analysis is included in 'Appendix 2 – Pariah Organisation Health Check' at the end of this book.

It is my hope that in the future we can increasingly predict the risk factors for organisations and provide their boards and regulators with accurate predictions of where the risks are highest.

Notes

1 http://www.38degrees.org.uk
2 See Morozov, 2013, p.116.
3 One of my friends recently pointed out to me how modish the very word and concept of outrage has become. Outrage is another word that has been devalued to the point where we have forgotten it means more than "temporarily angry".
4 In August 2015, Google announced a major restructuring that renamed the core holding company as Alphabet and separated out the core Google business from other ventures. This change echoes some of the suggestions I make in Chapter 4 regarding organisational brands. Note also that this chapter was written before Google's recent UK tax settlement with HMRC and the ensuing reputational crisis.
5 Google was 2nd in 2013 on Fortune's "Most Admired Companies" list, and top in Glassdoor's ratings for "Companies Hiring Interns Right Now" in the same year.
6 In Oakland, hostility to wealthy Googlers raising house prices and rents burst into violent protests in December 2013 featuring attacks on the shuttle buses that take employees to work in Silicon Valley. http://www.theverge.com/2013/12/20/5231758/protesters-target-silicon-valley-shuttles-smash-google-bus-window
7 Quoted in http://windowsitpro.com/windows-server/judge-jackson-exits-microsoft-discrimination-case
8 http://www.washingtonpost.com/politics/how-google-is-transforming-power-and-politicsgoogle-once-disdainful-of-lobbying-now-a-master-of-washington-influence/2014/04/12/51648b92-b4d3-11e3-8cb6-284052554d74_story.html

9 There are some parallels with the "Y2K problem". The absence of terrible computer-caused catastrophes in January 2000 either (depending on your viewpoint) a) justified the spend on upgrades and fixes made in the preceding years to avoid problems, or b) revealed the whole thing as a hoax hyped up by the IT industry to give it employment. The data fit both theories.

10 Some NGOs are brave enough to admit they failed, and thereby gain credibility for honesty and transparency (at least in the West). http://www.theguardian.com/global-development/poverty-matters/2011/jan/17/ngos-failure-mistakes-learn-encourage

11 The question of what constitutes "too much" can be a vexed one. Recent research suggests some of the most effective charities are also some of the least efficient on this measure. http://www.civilsociety.co.uk/finance/news/content/15065/low_admin_costs_do_not_mean_high_charity_performance_finds_study

12 In particular, note the issues surrounding the collapse of Kids Company in 2015.

13 See Chapter 1.

14 My perception is that Coke is a long way behind McDonald's in addressing its critics and embracing their concerns.

11

Employees of the Pariah Organisation

O NE OF MY original intentions for this book was to break the mould of contemporary fixation on the primacy of leadership as the only source of change in organisational systems. Throughout my career working with people at all levels in organisations large and small, I have observed that there are opportunities to change behaviour, culture and practice at every level; and although it is for leaders to define what they want and expect, it's reasonable that employees, unions, investors, regulators, customers and many other stakeholders can and will take part in such a dialogue. And perhaps it's time for us to ask whether the centralising tendency towards a standard, HQ-driven model of, well, just about everything, is really serving our countries and institutions well.[1]

We used to give extensive trust and control to managers and leaders at various levels in the organisation; now below the CEO level it's often hard to find a single general manager who has to string together the interests of the whole enterprise on behalf of everyone. Conversely, the overarching power of jobs at the top has increased, as globalisation has bloated the size of organisations, and modern technology and travel have meaningfully enabled day-to-day control of vast empires. Small wonder that in such structures there has been an increasing focus – to the point of obsession – on how leaders can set tone, design the future, manage customers and generally walk on water. But leaders are not the only ones who have a stake in the organisation and its future, and in this chapter I want to consider how everyone in the organisation reacts to crises and can be helpful and constructive in responding to them.

The Problem of Focus on Leadership

The over-reliance on leadership as the sole measure of success and failure of organisations is pernicious for two reasons. Firstly, it's pernicious to focus just on leaders because this places unreasonable expectations on what a single human being (the CEO) and other senior leaders can achieve. It's axiomatic – if you understand systems thinking – that you are very unlikely to change the behaviour of a large, complex and often multinational system by altering the attitudes and actions of a tiny minority of the system's participants, even if they are highly capable and hugely powerful. The dangerous myth that the leader can and must be all things to all people is itself creating huge stresses – for leaders. Erik de Haan and Anthony Kasozi have recently set out in their book *The Leadership Shadow* the impossible set of challenges facing contemporary bosses:

> As an executive today you have a multiplicity of factors to consider
> when taking even the simplest of decisions. You have to consider
> more stakeholders (internally and externally), more socio-political
> perspectives, more regulatory requirements, a greater range of cultural
> sensitivities, fuller transparency to the media and civil society, higher
> levels of accountability (for the decision as well as the consequences
> of the decision), more specific and rigorous governance standards, and
> more exacting performance criteria.
>
> (de Haan and Kasozi, 2014, p.9)

But they then note that biologically we cannot evolve sufficiently fast enough to cope with these changing demands:

> So undoubtedly we bring a lot less flexible, adaptive, learnable
> and malleable a person to the table than our 21st-century working
> environment is calling for. It would be no exaggeration to say that
> the main obstacle to meeting the challenges demanded by our
> present-day context is… us.
>
> (de Haan and Kasozi, 2014, p.10)

In other words, by focusing on the leadership of individuals in systems of great complexity we are setting ourselves up to fail – none of them can actually understand or manage these systems, and in pretending to do so they create dysfunctional stresses for themselves and those they lead. Secondly, an excessive leadership focus is pernicious because it is insulting and disempowering to those working in the organisation. Treating leaders as the source of all changes and solutions assumes the rest of the workforce has no point of view worth hearing, when in practice they often are the guardians of the organisation's spirit, heart and soul, as well as knowing more about the customers, processes and workings of the organisation than any single leader can ever do. As we reward an increasingly itinerant professional leadership class[2], we need to recognise – as the CEOs I have worked with did – that there is deep wisdom in the experience of the long-service rank and file workforce and mid-level leadership, so often dismissed by consultants as the "marzipan layer" who "resist change". But of course people don't resist change per se. They resist changes which seem to them bad for the organisation and/or for themselves (usually with the priority in that order for long-term staff, in my experience). In other words, they are highly rational and remarkably loyal to protecting the organisations they serve. Their conservatism is a good thing, as it protects against knee jerk and thoughtless destruction of things that may have taken years to create. By placing less emphasis on leadership and more on the system as a whole, we might perhaps get at a much more sustainable and meaningful set of shifts in organisational performance. And we might remind ourselves how to do change properly, with the active support and assistance of the workforce.

Implications for Pariahs

What does all that mean for pariahs? Well, it means we have to get much more serious about understanding and influencing those who work at every level in the pariah extended organisation; they are all going to be part of the problem and so deserve to be part of the cure. It's not that leaders don't matter – they are obviously critical. But we should spend a bit of time looking at the question of why people join or stay with organisations that have very difficult reputations. After all, one of the original reasons for writing this book was that I felt that pariah employees – more even than pariah leaders – are misunderstood, and also that they are potentially the salvation of their own organisations. In this chapter I am setting out a simple typology of "pariah employees" and also examining the emotional and psychological reactions each type has to crisis, nemesis and metamorphosis. We will see that there is much more work to be done on understanding these reactions and behaviours, and that there is also a powerful opportunity – usually missed – to leverage the good intent and positive motivations of many employees to far better advantage in the crisis recovery, metamorphosis and catharsis phases of the lifecycle.

Pariah Employees

Pariah employees come in many shapes and sizes, and any or all of them might be described as stakeholders in the organisation. My view is that they all matter and we forget that at our peril if we seek to reform pariahs or prevent new ones forming, **even if we are getting leadership at the top more or less right.** For HR and headcount reporting purposes, there tends to be a rigid formalisation of who is and who isn't an "employee" – for good legal and other reasons to do with things such as co-employment and tax and benefit entitlement. But it's essentially a bureaucratic distinction and it can be unhelpful. In the modern extended enterprise, it can be quite difficult to differentiate beyond these technical distinctions of "permanent staff" and "contractors" (or "badged" and "unbadged", or whatever the jargon of the organisation may be). Let me give a couple of examples to illustrate what troubles me about these crude markers of belonging.

Let's assume you are a newly hired "permanent" employee of an organisation. Perhaps on your first day you have relatively little sense of deep loyalty, attachment or ownership there, compared to the other longer-tenured employees. You may even perhaps remain quite sceptical about joining. Perhaps it was a marginal decision to come and work for this organisation rather than another one that made you a really good offer. Perhaps some of your friends and relatives have been disapproving or unsure. So initially you may be nervous, even suspicious, despite your apparent formal commitment to the organisation and its goals. In theory, the "hollowing out" of modern organisations (my own employers shed tens of thousands of staff over the years and will no doubt shed thousands more) should have led to those lucky enough to join as permanent staff having a greater degree of connection and commitment, but in practice that doesn't seem to be the case. If your employer is well known for hiring and firing quickly and easily, self-preservation will likely mean for some time even "permanent" employees protect themselves from potential disappointment by avoiding deep commitment to the organisation at an emotional level. They may work hard – indeed they will seek to "perform well" to give themselves organisational power and leverage – but they will avoid exposing their real feelings and concerns until they have built a basis of personal trust with close colleagues or people they have met socially. It's for these reasons that banks, consulting firms and others often encourage drinking and socialising: perhaps the employees won't trust the company and its leadership yet, but they can start to trust each other and their immediate team. In this first example, you are legally permanent, but until the years go by and you start to engage at a deeper level, you are anything but permanent and your level of belonging is actually quite low at first.

Alternatively, in a second example, let's imagine you are a third-party contractor with a long history of client service with the pariah organisation (perhaps for decades). You may share a strong set of emotional bonds and identify yourself deeply with the organisation's fate and reputation even though you have never been on the payroll. It's one of the great fallacies of modern life to assume that contractors don't care about their employers, or that consultants are objectively aloof from caring about their clients; on the contrary, the best of them care more than is good for them, or even perhaps for their own firms... But of course, because these are not "employees", their views are not usually heard or counted in surveys, or formally represented in staff councils or unions. This latter effect, where a large group of people – with a huge stake in the success of the organisation – is effectively marginalised and ignored, cannot be healthy for organisations. Some of the most useful and insightful observations I ever heard as an executive were from the insider–outsiders who worked alongside us on a non-permanent basis, and so could be critical friends making observations and sharing ideas from outside. Smart organisations are beginning to realise this and I predict that, in the future, the unfortunate legal apartheid of employees and contractors may come to an end.

As the categories of employment increase (e.g. permanent and temporary, full and part time, short-term contract and zero hours contract) so too does the complexity of managing these numerous "deals". As employers, we cannot have it both ways: we seem to want employees to act like loyal lifetime servants but treat them as flexible costs to be retrenched when the company has a bad quarter; to care and act in the long-term interests of the whole organisation, but to receive transactional rewards in return; to devote themselves to a brand that they know cannot keep its promises to them. In this regard, we recreate at the heart of the organisation some of the very pariah dynamics we need to oppose.

Because of these issues, we'll use the term "pariah employees" very loosely and inclusively in this context. Below, I set out what I hope is a more useful segmentation of employee types which can cut across these bureaucratic distinctions. Regardless of who is called what, it's worth knowing what employees want, if we are to avoid disappointing them.

Employee Segmentation

As companies become increasingly sensitive and smart about segmenting and understanding their own customers for marketing and other purposes, they are really struggling to achieve the same degree of insight into their own workforce, with predictable results in terms of lost opportunity, engagement and mutual understanding. In the 2014 *Towers Watson Global Workforce Study*,[3] drivers of attraction and retention were analysed from both employer and employee perspectives. In the study, job security had risen to become the number two reason why employees join an employer. No doubt that result is a sign of the times and indicates how unconfident employees still feel about the economic recovery globally. What is interesting is that 41 per cent of employees rate it as a key reason to join, but only 26 per cent of employers – an interesting mismatch of expectations. In the same survey, base pay turns out to be not only a key driver of attraction (as it always has been) but a key retention driver,[4] along with three drivers that employers themselves don't value as highly: trust/confidence in senior leadership, job security and length of commute. Such surveys are often relatively crude and can be skewed by current zeitgeist concerns or the interests of the questioners (in this case, my former employer, Towers Watson, has a vested interest in persuading clients they should be paying attention to pay and benefits issues, for example, so it tends to ask a disproportionate number of questions about them). But the overall concerns raised seem to me to be valid. Over the years, it's interesting to see how poorly most employers have understood employee priorities and concerns, and at least these surveys highlight the fact that this engagement gap exists as an opportunity for those willing to take an interest.

So, how can you communicate and connect effectively with employees when you still segment them crudely by distribution lists driven by legal employment status, location or (at best) optional self-selection? Well, you can't. Tomorrow's leading companies will become far savvier about combining the interests of like-minded groups across their organisations, rather than worrying about the legal liabilities of treating temporary workers as permanent staff. They will do this by using the same insights and segmentation techniques they are using on their customers, and as with customers, employees will largely remain oblivious to what is being done. How, then, are we to create a viable but simple taxonomy of employees that we can use to understand their responses and get them engaged to help the pariah organisation out? I am sure others will come up with far more sophisticated models and ideas, but I suggest that a great place to start would be the mountains of data that evolve, particularly on social media, at the time of a crisis and in its aftermath. I have looked at literally tens of thousands of pages of such views over the years and it's often hard to discern patterns in such complexity. However, there are some basic things going on at a time of crisis, some emotional responses, which cut through the normal babble of politically correct comms gibberish that we all endure in large organisations. Through looking at these reactions and talking to hundreds of employees in organisations big and small over the years, I have identified some patterns which might help us out.

Shock

It's surprising to many outsiders that pariah employees could be shocked when crises occur. They assume that those inside the tent "must have known" about financial irregularities, bad behaviour or product lapses. Or that they certainly were aware of a general culture in which such failings could occur. However, my own experience is that the vast majority of employees are absolutely stunned when the crisis occurs, unless something very similar has happened before. Why is this? Well, firstly it's impossible, unreasonable and inappropriate for everyone in the organisation to know everything that is going on. At the time of the LIBOR crisis we had about 140,000 people working for Barclays globally. A bank teller in a Barclays retail branch in Wigan is not going to know much about LIBOR, let alone be familiar with the traders involved in rate manipulation. As a result, such an employee is genuinely stunned when a crisis or scandal descends on their organisation with its origins in a part of the business they never knew existed. Obviously, such shocks are greatest in organisations with the highest degree of internal separation between specialisms,[5] and where few employees or leaders rotate between organisational areas. It's one of the best arguments for talent rotation and movement (between organisations and across countries) that fresh eyes bring fresh challenges, and that the cumulative experiences round out leaders and help them understand how the whole organisation runs. For these reasons and others,[6] during my time at Shell we persisted in managing relatively large numbers of expatriate employees, despite being criticised by some of our peers for the practice (an expensive and administratively complex business).

The second reason for the shock is that many employees in a pariah organisation will be suffering from a degree of individual or collective hubris. There is substantial cognitive dissonance as the beliefs about the organisation that the employee holds (such as, "It is a good organisation, really"; "I and the people I work with are decent and hardworking and technically capable"; "The outside world is critical, but it's basically envious of our success and competence, or high pay") come into conflict with data that suggests fellow employees are behaving badly, even criminally, or that millions of people distrust the organisation and its people. Many employees find themselves frozen in true, literal shock as they start to process the new data and assess their own beliefs. Like the proverbial deer in the headlights, they may literally stop dead and meaningful productivity may grind to a halt. Other employees, equally shocked, may continue to go through the motions of work, as though nothing has happened; they also cannot yet process what has occurred, but are essentially ignoring it.

Anger and Shame

The emotional upset that employees experience at these times of crisis has two primary outlets, which are closely interrelated: anger and shame. Anger may be externalised against those responsible or in angry denial of the facts and those criticising the organisation, including colleagues, relatives or friends. Alternatively, it may be repressed into intense tension and frustrations, surfacing in physical ailments such as headaches, migraines or even depression. As a crisis deepens, the upset may also be internalised and personalised as a shame response, particularly if the reputational impacts are felt personally by people who identify themselves closely with the organisation and its brand. Common shame reactions include: ceasing to identify with the organisation explicitly (perhaps by no longer carrying branded bags in public that identify one as an employee of the organisation); avoiding discussion of the organisation or industry in social situations or conversations to avoid being harangued or shamed publicly (it's been a brave banker who went to a comedy show and admitted what they did for a living since 2008); feeling depressed and lethargic; avoiding work friendships and avoiding spending time socialising with colleagues.

Unsurprisingly, some commentators have noted that these reactions are consistent with reactions to grief, and there are certainly some similarities.[7]

Generally speaking, leaders during a crisis are too busy firefighting to even experience their *own* reactions, let alone really notice what is going on for others. It's generally peer colleagues who support each other during the crisis period and often beyond, and indeed it's a good technique to encourage this during periods of highly unstructured change where assurance and answers cannot come from above.

Resurgent Loyalty

In any organisation with a strong sense of brand and identity, there is a strong felt need to "rally round the flag" at times of crisis. Employees look to their leaders (at least to the ones they trust) to tell them whether to believe – or not believe – data and interpretations of data that they are receiving through the press and social media. The instincts of many are defensive: they want to protect themselves, each other and the organisation and its reputation. The cumulative impact of seeing your organisation's name in lurid and negative headlines day after day is emotional, and triggers strong reactions, as we noted above. Again, there are complex issues here where there has been substantial hubris in the culture. Loyalty is a tremendously strong force, but if it is blind it can do more harm than good. Hubris creates a false pride, to which it is all too easy to become deeply attached. The employees of Lehman were deeply convinced they were the best firm on Wall Street even as they were going bankrupt. Some of them still believe it! As we will see when we look at proposed employee archetypes, loyalty is likely much stronger in some groups than others. But even in the loyalist groups it cannot be taken for granted. Once employees realise that their loyalty in the organisation has been misplaced or taken for granted, their response can be strongly negative against their own brand, even to the point of treachery and subversion.

Modern technology and social media certainly create new opportunities for the dissatisfied to air their grievances. Shell's corporate lawyers have struggled for years to manage the stream of anti-Shell sentiment on the royaldutchshellplc.com website, much of it emanating from the company's own employees. This extraordinary site was set up by an Englishman called John Donovan and his father, after a dispute with Shell over marketing ideas, which he claims were stolen by a Shell manager. For over two decades the site has provided disgruntled Shell employees (Donovan is heavily dependent on internal "moles") and external detractors with a place to publish their grievances and claims against the company. Donovan says that all he is doing is holding the company accountable to its own business principles, and exposing its hypocrisy and lack of integrity. The site is hugely popular within Shell, much to the annoyance of senior leaders and the amusement of the Donovans. Times of crisis provide sites like Donovan's with new sources inside the company; internal investigations into leaks at Shell often revealed that those who provided confidential material to the site (in breach of their own legal obligations) were usually frustrated by lack of a voice in the large bureaucracy, and believed that embarrassing revelations might cause a positive and useful impact. Organisations like Shell that trade on the loyalty and trust of long-term employees, and have large loyalist populations, potentially face severe downside risks, post-crisis.

Where the consequences for such disloyalty are more grave, as in the banking industry (where even former employees can have compensation clawed back or lose rights to deferred compensation), then the preparedness to criticise is more muted and subtle.[8] However, there is usually someone for any journalist to talk to, and rumour sites abound.[9] Employers are usually slow to realise that employees use such sites for one single reason: they find them more helpful and entertaining than the feeble and over-sanitised efforts of their own communications departments. During a proper crisis, internal comms tends to become even more of a joke; everyone relies on the press and externals to update them on gossip and rumour. Only the occasional formal announcement comes up internally as well as externally. This is not the fault of the comms people: it's just the nature of the beast. You won't share rumours or speculation with your own staff. You won't spread lies and misinformation. You may have long periods when there is nothing to tell them. But don't be surprised that they fill that gap. And certainly don't try to prevent them seeing what the outside world is saying in the vain hope they won't have alternative routes to that information, if you want to maintain any credibility with them.

Guilt, Responsibility and Denial

One of the other reactions one observes before, during and especially after a crisis is guilt. Many people feel responsible after a crisis occurs. Perhaps they feel they should have stopped bad things from occurring. They often believe they could have made a difference, had they only spoken up, or tried harder, or done something. For some, the feelings of guilt after a crisis, especially one in which a significant harm is caused to people or to the reputation of the organisation, are overwhelming. I witnessed grown men in tears on several occasions as they relived such difficult moments, particularly where safety incidents had occurred involving fatalities. All crises are traumatic, but some never leave you. There is no question that above and beyond the punishments that regulatory or legal processes may meet out, many diligent professionals torture themselves for months or even years over how they could have done things differently. Other insiders have no idea how they could have made any difference, yet feel a sense of shared guilt anyway, rather like the blameless survivors in some terrible accident, left wandering, shocked and bloodied, around the scene of an explosion.

Such guilt can lead to all sorts of psychological and emotional reactions. As noted above, many redouble their loyalty to the organisation and their efforts to fix the crisis, expiate the guilt and achieve personal – if not organisational – catharsis. Others deny their feelings of guilt; they cannot cope with the fact that this situation might have been something to do with them and, often, dissociate from the organisation. This dissociation may even go to the extremes of leaving the organisation, to get well away from any accusations or tainted reputation. Or they may redouble their bravado and efforts to pretend all is normal and that they have had no part to play in what has happened; one sees this a lot with bankers regarding the (actually very traumatic) events of 2008.

In some cases, of course, pariah organisations employ people who don't feel any guilt because they are ill-equipped to do so. Either they just don't feel guilt around any violation of a moral code (i.e. in a very few extreme cases, they are psychopaths) or, more commonly, they simply don't accept that what has occurred, and particularly their own role in it, is wrong (i.e. they don't accept the accountability others want them to take on for events, and their own narcissism may leave them unable ever to do so). More than anything else, it is the latter dynamic that has played out in the banking industry crises of recent years, and has been the main reason for the lack of catharsis and forgiveness.[10] To the majority of senior industry figures, including most of the highly paid investment bankers so disliked by the masses, what occurred in the period before, during and after 2008–9 (or at least their own role in it) was not particularly reprehensible, and they feel unfairly judged, blamed and persecuted for doing their jobs professionally in the spirit of the times. In their version of events, the debt bubble sanctioned by politicians and regulators, and enjoyed by all, went badly wrong at a systemic level. But they don't accept that this failure (and the massive public bailout that then occurred for their industry) entitles the general public to blame them individually or even collectively for the subsequent recession, or for much else. They therefore don't feel individually and personally accountable for bad behaviour, and they don't really believe that the organisations they were in were doing things wrong. Only in the most egregious cases of wrongdoing, where people were caught breaking the law in a fraud or deliberate manipulation, can they identify and admit serious wrongdoing.[11] Outside of these black-and-white cases, it's far harder for them – especially within cultures that encourage such limited self-examination – to take on the difficult accountability for systemic outcomes that the rest of the world regards as important and necessary.

The continued absence of such admissions of responsibility continues to undermine the industry's licence to operate, as far as many stakeholders are concerned.

Finally (and critically), financial leaders tend to focus more narrowly on the interests of only a few stakeholder groups, notably themselves and their own owners. The Economist Intelligence Unit undertook research in 2012[12] that came to the following, rather depressing, conclusions:

- Finance leaders attach the greatest importance to meeting short-term performance targets; being "socially responsible" is a much lower priority.

- C-level executives think they are most accountable to their boards, regulators and investors, and that is the way they think it should stay.

- Top managers in finance do not think their remuneration is excessive, and public criticism is having little impact on pay policies.

- Investment banking is becoming more sensitive to public perception, but its C-level still does not see accountability to society as a top priority.

- Corporate social responsibility weighs much less on finance leaders in North America than on their peers in other parts of the world.

- Attitudes towards accountability and risk management vary markedly between finance CEOs and CFOs.

In other words, it was not just Bob Diamond who felt by then that the time for remorse was over. The EIU research was completed at a time just before LIBOR, FX and other scandals, and while the full cost of Retail PPI mis-selling in the UK was still being revealed. It was quite clear then, and very obvious now, that these complacent attitudes were the classic interpretations of those trying to get back to the status quo, to restore order after a blip, not of bold and courageous leaders prepared to look systemically at what caused the issues to occur in the first place. Since LIBOR in particular, it needs to be acknowledged that much has changed. I doubt whether the same survey would get the same response today. A huge amount of deliberate effort is going into trying to change bank cultures. Much of this effort is intended to enable more of the highly paid to take on the true accountability commensurate with such a well-paid and powerful industry. Time will tell whether this effort has been effective on a long-term basis. Guilt, in and of itself, is not perhaps a particularly helpful emotion; but its absence is a real problem. An acknowledgement of the harm caused, the appropriate ownership of the relevant accountabilities, the ethical and moral responsibility for harm in the system: these are all things that employees of pariah organisations can and do take on, even when their own leaders, lawyers and others discourage it. And a good thing too.

Three Employee Tribes

To the best of my knowledge, very little (if any) research has been done on employee engagement within pariah organisations, except as part of wider employee engagement research by individual companies (with attendant flaws in sampling, objectivity, question selection and data integrity). Much more can and should be done to learn what real employees actually think and feel. Proper and in-depth research could help to cast a lot more light on employee segments and hence how to best engage them in the "good fight" towards catharsis, forgiveness and real new beginnings. Those who have worked in pariah organisations will likely recognise three broad archetypes. If these are correct, they might form the basis for targeted work in a number of fields, both to prevent pariahs forming and to deal with their toxic legacies once formed. Let's look at each of these three and observe who they are and their role in pariah organisational life.

Loyalists

Pariah organisations often have strong corporate cultures and business models that keep them going for long periods of time. Hence, the first tribe we need to understand within them are the loyalists – employees, often with long service, who have a deep-seated engagement with the organisation, its values and aims. These people don't wear the company colours as a joke; for them the brand and their own identity have become intertwined. Some of the strongest loyalties are felt and expressed low in the organisational hierarchy, perhaps because here jobs usually remain close to the customers, products and end purpose of the organisation. Many loyalists have an active memory of a time before criticism of the organisation started, and certainly before the current set of pariah crises developed. As we noted above, loyalty can blind employees to the seriousness of the situation or lead them to ignore or deny data that interferes with their world view. They are keen to restore the organisation to its rightful state in their own mind. They may not see it as perfect, but if they see it as fundamentally good, it will be deeply difficult to accept that the organisation has done harm to others. To accept such a claim would be to bring responsibility for harm too close to home. Usually loyalists will therefore engage willingly in ad hominem attacks on those bringing unwanted messages (for example, by criticising the news media or protest organisations bringing the data to public attention), insisting that the organisation has been misunderstood and misrepresented by outsiders. Where it is clear and undeniable that insiders have been individually or collectively to blame for what has occurred, loyalists will turn on these people as traitors to the organisation. Because loyalists find attacks on the organisation they love so painful, they tend to focus their attention onto their close colleagues, and stakeholders who accept them, engaging in the corporate equivalent of sticking their fingers in their ears and humming loudly for as long as possible to exclude what they don't want to hear.

Organisational failure after crisis is directly equivalent to deep personal failure for loyalists. They are shattered by it and may take years to recover. The psychological needs that have caused them to engage with and trust the organisation in the first place create deep ties, which cannot be destroyed without damage. In many cases, even where the organisation survives, we see people who are left with a damaged capacity to trust their employer, and this has subsequent impact on individual attitudes and performance. All too often, change agents (senior leaders, consultants, external commentators and pundits) treat loyalists as stupid, backward-looking, old-fashioned sheep, who must either be herded towards the new pastures of success or slaughtered in the downsizing ritual of the day. Smart leaders who want to achieve real metamorphosis have a natural suspicion of such patronising attitudes, and a natural respect for the wisdom and insights of loyalists. Loyalists are not necessarily unthinking conservatives; their loyalty is to the organisation and its values, and where they can see these being well served by change they will make extraordinary shifts in behaviour.

At their best, loyalists can be at the vanguard of efforts to fix the organisation and its culture. To do this they need to believe that the values they are connected with are not being abandoned, and that the future provides a place of safety for the organisation and perhaps also for themselves.

Mercenaries

Contemporary business models for both private- and public-sector organisations rely heavily on outsourcing and the use of temporary staff, consultants and contractors. To achieve such workforce flexibility (i.e. ability to reduce costs and shift long-term liabilities such as pensions from the balance sheets) a price has been paid, particularly in developed economies. The price includes the starkly obvious (the loss of jobs now performed elsewhere; less-favourable terms and conditions) but also less obvious costs for those left in the workforce, in terms of reduced confidence and gradual erosion of benefits, tenure and even pay levels.

It's therefore been a long-term aim of public policy in the UK since the time of Margaret Thatcher's administrations to create a workforce that was more independent of a parent–child relationship with employers. Supporters of such changes point to the growth in self-employment, entrepreneurial and flexible work arrangements of the last two decades, partly enabled by technology as well as social changes, in a positive light. Others see this as part of a "hollowing out" of our workforce and our society, where long-term relationships with employers have been replaced with zero hours contracts and reductions in benefits, and business has been simplistically absolved of its obligations to a wider society.[13] Regardless of these macro trends, the fact is that there have always been groups within the working population of any organisation (full or part time, permanent, temporary or contracted) whose emotional connection with the organisation is prosaic at best. They are doing the job for the money and as a result we will call this group "mercenaries".

Bankers as Loyalists or Mercenaries?

Some people seem to think everyone in pariah organisations is a mercenary. This is especially true for those who work in investment banks. Clearly, there are some good reasons for such beliefs: the high pay and the seeming indifference with which individuals – and even whole teams – decamp from firm to firm suggest there is no loyalty in banks to anything except self-interest and wealth. However, this is a crude misconception. Even in banking, a complex web of issues determines where people choose to work. Status – determined, it's true, partly by bonus (as a public and clear measure of worth and value) but also by rank and the perceptions of others – is often the dominant theme. Fierce identification with teams and individuals is common.

But recent years have demonstrated that even the most powerful of personal loyalties and bonds can be destroyed if the political and financial pressures are high enough. In her book *The Devil's Casino: Friendship, Betrayal, and the High-stakes Games Played inside Lehman Brothers,* journalist Vicky Ward details how the key players at Lehman Brothers created tight mutual loyalties while dealing with pressures on the firm during the '90s when it was sold to a unit of American Express. But later on, competition and money proved stronger than even these bonds:

> Even though he had made [Dick] Fuld[14] sign a $10 million severance deal, [Chris] Pettit never saw the coup coming. It never occurred to him that his old friends would betray him. Why? Because he would never have done it to them.[15]

At the time of his ousting in 1996, Pettit had become more of a liability than an asset to a ruling clique whose realpolitik was as unsentimental as the court of the Borgias.

The rules in operation inside the New York investment banks of the 1980s, 1990s and 2000s had their cultural roots in a mish-mash of Italian working-class mobsterdom, white shoe WASP superciliousness and chippy Jewish intellectualism, all stirred up with the pressures of long hours, ruthless commercial requirements and increasingly vast rewards for those who succeeded (or could be seen to have succeeded). Although many at Lehman's (and Barclays, and Goldman Sachs) paid lip service to "one firm" loyalties, under these pressures most turned out to do what was most expedient, good business sense or just plain self-interested. As people do, unless given higher things to aim at than this year's bonus.

The fact is that there are mercenaries in every organisation. Mercenaries are the pragmatists in the group, ruled by head not heart. In pariah organisations they tend to be quite cognisant of the issues and criticisms of the organisation. But they perform a calculus that accepts the personal and reputational risks they are running and deems them worthwhile. They therefore tend to be phlegmatic and often cool-headed during crises. They don't focus much on critics, preferring to spend their time and energy on supportive stakeholders. If and when the game is up, either for themselves personally or for their employer, they tend to accept defeat with reasonable grace, so long as their financial needs are met as they leave. Mercenaries can be seen in varied forms: as interim or short-term executives, as the skilled contractors surrounding the oil industry or as freelance journalists writing for a newspaper. There's nothing wrong with mercenaries. Just don't expect them to die for the organisation's good name or work for nothing. They are loyal to themselves. And if we dislike that, then perhaps we should ask ourselves what else we expect to see, given the way the organisations they work for behave. Do they really look after their people when they don't, strictly speaking, have to do so? Do they provide security over time and income in the future via pensions, even for widows and families? Do they go beyond their statutory obligations on providing health care? In short, we get the workforce attitudes we deserve as employers.

Heroes

The third and final group of employees is the heroes. These are the people who see themselves as the ones who are going to change the organisation – or perhaps even save it. Heroes are attracted even to quite toxic pariah organisations because they believe they can – even must – change them. Crises are not only not a problem for heroes, they are essential. Without a crisis, there is no opportunity for heroes to operate and demonstrate their heroism. Heroes get their energy, and often their sense of personal meaning and direction, from fighting crises.

Heroes can come from inside the organisation – cometh the hour, cometh the man or woman. But they are often from the outside and there remains a strong trend to bring in external leaders to "fix" things (especially after a crisis), despite considerable evidence that they perform, on average, no better than home-grown talent.[16]

Heroes are very different from pure loyalists, in that they define themselves in terms of what needs to change. This is a good thing, in that it makes them more receptive to hearing from those who are critical of the status quo, as well as listening to loyalists and mercenaries who may be less interested in accepting the negatives. They share with loyalists a desire to see the organisation succeed and, often, to maintain certain elements of the organisation's traditions or values (though those which are in the way of the required changes can be sacrificed more easily by heroes than loyalists).

Heroes are also different from mercenaries. They are less accepting of how things are, less prepared to fit in. And they are arguably less cynical: they actually believe in the possibility of change and improvement. They are sincere about their visions and values and mission statements, if only because these are essential vehicles for their own self-actualisation. They share with mercenaries the capacity to belong and yet to be critical, and to hold the fate of the organisation apart in their minds from their own individual fate.

If this description makes it sound as though all heroes are simply egotists, this is not the case. Many people are genuinely inspired to make a difference in their own organisations and others, and are glad of the opportunity to combine their loyalist tendencies with doing something to change and improve the organisation. What can be troublesome about heroes is that they may, at least subconsciously, want crises to happen. They know that the psychology of the crisis can give them authority and a mandate to act, as well as access to resources and extraordinary roles that would not be available without the crisis. Without a crisis, their frustrations or analytical criticisms of the status quo can remain without an outlet.

Here, I have to look hard in the mirror, as should many of my colleagues in the consulting and HR industries. We have long advocated that organisations and their leaders should get better at change, and suggested that up and coming leaders should be tested by their reaction to crises and their ability to achieve successful metamorphoses. But have we also created a cadre of adrenaline-hungry change junkies, who are only capable of temporary fixes (under the guise of restructuring, reengineering or whatever) that contain the inevitable seeds of the next cycle of destruction? Heroes certainly have become our archetype for successful leadership, particularly in CEOs. We love the idea that strong individual leaders can fix things, root out the rotten cores of failed organisations and make everything well. But of course, in taking on bold actions, these heroic CEOs are potentially creating the genesis of the next round of hubristic damage.

Pariah Worker Types in Crisis and Beyond

If we accept that there are these three major (and very different types) of worker in pariah organisations (and probably in non-pariah ones, too), then we can start to think about how they are likely to react to crises and also how those reactions may impact efforts to fix things.

Broadly speaking, **loyalists** are the least likely to accept the negative facts around a crisis, although their loyalty may make them rapidly effective in working hard to secure the organisation's future. However, what they really want is for the pain to go away and, if possible, to get back to the way things once were, where they felt safe. As a result, loyalists may not be the best people to lead deep investigations that might question a lot of the fundamentals of how the past system operated: they simply have too much to lose in terms of personal identity and investment. However, once a fact base has been established and they are convinced of the reality of the situation and the right course of action, loyalists are often superb at leading the organisation towards change because of their credibility to others and their orientation towards what is best for the organisation and the long term. Good organisations need loyalists, and lots of them.

Mercenaries tend towards pragmatism and in my experience are quite quick to understand what is really going on in a crisis, the level of existential threat it creates for the organisation, and what can or cannot be done about it where they work. They will also typically perform a rapid, selfish but objective calculus on whether they are going to invest more of their own time and effort to support the organisation. If they judge all is lost, they may switch away from any interest in efforts to analyse what has happened or rescue the organisation, and will focus on securing their own next role elsewhere, as well as perhaps their own exit package. For this reason, and others we will discuss later, we should be cautious how large a proportion of the workforce should be mercenaries, especially in senior ranks (where they often flourish). Mercenaries have high levels of connection and contact outside the organisation. This gives them the strength of understanding the organisation's role in the wider system and also means they tend to be at least psychologically ahead of their loyalist or hero colleagues in the rush to the lifeboats if things cannot be saved.

Heroes, as we have noted, love crises. Some of them hide this enjoyment, but the exhilaration and excitement of change, the dislocation of normal patterns of power and influence, as well as the long, tiring hours that tend to be demanded of those operating in a crisis can all be highly intoxicating things. There are many executives these days – particularly in corporate turnaround or support functions such as legal, communications/PR, HR and IT – who spend their entire careers chasing from one crisis to another, either within a large organisation or from company to company. At their best, heroes are the ones who deal realistically with the naysayers and externals while propping up internal morale, and then plan and execute the changes of true metamorphosis. Too often, though, heroes have feet of clay. Their action orientation and adrenaline addiction means that they take too little time over the complex and difficult work of understanding deeply what has occurred and why, and get bored before the deeper changes are fully planned, let alone implemented.

Of course, none of these archetypes is so pure in reality, and hopefully there can be some elements of the loyalist in all employees, even if they are principally mercenaries or heroes.

Pariah Workers before a Crisis

This chapter has principally focused on the impact of different worker types during and after a crisis. But what about before? If the workers are going to be part of the solution set, perhaps they have some accountability for the problem? In the important genesis and hubris stages of the pariah lifecycle, what are employees contributing to the roots of crisis?

Loyalists are formed in the genesis phase of new startups, where the creation of the new organisation and the hard scrabble of survival ties in employees at all levels to high levels of devotion. Such first-generation employees and leaders, particularly after long service, are among the most determinedly loyalist one can imagine, almost to the point of cult membership in some cases. There are interesting parallels between how cultures have evolved in startups in Silicon Valley and the creation of the new generation of investment banks in Wall Street and London during the last 30 years. What's different about the banks is that they were using the trusted brands of their (often relatively sleepy and conservative) corporate owners as host organisms to cloak – or even fund – innovation and growth. In both cases (banks and tech firms), the cultures created were – and remain – highly attractive to young, smart and ambitious people in a hurry to succeed and become insanely wealthy. But how do you keep growth rates high and encourage those climbing the ladder of these cultures? Beyond the first generation of "founders",[17] it rapidly becomes important for the fledgling organisation to be able to manufacture new loyalists on an industrial scale. This is usually achieved through carefully designed "onboarding" programmes at entry into organisations from schools or universities. Pariahs are famously careful about their hiring and talent-management processes. This is no accident: they *want* to screen out those less likely to become loyalists, and if they do this too efficiently they can sow the seeds of their own doom. It's therefore not a surprise that these loyalist-heavy, inwardly focused cultures in which workers learn only to question in certain, quite technical ways, become prone to hubris – particularly when the rest of the world joins in the mutual admiration society.

Mercenaries are present in these cultures, however much they may try and weed them out. Initially, they may be there because this is the only way to get a certain type of technical talent into the team. Later on, it is often the functional people (legal, IT, HR etc.) who can be tolerated as mercenaries because they are not "core". As we have observed, this could provide some opportunity for respected independents to challenge some of the hyper-loyalist norms of the organisations before they become dangerously hubristic. But too often what happens is that mercenaries are turned into loyalists: they drink the Kool-Aid and join in, with powerful impacts. The Salz Report into Barclays commented thus on the role HR had played:

> The role of human resources (HR), and the design and operation of
> the ways in which the bank managed and developed its people, did less
> than we would have wished to underpin desirable behaviours. The HR
> function was accorded insufficient status to stand up to the business
> units on a variety of people issues, including pay. This undermined any
> efforts to promote correlation of pay to broader behaviours than those
> driving individual financial performance. This mattered, because pay
> was seen as the primary tool to shape behaviour. The lack of serious
> attention to the consequences of individual behaviours was also

reflected in insufficient attention being given to personal development and leadership skills (as opposed to technical training). And there was too much emphasis on financial performance in recruiting, performance evaluation and promotion, with insufficient focus on values and behaviours.

(Salz, 2013, 2.25)

It would not be appropriate for me to comment on this paragraph further. But there are lessons to be learned here about the importance of keeping functions not only business savvy but also appropriately objective, externally oriented and technically competent.

Heroes tend to be less prominent in the pre-crisis phases of the pariah cycle, mainly because they will tend to look identical to loyalists. This is a shame, as it's during the genesis and hubris phases that the organisation could arguably most use heroes to put it right before crisis descends. Perhaps this is, in fact, what does occur in organisations that manage to avoid descending into hubris: heroes either within or outside the organisation are effective enough that they can divert the culture somewhere safer and less self-destructive.

I have suggested above that the three groups can come from a wide range of employment arrangements across the extended enterprise. Perhaps in the future we need to think harder about how we can encourage the development of more heroes in these stages of organisational development, people who can rise above the conformist herds of the loyalists, people who are more than just mercenaries. Perhaps that would be real leadership. What we definitely need to consider is how we develop and get the best from loyalists in a world where our employment practices and reward systems (especially our attitude to pensions) seem to be biased away from them. And if we are going to have so many mercenaries, especially in the senior ranks, we should be very sure we are paying them to fight in the right war and for the right side.

Notes

1 There is some debate between political commentators as to just how much prime ministers such as Thatcher and Blair have increased the centralisation of powers, but no real doubt in management literature that the dominant corporate parenting style of large corporations has become more centrally coordinated since the 1970s, particularly because of globalisation and techno-logical developments.

2 Booz + Company's 2012 CEO Turnover survey pointed out that the rate of outsiders taking over at the top had increased to 22 per cent. However, the same survey suggested that firms with insider appointments performed better, and had longer tenures.

3 Towers Watson Global Workforce Study 2014, http://www.towerswatson.com/en-GB/Insights/IC-Types/Survey-Research-Results/2014/08/the-2014-global-workforce-study

4 This finding held true across multiple demographics.

5 See Tett, 2015.

6 Although we did tighten up our requirements to ensure we were not wasting money, we chose to maintain relatively high expat numbers in order to ensure critical skills transfer/development and a breadth of experience for future leaders was maintained. I am certain this was also a key factor in Shell's consistency of values and behaviours globally, a form of cultural life insurance, if you will.

7 Elizabeth Kübler-Ross's infamous "stages of grief" model (denial, anger, bargaining, depression, acceptance) was outlined in her 1969 book *On Death and Dying*. Her theories were formed from interviews with dying patients, and subsequently her stages were applied to grief around the death of others, and then to other situations felt to be analogous to death (loss of a relationship, children in divorce etc.). Recent critiques of her work have suggested not only that the "stages" don't necessarily have to be worked through in order, but that they don't exist, and even that grief itself does not exist. It's beyond the scope of this book to argue out who is correct on this topic, but it seems valid to observe that employees are suffering a loss and experiencing cognitive disso-nance when crises occur. There are implications for "treatment" in terms of what leaders and others should do which may alter depending on one's theory of choice. My own view is that individuals experience these losses differently, and astute leaders will recognise this diversity of experience and not produce one-size-fits-all solutions. Some people are clearly helped by discussing the crisis openly and often; others just want to know facts or be reassured.

8 The dangers of this code of silence are well documented by Dutch journalist Joris Luyendijk in his investigation into the hidden world of the City. See Luyendijk, 2015.

9 A popular website when I worked at the bank was Here is the City: http://hereisthecity.com/en-gb/topic/barclays/

10 Many external observers seem wilfully incapable of distinguishing between two different worlds. In one world, everyone working on Wall Street is seen as psychopathic and hence merits no sympathy or empathy (an interesting move, given that lack of empathy is itself a psychopathic trait). The other world, where through cultural norms and self-protection the whole industry avoids seeing the harm it has perpetrated, is much less well understood, but is surely one which deserves greater research and understanding.

11 This was why LIBOR was such a big deal for Barclays and other banks: it was to a great extent the first time they had really been caught doing something blatantly illegal. Even the industry's cheerleaders could not excuse this behaviour, nor could it be blamed on a wider system.

12 Society, Shareholders and Self-Interest: Accountability of Business Leaders in Financial Services, 2012, London. http://www.exed.hbs.edu/assets/Documents/accountability-financial.pdf

13 Average job tenure in the UK remains quite high and has not shifted much in the last 13 years. In fact, it's gone up slightly (from 7.8 to 9.0 years between 2000 and 2013) and the proportion employed for 10 years and over has increased from 18.1 per cent to 19.0. However, the share of involuntary part timers as a percentage of part-time employment has more than doubled over the same period in the UK, from 8.1 per cent to 16.5 per cent of employment. Structurally, it would appear that more people are being thrust into work that offers them fewer hours and lower wages than they would like.

14 Fuld was CEO of Lehman Bros when it collapsed. Chris Pettit was a long-time friend and lieutenant of Fuld's.

15 See Ward, 2010, p.91.

16 Most studies on internals and externals are ambivalent at best about the ability of external senior leaders to outperform insiders. Some studies even show that external hires tend to disappoint in terms of both short- and long-term performance. Boris Groysberg at Harvard (Groysberg, 2010) demonstrated this for traders, and Matthew Bidwell at Wharton (Bidwell, 2011) for a range of workers in an investment bank (where the only thing externals were consistently better at than insiders was getting paid more money). However, Karaeveli and Zajac at Sloan MIT (Karaeveli and Zajac, 2012) found that, where the circumstances were right (poor performance or growth) then outsiders did outperform insiders.

17 People starting up digital companies these days love to refer to themselves as founders, presumably in the hope that they will be starting something important as well as to assert their roles. We should not forget that co-founders of many other companies have been unceremoniously dumped and lost their ownership rights, most notably at Facebook.

12

Final Conclusions

THIS BOOK HAS tried to set out a helpful model for considering the problem of pariah organisations, how they form, how and why they lose the trust they earn, and what we might do about these issues. Much remains to be done if these theories are to be proved as more than just an interesting way to gather this material together. In particular, I would be delighted if more serious research were devoted to trying to falsify (or prove) the assertions I have made based on my own experiences and the evidence that I have been able to bring together. We need to know from the basis of fact, not just opinion, whether or not hubris is really present before most major crises and if the genesis conditions are as dangerous as I suggest (without resort to circular arguments). In short, this theory needs more data, testing and challenge if it is to prove itself.

This, then, is a book that will probably frustrate some readers because it's not more sure of itself, more sure it is right and able to prove itself correct. But I did not want to write a conventional business tome that pushed everything back into a series of checklists and tables. What I did want to do was to make readers think about these things for themselves, consider different points of view and hence create conditions for us all to improve our capacity to trust each other more. In writing the book, I rediscovered once more how prescient classical authors have been about the topics that concern us today: power, leadership, living a balanced life, grandiosity, humility, behaving ethically, money, corruption, falls from grace, the power of diversity – it's all there. So I hope some readers will become more curious about this rich source of wisdom. Perhaps as we rediscover the classics we can even reclaim our civilisation and its moral philosophical roots.

We started this journey round the lifecycle with Greek tragedy and I think it's fitting we should end there too. At the end of the *Oedipus Tyrannus,* Sophocles' great play, the broken, blinded Oedipus – once a cocky king – is sent into exile and has his children taken from him:

Oedipus: Then it is time to lead me away.

Creon: Come, then, but let your children go.

Oedipus: No, do not take them from me!

Creon: Do not wish to be master in all things: the mastery which you did attain has not followed you through life.

Chorus: Residents of our native Thebes, behold, this is Oedipus, who knew the renowned riddle, and was a most mighty man. What citizen did not gaze on his fortune with envy? See into what a stormy sea of troubles he has come! Therefore, while our eyes wait to see the final destined day, we must call no mortal happy until he has crossed life's border free from pain.

(Sophocles, *Oedipus Tyrannus*, 1,520–31, translation by Jebb)

The Greek tragedies do not teach that one can avoid one's fate. Far from it. But they do teach that developing your *character* is a worthwhile activity and that, although nemesis awaits the hubristic, the more cautious, humble and wise can avoid such fates. And the tragedies also teach that to be powerful and mighty is something to take on carefully, and with due reverence for the gods. I don't want to wade into a religious minefield here, but perhaps we need to replace that sense of an all-powerful externality watching over leadership, above and beyond the board, the regulator and the state. Perhaps real leadership humility will come from the realisation we are all accountable to each other on this planet, and that no-one is too grand, clever or successful to be unveiled, deposed and shamed... Meanwhile, all of us who have the opportunity to keep our leaders honest, humble and decent should remind them of this, whenever we can, like the slave attending a Roman general's triumph:

"Respice post te! Hominem te esse memento! Memento mori!"

("Look behind you! Remember that you are a man! Remember that you'll die!")

(Quoted in Tertullian, *Apologeticus*, 33)

What an enticing and relevant picture that is: the Roman general, celebrating his victories with a lavish parade,[1] captives and looted treasures in front, family by his side, his unarmed troops behind him singing lewd songs in his honour. Such ego-boosting parades raised serious questions about how close the general in question might come to divine status.[2] Pompey, Caesar's famous rival, celebrated his forty-fifth birthday in 61 BC with his third triumph in Rome, accompanied by a gigantic portrait head of himself, studded with pearls. The ultimate bling-tastic moment, perhaps. The Republican Romans knew this sort of behaviour was too much, and the egotism and confusion of mortal and godlike qualities was ultimately disastrous for the Roman Empire. So knowing this stuff is not enough; we need to be prepared to act.

I am confident that we can support the talented people leading our largest and most influential organisations without putting up with too much of such nonsense. We can help support the servant–leaders, the reverent leaders, those who acknowledge that they are not the highest power, that they depend on others to be successful. If we can be successful, the prize is worth having. A society based on institutions that inspire trust in other individuals and organisations is surely a better place to live in, one that can evolve beyond the cynical negativity of the present age and provide hope and opportunity, sustainably, for everyone.

Notes

1 So huge were the expenditures on Roman Triumphs they had a defining impact on GDP and released so much money into the economy that they reduced interest rates. An early form of Keynesianism, perhaps?

2 Mary Beard devotes a whole chapter to this question of men as gods in her book *The Roman Triumph* (2007).

List of Recommendations

There are 13 core recommendations contained in Part Two of this book:

A – Avoiding Pariahdom (Genesis and Hubris)

1. Manage Genesis Conditions Mindfully
2. Get Purpose and Values Right
3. Monitor Status Broadly
4. Make Your Culture Unfriendly to Hubris
5. Get Leadership Right

    5.1 Definitions of Leadership Potential and Capability

    5.2 Long-term and Intentional Leadership Development

    5.3 Critical Promotions and Developmental Moves

    5.4 Performance Management and Reward

B – Preparing For and Coping With Pariahdom (Crisis)

6. Assume It Will Happen
7. Prepare and Practise for Crises
8. Develop a Broad and Supportive Coalition
9. Communicate by Listening not SHOUTING

C – Curing Pariahs (Nemesis, Metamorphosis and Catharsis)

10. Redefine Nemesis as Organisational Learning

11. Avoid False Metamorphosis

12. Ask for Forgiveness – Candour and Catharsis

13. Maintain Healthy Paranoia

Pariah Organisation Health Check

Organisations wishing to assess their current pariah status have no single baseline for data. However, an initial review will usefully combine for the board and CEO perspectives from both an internal and external perspective, aimed at providing critical but informed feedback on areas of concern.

INTERNAL PERSPECTIVE	EXTERNAL PERSPECTIVE
Crises – internal reviews and audit reports etc. – identify themes and recurring issues	**Crises** – news reports, share price and reputation tracker impacts (including social media)
Genesis – check which organisations/ countries etc. have experienced rapid growth and who is leading them	**Genesis** – measures of growth and success (inc. press)
Hubris – leadership development and talent review data (including psychological profiles focused on narcissism), whistleblowers, employee engagement data	**Hubris** – cultural signifiers in external presentation and behaviour; views of commentators and analysts, customers, ex-employers, whistleblowers
Metamorphosis – objectives and achievements of "transformation" projects relative to scale of issues and crises	**Metamorphosis** – third-party verification of claimed changes

Bibliography

Aeschylus (1984) *The Oresteia*, trans. Robert Fagles, London: Penguin.

Aitken, Robin (2007) *Can We Trust the BBC?* London, New York: Continuum.

Ante, Spencer E., and Lublin, Joann S. (2012) Young CEOs: Are They Up to the Job? It's Creativity vs. Experience as a New Flock of Leaders Take Their Companies to Public Markets, *Wall Street Journal*, 7 February 2012.

Arendt, Hannah (1963) *Eichmann in Jerusalem: A Report on the Banality of Evil*, London: Penguin Books.

Babiak, Paul, and Hare, Robert D. (2006) *Snakes in Suits: When Psychopaths Go to Work*, New York: Regan Books.

Bakan, Joel (2012) *The Corporation: The pathological pursuit of profit and power*, UK: Hachette.

Baker, James A. III (Chair) (2007) The Report of The BP US Refineries Independent Safety Review Panel.

Barclays (2013) Barclays' Response to the Salz Review.

Barnes, Jonathan (ed.) (2014) *Complete Works of Aristotle, Volume 1: The Revised Oxford Translation*, Princeton University Press.

Baron-Cohen, Simon (2004) *The Essential Difference*, Penguin UK.

Baron-Cohen, Simon (2008) *Autism and Asperger Syndrome*, Oxford University Press.

Bazerman, Max and Watkins, David (2004) *Predictable Surprises: The Disasters You Should Have Seen Coming, and How to Prevent Them*.

Beard, Mary (2009) *The Roman Triumph*, Harvard University Press.

Beinart, Peter (2010) *The Icarus syndrome: A history of American hubris*, Melbourne University Publishing.

Benn, Tony (1995) *The Benn Diaries*, Vintage.

Benn, Tony (2007) *More Time for Politics: Diaries 2001–2007*, Random House.

Benn, Tony (2009) *Free At Last: Diaries 1991–2001*, Random House.

Benn, Tony (2012) *Out of the Wilderness: Diaries 1963–67*, Random House.

Benn, Tony (2013) *A blaze of Autumn Sunshine*, Random House.

Bernstein, George Lurcy (2004) *The Myth of Decline: The Rise of Britain since 1945*.

Bidwell, Matthew (2011) Paying more to get less: The effects of external hiring versus internal mobility, *Administrative Science Quarterly*.

Bonini, Sheila, Court, David, and Marchi, Alberto (2009) Rebuilding Corporate Reputations, *McKinsey Quarterly*, June 2009.

Box, George (1987) *Empirical Model-Building and Response Surfaces*, Wiley.

Brizendine, Louann (2010) *The Male Brain*.

Brown, Archie (2014) *The Myth of the Strong Leader: Political leadership in the modern age*, Basic Books.

Burkert, Walter (1992) *The Orientalizing Revolution: Near Eastern Influence on Greek Culture in the Archaic Age*, Harvard.

Cairns, Douglas L. (1992) *Aidos: The Psychology and Ethics of Honour and Shame in Greek Literature*, Blackwell Publishing Ltd.

Cairns, Douglas L. (1996) Hybris, Dishonour and Thinking Big, *Journal of Hellenic Studies*, Vol. 116.

Claxton, Guy, Owen, David, and Sadler-Smith, Eugene (2015) Hubris in leadership: A peril of unbridled intuition?, *Leadership* 11(1): 57–78.

Coates, John M., and Herbert, Joe (2008) Endogenous steroids and financial risk taking on a London trading floor, *Proceedings of the National Academy of Sciences* 105(16): 6,167–72.

Coggan, Philip (2009) *The Money Machine: How the City Works*, Penguin.

Coggan, Philip (2013) *Paper Promises: Debt, money, and the new world order*, PublicAffairs.

Cohen, David (1995) *Law, Violence, and Community in Classical Athens*, Cambridge University Press.

Collins, James (2009) *How the Mighty Fall*, Random House.

Collins, James C., and Porras, Jerry (1994) *Built to Last*, Random House.

Conquest, Robert (2007) *The Great Terror: A Reassessment*, 40th anniversary edition, OUP.

Coombs, Timothy (2007) *Crisis Management and Communications*, Institute for Public Relations.

Coombs, Timothy, and Holladay, Sherry J. (2006) Unpacking the halo effect: reputation and crisis management, *Journal of Communication Management*, Vol. 10, Iss. 2, pp.123–37.

Darling, Alistair (2011) *Back from the Brink: 1000 days at number 11*, Atlantic Books Ltd.

Davenport-Hines, R.P.T. (2013) *An English Affair*, HarperCollins.

Davies, H. (2010) *The Financial Crisis: Who Is to Blame?* Cambridge: Polity Press.

Davies, Nick (2014) *Hack Attack*, Faber.

Davis, Simon (Clifford Chance), Report into the events of 27/28 March 2014 relating to the press briefing of information in the Financial Conduct Authority's 2014/2015 Business Plan.

de Haan, Erik, and Kasozi, Anthony (2014) *The Leadership Shadow*, Ashridge.

Denniston, John Dewar, and Page, Denys (eds), Aeschylus (1957) *Agamemnon*, OUP.

D'Souza, Stephen, and Renner, Diana (2015) *Not Knowing: The art of turning uncertainty into opportunity*, LID Publishing.

Dowling, Grahame (2000) *Creating Corporate Reputations: Identity, Image and Performance*, Oxford: OUP.

Economist Intelligence Unit (2012) *Society, Shareholders and Self-Interest*.

Eggers, Dave (2013) *The Circle*, Knopf Canada.

Euripides (1954) *The Bacchae and Other Plays*, Vol. 44, Penguin.

Fine, Cordelia (2006) 'A Mind of its Own': How our brain distorts and deceives, Thriplow, England: Icon Books.

Fine, Gary Alan (2001) *Difficult Reputations*, Chicago.

Fisher, Nicolas R. (1992) *Hybris: A study in the values of honour and shame in Ancient Greece*, Aris & Phillips.

Forsdyke, Sara (2005) *Exile, Ostracism, and Democracy: The Politics of Expulsion in Ancient Greece*, Princeton.

Francis, Robert (Chair) (2013) *Report of the Mid Staffordshire NHS Foundation Trust Public Inquiry*, HMSO.

Freshfields Bruckhaus Deringer (2012) *Knowing the Risks, Protecting Your Business – Crisis Management*.

Freshfields Bruckhaus Deringer (2014) *Containing A Crisis*.

Friedman, George (2010) *The Next 100 Years: A forecast for the 21st century*, Anchor.

Fukuyama, Francis (1995) *Trust: The Social Virtues and the Creation of Prosperity*, London: Hamish Hamilton.

Furnham, Adrian (2010) *The Elephant in the Boardroom*, Palgrave Macmillan.

Garrard, Peter, and Robinson, Graham (eds) (2015) *The Intoxication of Power: Interdisciplinary Insights*, London: Palgrave Macmillan.

Geithner, Timothy (2014) *Stress Test: Reflections on financial crises*, Random House.

Girard, René (1977) *Violence and the Sacred*, trans. Patrick Gregory, Baltimore, 49.

Goldman Sachs (2011) Report of the Business Standards Committee.

Goldman Sachs (2013) Business Standards Committee Impact Report.

Gottman, John Mordechai (2014) *What Predicts Divorce?: The relationship between marital processes and marital outcomes*, Psychology Press.

Graham, Bob, and Reilly, William E. (2011) *Deep Water: The Gulf Oil Disaster and the Future of Offshore Drilling Report to the President*, National Commission on the BP Deepwater Horizon Oil Spill and Offshore Drilling.

Greene, Joshua (2014) *Moral Tribes: Emotion, reason and the gap between us and them*, Atlantic Books Ltd.

Grene, David, and Lattimore, Richmond (eds) (1953) *Aeschylus*, University of Chicago Press.

Griffin, Andrew (2014) *Crisis, Issues and Reputation Management: A Handbook for PR and Communications Professionals*, Kogan Page Publishers.

Grove, Andrew S. (1996) *Only the Paranoid Survive: How to Exploit the Crisis Points that Challenge Every Company and Career*, Broadway Business.

Groysberg, Boris (2010) *Chasing Stars: The Myth of Talent and the Portability of Performance*, Princeton.

Haig, Matt (2011) *Brand Failures: The truth about the 100 biggest branding mistakes of all time*, Kogan Page Publishers, 2nd edition.

Haldane, Andy (2014) Central Bank Psychology – Speech given at a conference on leadership, stress and hubris at the Royal Society of Medicine, 17 November.

Harrison, Alick Robin Walsham (1968) *The Law of Athens*, 2 vols, Indianapolis: Duckworth.

Hayward, M.L A. (2007) *Ego Check*, Chicago, Il: Kaplan.

Hayward, Mathew L.A., and Hambrick, Donald C. (1997) Explaining the premiums paid for large acquisitions: Evidence of CEO hubris, *Administrative Science Quarterly*: 103–27.

Heffernan, Margaret (2011) *Wilful Blindness: Why We Ignore the Obvious*, Simon and Schuster.

Hennessy, Peter (2014) *Establishment and Meritocracy*, Haus Publishing.

Hennessy, Peter (1986) *The Great and the Good: An Inquiry into the British Establishment*, no. 654, Policy Studies Institute.

Hesiod (1978) *Works and Days*, ed. West, Oxford.

Hill, R.W., and Yousey, G. (1998) Adaptive and maladaptive narcissism among university faculty, clergy, politicians and librarians, *Current Psychology*, 17(2/3): 163–9.

Hopkins, Andrew (2009) *Failure to Learn: the BP Texas City Refinery Disaster*.

Hosking, Geoffrey (2010) *Trust: Money, Markets and Society, Manifestos for the 21st Century*, London: Seagull Books.

Ignatieff, Michael (2013) *Fire and Ashes*, Harvard University Press.

Independent Commission on Banking (2011) *Final Report*, London: HMSO.

Jacobs, Alan (2008) *Original Sin – A Cultural History*, Zondervan.

Jensen, Michael C., and Meckling, William H. (1976) Theory of the firm: Managerial behavior, agency costs and ownership structure, *Journal of Financial Economics* 3(4): 305–60.

Kahneman, Daniel (2011) *Thinking, Fast and Slow*, Macmillan.

Kaplan, Robert S., and Norton, David P. (1996) *The Balanced Scorecard: Translating strategy into action*, Harvard Business Press.

Karaevli, Ayse, and Zajac, Edward J. (2012) When Is an Outsider CEO a Good Choice?, *MIT Sloan Management Review* 53(4): 15.

Kellerman, Barbara (2006) When should a leader apologize and when not?, *Harvard Business Review* 84(4): 72–81.

Kershaw, Ian (1998) *Hitler 1889–1936: Hubris*, London.

Kershaw, Ian (2000) *Hitler 1936–1945: Nemesis*, London.

Kietzmann, Jan H., et al. (2011) Social media? Get serious! Understanding the functional building blocks of social media, *Business Horizons* 54(3): 241–51.

Kohn, Marek (2008) *Trust: Self-interest and the Common Good*, Oxford: Oxford University Press.

Kontes, Peter W., and Mankins, Michael C. (1994) *The Value Imperative: Managing for superior shareholder returns*, Free Press.

Kübler-Ross, Elisabeth (2009) *On Death and Dying: What the dying have to teach doctors, nurses, clergy and their own families*, Taylor & Francis.

Lawrence, Dena Y., Pazzaglia, Federica, and Sonpar, Karan (2011) The introduction of a non-traditional and aggressive approach to banking: the risks of hubris, *Journal of Business Ethics* 102(3): 401–20.

Levy, Steven (2011) *In the Plex: How Google thinks, works, and shapes our lives*, Simon and Schuster.

Lewis, Michael (2014) *Flash Boys: A Wall Street Revolt*, New York.

Lieberman, Matthew D. (2013) *Social: Why our brains are wired to connect*, Oxford University Press.

Love, John F. (1995) *McDonald's: Behind the Golden Arches*, Bantam.

Luyendijk, Joris (2015) *Swimming with Sharks: My Journey into the World of the Bankers*, London.

Maccoby, Michael (2000) Narcissistic leaders: The incredible pros, the inevitable cons, *Harvard Business Review* 78(1): 68–78.

MacDowell, Douglas M. (1976) 'Hybris' in Athens, *Greece and Rome*, Second Series 23(1).

Malkin, Craig (2015) Rethinking narcissism: the bad – and surprising good – about feeling special, New York.

Marr, Andrew (2008) *A History of Modern Britain*, Pan.

Martin, Iain (2013) *Making It Happen: Fred Goodwin, RBS and the men who blew up the British economy*, Simon and Schuster.

McKeon, Richard (ed.) (2009) *The Basic Works of Aristotle*, Modern Library.

Meadows, D.H., Meadows, D.L., Randers, J., and Behrens, W.W. (1972) *The Limits to Growth*, New York.

Menke, Christoph (2010) Law and Violence, *Law & Literature* 22(1).

Mishina, Yuri, Dykes, B.J., Block, E.S., and Pollock, T.G. (2010) Why 'good' firms do bad things: The effects of high aspirations, high expectations, and prominence on the incidence of corporate illegality, *Academy of Management Journal* 53(4): 701–22.

Morozov, Evgeny (2013) *To Save Everything Click Here*, New York.

Morris, Nicholas, and Vines, David (2014) *Capital Failure: Rebuilding Trust in Financial Services*, edited by Nicholas Morris and David Vines, Oxford: Oxford University Press.

Mourkogiannis, Nikos (2006) *Purpose: The starting point of great companies*, Macmillan.

Nadler, David A. (2005) Confessions of a trusted counsellor, *Harvard Business Review* 83(9): 68–77.

Nolan, Lord (1995) *Public Life – First Report of the Committee on Standards in Public Life*, HMSO.

Ovid (1963) *Tristia, etc.* edited by S.G. Owen, Oxford.

Ovid (2004) *Metamorphoses*, edited by R.J. Tarrant, Oxford.

Owen, David (2012) *The Hubris Syndrome: Bush, Blair and the Intoxication of Power*, Methuen.

Owen, David, and Davidson, Jonathan (2009) Hubris syndrome: An acquired personality disorder? A study of US Presidents and UK Prime Ministers over the last 100 years, *Brain* 132(5): 1,396–406.

Page, J.D., and Denniston, D. (1957) *Aeschylus: Agamemnon*, Oxford: Oxford University Press.

Parkinson, C. Northcote (1958) *Parkinson's Law*, London: John Murray.

Parliamentary Commission on Banking Standards (2013) *Changing Banking for Good*, London: HMSO.

Perman, Ray, and Darling, Alistair (2013) *Hubris: How HBOS wrecked the best bank in Britain*, Birlinn.

Perry, Gina (2013) *Behind the Shock Machine: The untold story of the notorious Milgram psychology experiments*, New Press.

Peston, Robert (2012) *How Do We Fix this Mess?: The Economic Price of Having it All, and the Route to Lasting Prosperity*, Hachette UK.

Petit, Valérie, and Bollaert, Helen (2012) Flying too close to the sun? Hubris among CEOs and how to prevent it, *Journal of Business Ethics* 108(3): 265–83.

Piketty, Thomas (2014) *Capital in the 21st Century*, Cambridge: Harvard University Press.

Pink, Daniel H. Drive (2011) *The Surprising Truth about What Motivates Us*, Penguin.

Plato (2003) *Republic*, edited by S.R. Slings, Oxford: OUP.

Posner, Richard A. (2009) *A Failure of Capitalism*, Cambridge: Harvard University Press.

Regester, Michael, and Larkin, Judy (2008) *Risk Issues and Crisis Management in Public Relations – A Casebook of Best Practice*, 4th edition, London/New York.

Reyner, Michael et al. (2013) *Taming Narcissus: Managing Behavioural Risk in Top Business Leaders*, MWM Consulting.

Riddell, Paul (2013) Rallying the troops: Crisis communication and reputation management in financial services, *Journal of Brand Strategy* 2(3): 222–7.

Rogers, W.P. (Chair) (1986) Presidential Commission on Space Shuttle Challenger: Report of the Presidential Commission on the Space Shuttle Challenger Accident, Washington D.C.

Ronfeldt, David (1994) Beware the Hubris–Nemesis Complex – A Concept for Leadership Analysis, RAND National Security Research Division.

Ronson, Jon (2015) *So You've Been Publicly Shamed*, London: Picador.

Rose, David C. (2011) *The Moral Foundation of Economic Behavior*, Oxford: Oxford University Press.

Ryde, Robin (2012) *Never Mind the Bosses: Hastening the Death of Deference for Business Success*, John Wiley & Sons.

Sadler-Smith, Eugene, and Shefy, Erella (2004) The intuitive executive: understanding and applying 'gut feel' in decision-making, *The Academy of Management Executive* 18(4): 76–91.

Salz, Anthony (2013) Salz Review – An Independent Review of Barclays' Business Practices.

Scharmer, C. Otto (2009) *Theory U: The Social Technology of Presencing*, San Francisco.

Scharmer, C. Otto, and Kaeufer, Katrin (2013) *Leading from the Emerging Future: From Ego-System to Eco-System Economies*, San Francisco.

Schein, Edgar H. (2006) *Organizational Culture and Leadership*, John Wiley & Sons.

Schein, Edgar (2009) *Helping: How to offer, give, and receive help*, Berrett-Koehler Publishers.

Schultz, Kathryn (2011) *Being wrong: Adventures in the margin of error*, Granta Books.

Schwartz, Howard S. (1992) *Narcissistic Process and Corporate Decay: The theory of the organizational ideal*, NYU Press.

Short, Philip (2007) *Pol Pot: Anatomy of a Nightmare*, Macmillan.

Smith, Adam (1776) *The Wealth of Nations*.

Smith, Sarah Francis, Watts, Ashley, and Lilienfeld, Scott (2014) On the trail of the elusive successful psychopath, *Psychologist*.

Sommerstein, Alan H. (1989) *Aeschylus: Eumenides*, Cambridge University Press.

Sophocles (1990) *Plays*, ed. Lloyd-Jones and Wilson, Oxford.

Sorkin, Andrew (2009) *Too Big to Fail: The inside story of how Wall Street and Washington fought to save the financial system*, New York: Penguin.

Stadler, Christian (2011) *Enduring Success: What We Can Learn from the History of Outstanding Companies*, Stanford.

Stadler, Christian, and Dyer, Davis (2013) Why Good Leaders Don't Need Charisma, *Sloan Management Review*, Spring.

Stanford, Naomi (2012) *Organizational Health: An integrated approach to building optimum performance*, Kogan Page Publishers.

Stanford, Naomi (2014) *The Economist: Organisation Culture: How corporate habits can make or break a company*, Profile Books.

Steare, Roger (2006) *Ethicability*, Roger Steare Consulting Limited.

Stein, Mark (2013) When Does Narcissistic Leadership Become Problematic? Dick Fuld at Lehman Brothers, *Journal of Management Inquiry*.

Syed, Matthew (2015) *Black Box Thinking – The Surprising Truth About Success*, London: Hodder & Stoughton.

Szemerenyi, O. (1974) The origins of the Greek lexicon: Ex oriente lux, *Journal of Hellenic Studies*, 94: 144–57.

Taleb, Nassim Nicholas (2001) *Fooled By Randomness*, New York.

Tett, Gillian (2015) *The Silo Effect: Why putting everything in its place isn't such a bright idea*, Hachette UK.

U.S. Chemical Safety and Hazard Investigation Board (2005) Investigation Report, Refinery Explosion and Fire, BP Texas City, 23 March.

Vander Weyer, Martin (2000) *Falling Eagle: The Decline of Barclays Bank*, Weidenfeld & Nicolson.

Viswanath, Rupa (2014) *The Pariah Problem: Caste, Religion, and the Social in Modern India*, Columbia University Press.

Wang, Zhongmin, Lee, Alvin, and Polonsky, Michael (2015) Egregiousness and Boycott Intensity, Resources for the Future Discussion Paper.

Ward, Vicky (2010) *The Devil's Casino: Friendship, Betrayal, and the High-stakes Games Played inside Lehman Brothers*, John Wiley & Sons.

Watson, Tom, and Hickman, Martin (2012) *Dial M for Murdoch: News Corporation and the corruption of Britain*, Penguin UK.

Winnington-Ingram, R.P. (1971) The Second Stasimon of the Oedipus Tyrannus, *Journal of Hellenic Studies*, Vol. 91.

Wolmar, Christian (2001) Broken Rails: How Privatisation Wrecked Britain's Railway, London: 2001.

Young, Michael Dunlop (1958) *The Rise of the Meritocracy*, Transaction Publishers.

Ziegler, Philip (1993) *Wilson: The Authorised Life of Lord Wilson of Rievaulx*, Weidenfeld & Nicolson.

Index